Reframing Educational Research

Possibilities for the use of research in educational practice are often written off due to the history, politics and interests of the ostensibly separate worlds that researchers and practitioners occupy. However, a more optimistic account highlights the ways these communities share a common need for practice-based theories, which enable them to make sense of a wide range of issues in education, including pedagogy, learning and educational equity.

In applying theory to situated accounts of various educational practices and learning contexts, this book explores mistaken assumptions about the ways that research can 'inform' or otherwise impact practice. It problematises a 'what works' agenda but also points to potentially more productive research–practice relationships in education. Experienced contributors describe how they have used a variety of context-sensitive theoretical approaches in the sociocultural and discursive traditions to both understand practice and address a wide range of practical issues in education.

At its core *Reframing Educational Research* challenges two commonly held assumptions:

- that 'best practice' is readily identifiable in a way that is then transferrable to new contexts for use by practitioners more widely, and
- that theory will not help with what to do on Monday morning in the class-room or in developing policies with direct and visible impact.

Drawing on the experience of a number of highly respected expert contributors, including Mel Ainscow, Harry Daniels, Anna Sfard and Etienne Wenger-Trayner, the book discusses a range of issues that must be explicitly addressed if we are to make headway in developing a sustainable and productive relationship between research, policy and practice. The authors make it clear that the politics, policies, institutional practices, market systems and social dynamics currently at play in education have a tendency to derail the idealised pathway from research to reform. This book aims to move the discussion towards alternative, and potentially more fruitful, ways of linking research with practice.

Reframing Educational Research is an invitation to all researchers to identify new opportunities for advancing theory and practice in education. It is a must-read for all practitioners and researchers in education.

Valerie Farnsworth is a Research Fellow at the University of Leeds in the School of Education's post-14 education research group, where she focuses on the intersections of curriculum, policy and identity.

Yvette Solomon is Professor of Education in the Education and Social Research Institute, Manchester Metropolitan University, and Professor II in Mathematics Education in the Faculty of Education and International Studies, Oslo and Akershus University College of Applied Sciences.

Reframing Educational Research

Resisting the 'what works' agenda

Edited by Valerie Farnsworth
and Yvette Solomon

Routledge
Taylor & Francis Group

LONDON AND NEW YORK

First published 2013
by Routledge
2 Park Square, Milton Park, Abingdon, Oxon OX14 4RN

Simultaneously published in the USA and Canada
by Routledge
711 Third Avenue, New York, NY 10017

Routledge is an imprint of the Taylor & Francis Group, an informa business

© 2013 Valerie Farnsworth and Yvette Solomon

British Library Cataloguing in Publication Data
A catalogue record for this book is available from the British Library

Library of Congress Cataloging in Publication Data
Farnsworth, Valerie.
Reframing educational research : resisting the 'what works' agenda / Valerie
Farnsworth and Yvette Solomon.
pages cm
1. Education--Research. 2. Education--Research--Methodology. I. Solomon,
Yvette. II. Title.
LB1028.F29 2013
370.72--dc23
2012046785

ISBN: 978–0-415–52915–0 (hbk)
ISBN: 978–0-415–52917–4 (pbk)
ISBN: 978–0-203–59073–7 (ebk)

Typeset in Galliard
by GreenGate Publishing Services, Tonbridge, Kent

Printed and bound in the United States of America by Publishers Graphics,
LLC on sustainably sourced paper.

Contents

    designing hybrid activities in third spaces   200
    JULIAN WILLIAMS AND JULIE RYAN

    Bibliography   213
    Index   236

Figures, tables and boxes

Figures

Tables

Boxes

Contributors

Mel Ainscow is Professor of Education and co-director of the Centre for Equity in Education at the University of Manchester. Between 2007 and 2011 he was the Government's Chief Adviser for the Greater Manchester Challenge, a £50 million initiative to improve educational outcomes for all young people in the region.

James Avis is Director of Research and Professor of Post-Compulsory Education and Training at the University of Huddersfield. He has written extensively on the policy contextualisation of Further Education, curriculum issues, research methodology and teacher professionalism, as well as the lived experience of teachers and learners.

Yvonne Barnes is a Senior Lecturer in Primary Mathematics Education at Manchester Metropolitan University. Her doctoral research interests focus on how continuing professional development programmes within mathematics education impact on the pedagogical practices of participants and their identities as learners, researchers and classroom practitioners.

Janine Carroll completed her first degree at Liverpool John Moores University in Applied Psychology in 2001. She worked in the civil service and then at the University of Liverpool as a Communication Skills Technician before embarking on her PhD at the University of Manchester, focusing on the contextual and psychological factors that influence personal and professional development in medical education and she received her award in 2011. She has subsequently worked as a research associate at the University of Liverpool and is currently a Lecturer in Psychology at the University of Chester.

Seth Chaiklin is a Reader in the Department of Education at the University of Bath. His research interests include cultural–historical science, subject-matter teaching, strategies for developing professional practice and methodological development of cultural–historical theory. He has published widely on cultural–historical approaches within these areas.

Fiona Cockerham is a Senior Lecturer in Secondary Mathematics Education at Manchester Metropolitan University in the Faculty of Education. She is interested in the mathematical understanding of student teachers and the application of sociocultural theory to understand the conflicting demands on postgraduate and newly qualified teachers.

Harry Daniels is Professor of Education at the Department of Education, University of Oxford. He is also affiliated with universities in Australia, Japan and Russia. He has published widely on sociocultural and activity theory, educational reform and special educational needs and inclusion.

Tim Deignan is a freelance consultant and contract researcher. He works for a range of clients, including universities, general and specialist colleges, trusts and non-governmental organisations. His approach typically involves modelling different values and perspectives on complex issues in order to improve system performance.

Tim Dornan is Professor in the Department of Educational Development and Research, Maastricht University, the Netherlands and Honorary Professor, University of Manchester and Peninsula Medical School. Previously a specialist internist and endocrinologist, he has turned to reconciling theory and practice in another domain, the education of medical students and qualified doctors.

Valerie Farnsworth is a Research Fellow at the University of Leeds in the School of Education where her work focuses on post-14 education, curriculum and opportunities for progression in education and training, with a particular interest in research that identifies systemic injustices in order to inform reforms in policy and practice.

Una Hanley has recently retired from Manchester Metropolitan University where she was Senior Lecturer in Mathematics Education. Her interests and research lie in exploring the ways in which teachers elucidate their practices in the context curriculum innovations and accountability systems.

Cormac Lawler has worked with learning networks and communities in various contexts, including teaching at the University of Manchester. His research has been primarily in online, wiki-based contexts, having been centrally involved in setting up a Wikimedia Foundation project, Wikiversity. He is also interested in locality and community development.

Erica McAteer is a Visiting Fellow in Psychology and Human Development at the Institute of Education, London. With a history of research into the educational uses of Information and Communication Technologies, her work now focuses on ethnic identity, school and social engagement and the potential of multi-modal representations for classroom learning.

Emma Pearson completed her first degree at the University of Manchester in Psychology and Neuroscience in 2006. She went on to complete her PhD at the University of Manchester, applying psychological theory to explore the emotional development of medical students engaged in workplace learning. She is currently pursuing a teaching qualification at Manchester Metropolitan University.

Julie Ryan is a teacher, tertiary educator and researcher. She is a senior lecturer at Manchester Metropolitan University. She has worked in schools and universities in Australia and England and is currently working on a long-term project to develop a dialogic pedagogy for mathematics.

Anna Sfard is Professor of Mathematics Education at the University of Haifa and a Visiting Professor in the Institute of Education, University of London. Her research focuses on the development and role of mathematical discourses in individual lives and in the course of history. She has published widely on theory and practice in mathematics education.

Yvette Solomon is Professor of Education in the Education and Social Research Institute, Manchester Metropolitan University, and Professor II in Mathematics Education in the Faculty of Education and International Studies, Oslo and Akershus University College of Applied Sciences. She researches the development of mathematics learner identities in secondary school and undergraduate students, and mathematics teachers' developing professional identities.

Mary Thorpe is Professor of Educational Technology in the Institute of Educational Technology at the Open University. She has extensive experience in course teams, student support and quality assurance and enhancement. Her research focuses on technology-enhanced learning, online and distance learning and the evaluation of mediated teaching and learning.

Geoff Wake is an Associate Professor at the University of Nottingham, School of Education. His research focuses on mathematics education, particularly on applications of mathematics in a range of settings including schools/colleges and workplaces. He is actively involved in exploring curriculum and assessment issues at a national level.

Sue Webb is a Professor in the Faculty of Education, Monash University. Her research and teaching interests are in adult education and lifelong learning, particularly educational policies and practice to widen participation and access to higher education by focusing on mature learners' experiences and narratives.

Etienne Wenger-Trayner is an independent consultant. He is author and co-author of seminal articles and books on 'communities of practice' theory, including *Situated Learning*, where the term was coined, and *Communities of Practice: Learning, Meaning, and Identity*, where he lays out a theory of learning based on the concept of communities of practice.

Julian Williams is a Professor of Mathematics Education at the University of Manchester. After a career in mathematics teaching, he spent a decade in curriculum development and mathematics teacher education, and then another decade in teaching about research, research design and methodology. His current interests span sociocultural and Cultural Historical Activity Theory, educational measurement and mathematics education.

Acknowledgements

The idea and opportunity for compiling this book came from a series of seminars funded by the Economics and Social Research Council (ESRC) (RES-451-26-0576). The series was developed by Valerie Farnsworth in collaboration with Julian Williams, and was one of many undertaken under the auspices of the Socio-cultural Theory Interest Group (ScTIG) at the University of Manchester. The series, together with an international conference, regular reading groups, small conferences and a postgraduate module on Social Theories of Learning in Research and Practice, has played a key role in enabling the development of an extensive network. The range of authors and perspectives represented in this book is a direct result of this network and the many discussions we have had on theory, research and practice.

We wish to thank all the authors for diligently working with us to ensure the chapters cohered around the common theme of the book. They took seriously the task of representing their research in a way that engaged explicitly with a dialogue about 'what works' in education research and the relationship between research, policy and practice. We are also grateful to all the seminar participants, whether speakers, group chairs, note-takers, 'ordinary' participants or some combination of these. Their participation made the seminars a productive space within which to work through the ideas that are presented in this book, and to identify the issues that were pertinent and needed to be addressed in it. We would especially like to thank the 'learning unit' – a group of individuals who met (often by phone) to plan the seminars – including James Avis, Alan Bleakley, Gill Boag-Munroe, Tony Brown, Valerie Farnsworth, Peter Jones, Cormac Lawler, Erica McAteer, Yvette Solomon, Sue Webb, Etienne Wenger-Trayner and Julian Williams.

For all of us engaged in educational research, the 'what works' agenda is real in its influence on funding of research and the value of research. Ultimately, our underlying concern for the direction we seem to be heading, where research is defined more and more narrowly in terms of 'what works', provided the motivation for completing this project. We hope the arguments and ideas presented in this book contribute to an ongoing dialogue about the role of research, theory and practice in educational reform.

We would like to thank our editors at Routledge for taking this project on. We each have some personal thanks ...

Valerie Farnsworth writes: I would first like to expressly thank my co-editor, Yvette, for her energy, enthusiasm, commitment, support and guidance. I would like to thank Professor Michael Olneck, now retired from the University of Wisconsin-Madison, for supporting my desire to investigate the issues around research use. I would like to give special thanks to Julian Williams for forming the ScTIG which was the basis for my engagement with sociocultural and cultural–historical theory, and for inviting Etienne Wenger-Trayner to be Visiting Professor to the University of Manchester, providing me with the opportunity to learn more about 'communities of practice' first hand. I would also like to thank Jeremy Higham for reading and commenting on drafts of my chapter and for always being supportive. I am forever grateful to my family and especially my parents, Diana and Edward Farnsworth, for encouraging me to pursue my interest in education, even if they would have preferred that I was a doctor or an engineer. My sister, Gwen Farnsworth, will always be one step ahead as I follow in her footsteps. The true support comes from knowing all my family and friends believe in me, and the one who has stuck with me, Pauline Whelan.

Yvette Solomon writes: my thanks to Valerie for asking me to share this project with her, and her enthusiasm about making this book 'work'. I have learned a great deal from the opportunity this has given me for thinking through the wider arena in which my own research takes place, and for engaging with researchers and practitioners in other areas of education. Not for the first time, I would like to express my sincere thanks to Julian Williams for his generous inclusion of me in the activities of the Manchester University ScTIG, which continues to be a source of inspiration and friendship. Closer to home, as ever I am grateful to my family – John, Bridie and Rosie – for their support and interest in my work.

Finally, we acknowledge the publishers of the following for granting reprint permissions to include figures from these previously published works:

Deignan, T. (2012a). Modeling and developing a dyslexia support system. In D. Moore, A. Gorra, M. Adams, J. Reaney and H. Smith (eds), *Disabled students in education: Technology, transition and inclusivity* (pp. 239–271). Hershey, PA: IGI Global.

Deignan, T. (2012b). A novel way to develop policy and practice. *Operant Subjectivity: The International Journal of Q Methodology*, 35(2), 102–128.

Engeström, Y. (2001). Expansive learning at work: toward an activity theoretical reconceptualisation. *Journal of Education and Work*, 14(1), 133–156.

Engeström, Y. (2010). *From teams to knots: Activity-theoretical studies of collaboration and learning at work*, Cambridge: Cambridge University Press.

Abbreviations

APE	average points per entry
APS	average points score
AS	activity system
BEME	Best Evidence Medical Education
BIS	Department for Business, Innovation and Skills
CAME	Cognitive Acceleration in Maths Education
CBL	community-based learning
CHAT	Cultural Historical Activity Theory
COP	community of practice
CPD	continuing professional development
DSA	Disabled Students' Allowance
DWR	Developmental Work Research
EBM	Evidence-Based Medicine
ESRC	Economic and Social Research Council
FE	Further Education
HEFCE	Higher Education Funding Council for England
HEI	Higher Education Institution
ICT	Information and Communications Technology
LAs	Local Authorities
LEA	Local Education Authority
LIW	Learning in and for Interagency Working
LPP	legitimate peripheral participation
MaST	Mathematics Specialist Teacher
MEC	Mathematics Enhancement Course
M.Eng.	Master of Engineering
NCLB	No Child Left Behind
NICE	National Institute for Health and Clinical Excellence
OER	open educational resources
PBL	problem based learning
PDS	Professional Development School
PFM	personal financial management

ScTIG	Socio-cultural Theory Interest Group
SFE	Student Finance England
SLC	Student Loans Company
STEM	science, technology, engineering and mathematics
TAFE	Technical and Further Education Colleges
UoM	Use of Mathematics
VI	visual impairment
VLE	virtual learning environment

Introduction

Much of the discourse surrounding research in education sets up a false dichotomy between 'applied' and 'pure' research (Stokes, 1997). One result of this discourse is that those who advocate a 'what works' approach are seen as 'pragmatists' (Furlong and Oancea, 2006), while 'theorists' are positioned in opposition to this practical stance as those who pontificate about ideas but do not have much to say about what a teacher should do on Monday morning. The authors in this book challenge this dichotomy, and show how an explicit theoretical stance can be combined with a practice-based, practice-informed and practice-informing approach to educational research. As they apply contextually sensitive theories to account for the local and situated enactments of practice, from the micro level of the classroom to the macro level of national policies, they also reveal the many impracticalities of several assumptions of the 'what works' agenda. Together, the arguments developed by the authors have implications not only for educational practice but also for the reframing of educational research and our expectations for social science.

The diversity of perspectives found across the chapters, afforded by the range of educational contexts that authors know and the positions they hold within these educational systems, along with their applications of different contextually sensitive theoretical lenses, indicate both the wide-reaching influence of the 'what works' agenda and the many ways it can be resisted. Theory is positioned as an important tool enabling them to challenge 'what works' assumptions and to redefine the ways in which research can be useful in policy and practice. However, theory is viewed as necessarily linked to practice, dialectically, so that they both inform and enhance one another. As such, the authors point out what theory can do for practice (and indirectly, policy), but also reveal the ways that practice can inform advances in theory, which can then in turn feed back into practice. 'Research use' is portrayed as a recursive cycle rather than a one-directional relationship of research informing practice and policy.

Our aim in developing this book, as editors, has been to provide a foundation for a dialogue about alternative ways of framing a research agenda which, while it shares the aim of developing greater synergies between research, policy and practice in education, still recognises the complexities of teaching, learning and educational contexts. What is distinctive about this book is its focus on the use of theory, filtered through the lens of practice. That is, the authors both *apply* theory to make sense of complex issues of education reform, and *develop* theoretical understandings of practices in education as a way of extrapolating what our research findings mean (or don't mean) for other apparently similar contexts and practice goals.

The book was developed out of a series of seminars held at universities across England in 2009, funded by the Economic and Social Research Council (ESRC). The seminars were structured to enable those engaged in education, research and theory to systematically and collaboratively examine the ways that theory could inform understandings of teaching and learning practices. Our objectives were:

- to better understand theoretical perspectives in terms of their relevance for questions about practice in education; and
- to better understand practice questions that could be addressed from various theoretical perspectives.

The series provided structure for these discussions by focusing on two theoretical perspectives at each session (e.g. activity theory, communities of practice theory, Cultural Historical Activity Theory (CHAT), Bernstein and Bourdieu) in relation to a level of the educational system (e.g. individual, classroom, school, district and national levels). These theories were chosen because they typically take 'learning environments' and systems as the unit of analysis, as opposed to individual learners and teachers. Activities and practices, from these perspectives, are thus understood to take place in social, cultural and/or historical contexts: educational practices are fundamentally socioculturally situated. Our starting assumption was that such an approach not only foregrounds those aspects of education that are most amenable to redesign by education practitioners, managers and policy makers (e.g. by reconfiguring classroom, institutional or policy environments), but also provides a way of capturing and understanding the complexity of education contexts, without which change can only be superficial.

Seminar participants were asked to put these theories to the test, using them to address macro-level policy concerns about equity and access, as well as micro-level questions regarding pedagogy and curriculum. This book brings the various issues discussed to a wider audience, with a focus on re-presenting the perspectives that we, as editors, thought could contribute to a dialogue about how research can play a role in improving teaching, learning and equity in education. While some chapters are versions of papers presented at the seminars, others have been written specifically for this book in order to engage directly with the problematic assumptions of a 'what works' research agenda and to propose alternative directions for research. The book is divided into four parts, or 'dialogues', each representing at least two 'voices' or perspectives on the issue and hence following a particular line of argument with regard to 'what works'. Together the chapters initiate a much-needed dialogue around the purpose of and expectations for educational research.

The 'what works' agenda

In this book, the 'what works' agenda refers to a movement still strong in the US and UK, following years of distinct but interlinked histories of government involvement in educational research. Such involvement is not surprising given that the topic we research – education – is widely considered a public good. What is of concern, however, are the ways in which the links between research, policy and practice have been framed in discourses on education. Central to this framing in the US have been the numerous government reports and policies (National Research Council, 1999; U.S. Department of Education, 2002; U.S. House of Representatives, 2000) which call for the use of quality research in education, often characterised through the call for 'evidence-based practice'. First promoted in medicine and proliferated through the Cochrane Collaboration, the term 'evidence-based' was applied to social scientific research by the Campbell Collaboration (Bridges, Smeyers and Smith, 2009). In the UK, the importance of 'evidence-based practice' has been amplified by the Hillage report, commissioned by the Department of Education (Hillage, Pearson, Anderson and Tamkin, 1998), and a critique of educational research in a report (Tooley and Darby, 1998) commissioned by OFSTED, the UK's educational quality assurance agency.

We use the term 'what works' because we see this as the current dominant construct used to frame a research agenda for those concerned with education. We add our contribution to the heated debates that have ensued since the publication of these US and UK government sponsored reports (e.g. Atkinson, 2000; Biesta, 2007; Erickson and Gutierrez, 2002; Feuer, Towne and Shavelson, 2002; Hammersley, 1997, 2000, 2003; Oancea, 2005).

Resisting 'what works': shifting the debate to a dialogue

A fundamental critique of the 'what works' agenda relates to beliefs and expectations for research, and we turn here to a brief consideration of these issues. First, we note that biases are inherent in the nature of social research when the topics of study are complex and changing (Scott and Shore, 1979). Such biases can be revealed, for example, through researchers' choices of the object of study and their research questions. The questions that drive research in the first place are founded on ontological and epistemological beliefs about the world and ways of knowing it, which are privileged according to the researchers' philosophies, as Anna Sfard notes in her chapter. The bias of the researcher leaves no guarantee that an important variable will not be left out of a given study. Thus, a single study cannot tell 'The Truth' about what works or doesn't work in education. Moreover, given the various actors and stakeholders involved in education, who are all positioned in different ways to carry out different goals and with different practice histories, there will always be more than one way to 'see' a problem and its solution, as Tim Deignan's chapter demonstrates. In summary, subjectivity as well as politics are inherent aspects of education, as Julian Williams and Julie Ryan note in the final chapter of the book.

A 'what works' agenda that fails to recognise these aspects of research gives the false impression that educational research can be a substitute for democratic, moral debate about important education decisions that affect learners at all levels, ages and disciplines (Hammersley, 2003). These unfounded assumptions of objectivity, together with a tendency to conflate science and methods that make 'scientific research' a code word for randomised experiments (Berliner, 2002), unnecessarily limit the possibilities of what research can tell us about teaching and learning and what research is worth doing. Moreover, only in taking account of external factors, such as the politics of education (Apple, 1996), through our theories and methods, will we take notice of the ways in which educational policies 'work' to produce unintended consequences, an issue demonstrated by both Sue Webb and Geoff Wake, or begin to understand why particular interventions don't 'work' in accordance with a blueprint, as Yvonne Barnes, Fiona Cockerham, Una Hanley and Yvette Solomon argue.

The authors in this book show us that research can offer theoretically informed interpretations of practice that bring critical issues to the attention of decision makers and provide principles for curricular design, as exemplified in Erica McAteer, Mary Thorpe and Cormac Lawler's chapter. The complexity and situated aspects of curriculum design, teaching and learning that are insightfully portrayed through all the chapters point to a particularly problematic assumption of the 'what works' agenda – the false expectations of research providing confirmed results on what works in educational practice. This expectation carries with it the 'transfer' metaphor which expects research to be 'translated' into 'evidence-based practice'. An alternative expectation, argued by Valerie Farnsworth in her chapter, is that theorising in the context of empirical research enables the extraction of principles and perspectives on a specific phenomenon which can then be 'transferred' to other contexts.

As the chapters progress through the book, we develop an alternative conceptualisation for research that positions it more directly in relation to practice. The case for theoretically informed, practice-based research is made from a variety of angles and in relation to various aspects of a researcher's practice. For example, Etienne Wenger-Trayner reflects on the job of a theorist who makes decisions about the application of theory in relation to practice. In their chapters, Seth Chaiklin and Anna Sfard consider the importance of educational practice and epistemology, respectively, in relation to achieving one's research agenda. Policy makers are not left out of the dialogue, as Tim Deignan shows how research can be a channel through which the multiplicity of voices – such as those of practitioners and students – are identified and can be accounted for in policy decision making.

Many of the chapters in this book illustrate that the 'what works' agenda tends to restrict research to addressing certain kinds of questions – questions about what pedagogy or innovation 'works best', following the line of questioning in medicine 'what is the best treatment for condition x?', as Emma Pearson, Janine Carroll and Tim Dornan's chapter reminds us. But this approach excludes examinations of a historical, philosophical, sociological, political and economic nature. The 'what works' focus may also exclude or divert attention from questions about *how* things work as well as how things *do not* work (and hence maybe should be reformed), or how things work for some people and in some contexts, but not for all or in all contexts. The exclusions constructed by this discourse are highlighted in this book by asking: 'what kinds of questions about education are researchers driven to ask if they take a practitioner perspective and/or a particular sociocultural theoretical perspective?'

This approach engages with the alternative 'enlightenment' model of research use (Hammersley, 1997; Lindbloom and Cohen, 1979; Weiss, 1995) whereby research does not tell teachers what to do, but instead provides resources that practitioners can use to make sense of their situations and behaviours. Thus, a better expectation for research is that it 'calls attention to the existing conflicting positions, sometimes elaborates them, and sometimes generates new issues altogether' (Cohen and Garet, 1983, p. 315). In this model, research is positioned as one voice in 'the debate about social problems and their solutions' (Cohen and Garet, 1983, p. 315). As Harry Daniels' chapter illustrates, one important contribution that research can make to such debates is the development of a common language and concepts for discussion.

The value of contextually sensitive theories becomes particularly salient to discussions of research use where the assumption is that their application will improve educational practice. To initiate sustainable and deep change means taking account of the dynamic relationships between individual agents, school structure, school culture and the larger structures and cultures of which they are a part (Datnow, Hubbard and Mehan, 2002). Given the sense-making processes involved in a teacher's implementation of a policy or practice (Spillane, Reiser and Reiner, 2002), it follows that a more effective approach to educational reform is one that allows for 'mutual adaptation, or the adaptation of a project and institutional setting to each other' (McLaughlin, 1991). The implication is that research needs to be contextualised and systemic in order to identify the different layers at which resources might be relevant to promoting change, and how (Talbert and McLaughlin, 1993). Action-oriented research projects, such as those described by Mel Ainscow and Harry Daniels in their chapters, demonstrate the ways theory and practice can be integrally connected in ways that reform practice and transform institutional contexts. The 'research path' idea proposed by Seth Chaiklin and the suggestion made by Julian Williams and Julie Ryan that we design 'hybrid activities' also provide ways we might improve the relationship between research and practice. However, as James Avis points out, even a theory such as CHAT, which can support radical changes where such change is needed, may simultaneously downplay wider structural relations of capital and production.

The underlining argument presented in the book is that research can be both practice based and theoretically sophisticated, and that such research holds greatest potential for being used in educational practice. Together, the chapters build a reconceptualisation of how we do research, how we envision evidence-based practice 'working' and how we find value in educational research. The book ultimately calls on the social science research community to continue the dialogue that has been initiated here.

Dialogue I

Using context-sensitive theories to rethink the 'what works' research agenda

We have chosen to begin the dialogue by unpacking some of the problematic assumptions raised by a 'what works' approach to educational policy, practice and research. The authors here use theory to reveal the political and social complexities of education as they draw on specific accounts of interventions in practice. Hence, they engage with the dual purposes of the book – to resist 'what works' and to develop a new research agenda.

A primary 'what works' assumption, levied most often in relation to political needs, is that 'best practice' is readily identifiable in a way that is then transferrable to new contexts for use by practitioners more widely. The authors in this first dialogue engage head on with this assumption in a variety of ways: by presenting novel ways of thinking about practice in context; by foregrounding the perspectives and voices of students and practitioners at the receiving end of policies informed by 'what works' initiatives; by applying theory to explore histories of inequity; by recognising the forms and functions of contradictions within and between systems; and by engaging with the very complexity of practice.

Thus Sue Webb begins the dialogue with a demonstration that the lifelong learning agenda is both political and personal, and that policy works in different ways for different people located in different parts of the education and qualification markets. She shows how unintended consequences can arise when individuals who locate themselves firmly within the policy construct of 'responsible learner' are nevertheless disenfranchised in terms of their relationship to social structures and engagement with powerful discourses. Her demonstration of the fractures in the assumption that 'what works' can be effectively, or equitably, implemented in practice are echoed in Geoff Wake's chapter. Again focusing on the theme of widening participation, this time in terms of access to post-compulsory mathematics qualifications, he shows how policy and practice become distorted in the context of performativity and marketisation. Like Sue, he also explores the teaching and learning context from the perspectives of multiple players, taking us further into the contradictions that can result in this context. He shows how the application of theory can make sense of the multiple voices within education, and how expectations at both individual and institutional level are able to influence the implementation of a curriculum intervention designed to increase participation but that ultimately fails.

The theme of performativity and accountability is taken up in the next chapter by Yvonne Barnes, Fiona Cockerham, Una Hanley and Yvette Solomon. They shift the focus to teacher education programmes designed to change practice, again in mathematics teaching, with the aim of calling into question what it means for these programmes and others like them to 'work'. Recognising the role of power relationships within education and associated tensions that are experienced at a personal level, they aim to challenge the assumption that success in such programmes is a matter of 'progress' towards an 'ideal' state of affairs. For them, understanding 'what works' must include an understanding of the learner's developing professional agency.

Thus, the first three chapters in this dialogue present the case for the untenability of 'what works' approaches, given the challenge of *implementing* generic/ generalised 'best practices' as a strategy for improving educational practice in what is undeniably a very diverse and highly politicised context. Practices in education are complex, and shaped by the local policy and institutional contexts in which they are embedded. In the next chapter, Emma Pearson, Janine Carroll and Tim Dornan pick up on the theme of the complex relationship between learner and context where the goal, from the learner's perspective, is to become a doctor. They explain how medicine itself championed the 'what works' agenda within the evidence-based medicine movement, influencing contemporary, competency-based medical education. Proposing a different focus on practice, away from competency towards a view of medical training as a process of identity formation, they argue for a radical (re)view of 'what works' which makes identity formation an explicit educational process in medicine. In the final chapter of this dialogue Erica McAteer, Mary Thorpe and Cormac Lawler also illustrate the complexity of practice, this time in online learning. Drawing on case studies involving learners in very different contexts, they return us to the issue of 'participation', noting that research advances our educational knowledge and practice only if it continues to study, *in situ*, how people participate (or do not participate) and why.

These five accounts of linking research to practice come together in this first dialogue to show how research can identify what is *not* working and how theory can be used to explain *how* things *are* working, often in ways not initially expected or intended. They also illustrate how practice-based theorisations can be useful in conceptualising change and reform in educational practice, curriculum and policy. As later chapters in this book will show, the value of research lies in the questions it can raise and the new practice storylines that it engenders, rather than in the production of recipes for duplicating and implementing 'best practices'.

Chapter 1

Narratives of learning and the unintended consequences of lifelong learning policy

Sue Webb

This chapter takes a case study approach to examine the relationship between narratives of learning, institutions and policy, and individual identities and decisions to engage in lifelong learning. By means of a comparison of two individuals' narratives of their recent (re-)engagement with formal education, I discuss the way that lifelong learning policy constructs its policy object, the individual learner, to be a 'responsible learner'. Both individuals appear to have taken responsibility for increasing their skill levels and for making themselves more employable. Yet, as the chapter will show, their accounts of learning and its place in their lives are very different. Building on Bourdieu's (2002, 2003) concepts of practice and habitus, I will argue that these learners' accounts need to be understood as socially organised narratives. Thus, this empirical exploration of the 'responsible learner' reveals that policy works in different ways for different people located in different parts of the education and learning markets. Unintended consequences reveal the fractures in the assumption that 'what works' can be effectively or, more importantly, equitably, implemented in practice.

The starting point for this research[1] was the question: how can we adequately capture the formation of adult learner identities in a context of rapid social, cultural and economic change? The question concerns the relationship between individual agency and identity and the troubling effects of policies. It also involves exploring how the practices of particular institutions become structuring structures (Bourdieu, 2002, 2003) that might organise social life and personal narratives differently for different individuals. Two learning sites were selected to examine this research question: one involved learners on a part-time modern foreign languages course in a university adult education department, and the other involved learners on a full and part-time vocational social care and health course in a Further Education (FE) college.[2] The initial data gathering focused on adult learners' decision-making processes in terms of their understanding of how they became involved in formal learning and the meaning of this in their lives now and in the future. We used a recursive methodological approach involving repeated visiting to the field site to present and discuss our initial analytical accounts, extrapolated from interviews with learners, so that we could rework the analysis of their narratives to acknowledge the effects of other accounts held by people at different levels and positions in the nexus of practices of educational organisations.

The research was situated in a former industrial city in northern England which has witnessed major economic restructuring involving the demise of much of its heavy industry and its replacement by service industries, although some highly specialist industrial production continues. Changes in the city over the past 15 years have resulted in structural inequalities that the policies under discussion were designed to address, and in selecting learners we sought to identify people who would appear to exemplify the object of these policies. The two case studies discussed here include a 40-year-old woman returning to learning to improve her labour market position, and a young man engaged in both a leisure learning course and an employer-sponsored postgraduate degree, while working in an international high-tech engineering industry.

The policy construct of the 'responsible learner'

Lifelong learning policy aims to enable the emergence of a new social agent – the 'responsible learner'. What does this character, developed within the policy discourse, look like in reality? Arguably, the 'responsible learner' has emerged out of a series of related assumptions underlying the reform of post-compulsory education and training, and higher education. Much of the rationale for policy reform under the New Labour government in Britain between 1997 and 2009 was presented as justified by the need to modernise major social institutions, and the discourse of policy and politics was dominated by a language of modernisation (Fairclough, 2000). Previous structures of social provision and their content were determined inadequate for dealing with the requirements of a modern society in the global age, including the need for new dispositions to learning. British education policy during this period can also be understood as forming a taken for granted 'commonsense' view of the world – the world as global (Department for Education and Employment, 2001; Department of Trade and Industry, 1998).Within this new commonsense view, education became more closely tied to economic outcomes; it became a commodity to be exchanged for economic capital in labour markets, as well as contributing to Britain's economic competitiveness. The economisation of education is spelt out explicitly in almost every policy paper produced by the Department for Education and Skills between 1997 and 2009. For instance the *Skills* White Paper made it clear that the development and acquisition of skills 'are central to achieving our national goals of prosperity and fairness' (Department for Education and Skills, 2005, p. 5), while the reform of the FE sector during this period was premised upon the need to be 'focused on the employability and progression of learners' and 'to delivering the skills and qualifications which individuals, employers and the economy need' (Department for Education and Skills, 2006, p. 20). In universities, 'high level skills – the skills associated with higher education – were seen as the drivers that add value for everyone (Department for Industry, Universities and Skills, 2008).

These policy texts illustrate a neoliberalist approach that requires the construction of new forms of agency (Rose, 1999; Rose and Miller, 1992). Rose suggests that neoliberal policies seek to hollow out the state and its responsibility for social welfare by shifting social responsibility onto individuals, so that a 'responsible', more entrepreneurial, individual needs to be constructed (see also Dean, 1999; Du Gay, 2000). This process of 'responsibilisation' over the past 15 years has prompted some to argue that hegemonic policy formations in the field of post-compulsory education and training specifically constituted new forms of domination and governmentality within capitalist society in which learners are expected to work upon themselves to become more amenable to demands of mobile capital (Avis, 2000; Crowther, 2004; Martin, 2003).

While the policy texts discussed above suggest that the 'responsible learner' exists at a discursive level, it is a matter for empirical investigation to discern how it is lived out in practice. In particular, for individuals who appear to be engaging in reflexive practices – adults who 'choose' to engage with formal learning – what is it that they do and what is it about their practices and understandings of these that make them a 'responsible learner'? Rather than simply accepting the notion of the economically rational agent seeking to maximise both their capacities and interests, the research discussed here sought to enquire into the complex ways in which individuals' personal, family and structural histories and their understandings of these articulate with a global economic restructuring of capitalism, mediated through policy discourse and implementation. In sum, it is an interest in how things work in order to critically consider what works for whom and under what circumstances.

Narratives of responsible learners

Viewing the effects of policy on individuals through narrative is a feature of much contemporary social science writing on identity. Jenkins (2004) reminds us that identity is not something that just *is* – identity is always provisional and in the making and always relational. Thus I have been drawn to Bourdieu's (2003) *Practical Reason* as a way of thinking about how to locate learners' identities within relational and ecological accounts of social practice. Their identity work and narrative accounts of these processes and perspectives are thus located within the social spaces and organisations within which practices are performed and given meaning.

A narrative-based methodology is an appropriate way to explore learners' identities because it gives primacy to the ontological work people do in storying their lives to provide coherence to their accounts (Erben, 1998; Ochberg, 1994; Somers, 1994; Stronach and MacLure, 1997). Furthermore, as Somers argues, the focus on the ontological dimension of narrative enables us to engage with the 'temporal, relational and cultural, as well as institutional, material and macro-structural' (Somers, 1994, p. 607). By locating narratives in the relational and historical context of their production, life stories can be understood as life histories that locate identities in networks of interventions that shift over time and space (Goodson and Sikes, 2001). Narratives involve emplotment that draws on different genres, providing a glimpse into the relational intersections of institutions, public narratives and individuals.

In choosing to compare two cases taken from contrasting relational and institutional settings exposed to the same policy discourse, I focus on the different contingencies that arise in their narratives of meaning in order to explore how policy has constructed differently the learning opportunities to become a 'responsible learner'.

Narratives of responsibility

'Jenny' was a 40-year-old white mother of four children, recently separated from her husband. When we first met her she was enrolled on a part-time vocational GCSE (Level 2) Health and Social Care course at an FE college. Although at the time Jenny was in receipt of welfare benefits, she had previously worked in the care sector looking after older people, and her family background involved self-employment in the catering and hospitality sector. At the time of our first interview, Jenny had just completed the first of three semesters, and was close enough to her entry onto the course to reflect back on her motivations, and far enough through to project forward into a possible future.

'Pierre' was a 24-year-old white man from southern France living and working in England, who we met through his enrolment on a university part-time degree programme in Hispanic Studies. At the time of interview he was employed full time as a production manager at an engineering company, and was sponsored by his employer to undertake a part-time master's programme in Engineering Management at another university in the city. He had just completed the first semester of this postgraduate degree and was halfway through his part-time undergraduate study. This juxtaposition of voluntary formal learning to increase high skills and knowledge, alongside employer-sponsored formal learning and employment, provided contrasting relational and institutional settings that the interview sought to explore.

Underlying identity as a 'carer'

Jenny's story appears to be a notably reflexive and rational account of the opportunity to realise a 'caring' identity. 'Caring' appeared as a central feature of her narrative, while in part this is imposed by the fact that she was being interviewed about her participation in a 'caring' course. We argue that 'caring' provided Jenny with symbolic resources with which to construct a particular gendered identity, in part echoing the women in Beverley Skegg's study of 'respectability' (Skeggs, 1997). However, this is not to suggest that an unconscious habitus was driving her towards particular options. Instead, Jenny presents herself as a knowledgeable game player in the field of lifelong learning, making strategic choices, negotiating obstacles and taking up opportunities. We can detect in the narrative five distinct 'caring' periods through which Jenny 'stories' her life.

The first period covers her post-school transition into employment. Jenny informed us that when leaving school she had wanted to work with children, though she was encouraged by her parents to go into the family occupation of catering. Yet, Jenny claims, she held on to the idea of working with children, marriage and pregnancy as offering a way out of catering. The shift to the second period, where 'caring' could predominate, began when she became a stay-at-home mother. While this was partly pragmatic, since looking after four young children was incompatible with the work patterns of catering, providing good caring was central to this part of her story. For Jenny, to be a 'good' mother meant being a full-time mother, and this moral and normative aspect would reappear later in her account of her role as a care worker.

Being good at caring was reinforced in the third period by her experience of looking after her dying aunt who, Jenny recounted, commented that she had a natural aptitude for it. Caring for her aunt appeared to be directly connected to taking up working with the elderly in community care settings. In retrospect, this fourth period of 'caring' appears to have set down roots that would flourish later in her decision to participate in formal adult learning. Jenny's account of working for private sector care companies was anchored around the moral struggles she found herself engaged in at work, and she disagreed with the way many people were treated in the community care settings by other staff and by the rules of engagement set by the management. She felt strongly that people should be treated with dignity, as she had done with her aunt. She was unhappy with the level of training provided and said that she found herself in situations she knew intuitively were wrong, but did not have the relevant skills or knowledge to question and be taken seriously by those in more powerful positions. These experiences simultaneously reinforced her sense that a more appropriate form of caring was required, and of herself as a good 'carer'. Without the authority of higher qualifications in this field, she would not gain employment at a level where she could realise this 'caring' role, and so the narrative is set up as the rationale to the fifth period, her return to education.

The part-time nature of the health and social care course fitted around Jenny's childcare commitments and her perception that she did not have the capacity to engage with the academic content and workload of a full-time course. Jenny views the course as a 'life-changing' experience, and she has confirmed her sense as a 'carer', and more specifically as somebody who can make a difference to children in care. Her narrative also describes the course as raising of her self-confidence in her academic abilities, and she talks about looking forward to continued study. Indeed, she took on a counselling course, which she sees as enhancing her 'caring' identity and providing important vocational skills.

Jenny's narrative clearly 'stories' her life, placing events in a particular chronological order so that she conveys a life that is temporally coherent and meaningful. Importantly, there are a number of key motifs of 'caring' within the narrative that organise it as a whole, and key points where Jenny has been able to take responsibility for realising her caring identity through, for example, standing up to her employer and taking the responsibility to become more qualified.

Underlying identity as a 'communicative cosmopolitan'

Pierre's narrative contains a number of themes such as 'communication', 'learning by doing' and 'travelling and movement' which were repeated in an underlying thread running through his accounts of his early family life, his education, his employment and his future plans, and expressed as a desire to move between different places and cultures and be able to use languages to communicate with people like a native. Brought up in a middle-class professional family in southern France, the family lived in a rural area, but commuted daily for employment and the children's schooling to the nearby city. Pierre identified the importance of family holidays abroad when he was a child and of the memory of his father communicating easily in other languages. His father spoke four languages and, as a young boy, Pierre grew up wanting to learn languages too. The narrative described a number of phases where Pierre suggested a 'cosmopolitan' identity, which he sought to realise through travel and fluency in languages. He often contrasted the pleasure he gained through this wanderlust to explore and be comfortable in different contexts with the staidness and stability of French society.

Schooling and tertiary education in France were described by Pierre as fairly rigid with set pathways and types of students. Rather than follow a normal biography (to borrow a metaphor from Ball, Davies, David and Reay, 2002) from the school Baccalauréat through the university bachelor's programme, he opted for a riskier path. He viewed himself as someone who liked technical things and understanding how they worked. Therefore, after gaining his Baccalauréat, he completed a two-year university technology diploma and then decided he would like to work rather than continue studying. He did not reject learning, however, regarding employment as an opportunity to learn by doing, and also develop his language skills. He sought out his first job outside France, in England, working for a small French-owned engineering company just outside London. At first this seemed to be the perfect position, but small town life in England where attitudes to strangers from abroad were far from cosmopolitan, and working in a job that did not stretch his knowledge and skills, meant that he soon became bored. After 18 months he returned to France and unemployment.

Nevertheless, the experience did not dampen Pierre's desire to travel as a 'communicative cosmopolitan'. France was presented as a temporary location, and Pierre described French life for people from his family background as too staid: he enjoyed the more precarious environment in England, and the riskier approach to life he noticed many younger people adopted. Specifically, he found the approach to consumption, debt and the use of credit cards extraordinarily liberating. He reflected on the differential effects on adult participation of the largely publicly funded French university system, and the shift in responsibility for funding higher education in the English system away from the state to other supposed beneficiaries, such as employers and individuals. Although French students do not pay large fees compared to English students, he perceived the provision in France as primarily for young people, whereas he felt there were more opportunities to be an adult student in England. Participation in England may involve large debts, but adults who wish to invest in themselves could participate easily.

We first encountered Pierre after he had returned to England for a second time, motivated to improve his English. His previous employer was starting up a new operation in the northern city where this research was conducted, and Pierre commented that the driving forces in accepting the position were the work and learning opportunities the company provided and the friendliness of the people. As a production manager in this specialist engineering company producing materials for the oil industry, Pierre seems to have found a base from which to develop his 'communicative cosmopolitan' identity, taking on new responsibilities for both production and liaison with customers and suppliers, not only in England, but in several other countries. Pierre was studying a Master's in Engineering Management, part time, sponsored by his employer. His cosmopolitan theme came through in his reflections on the diversity of the students in this course: he was surprised and pleased to find that about a quarter of the full-time students are international students from a wide range of countries and age ranges. Once again he drew positive contrasts from this experience in which adults take up learning and students cross borders to study, with his experience of learning in France.

Pierre's personal life has also helped enable him to realise his communicative cosmopolitan identity. He now has a Spanish girlfriend and he is studying part time in the evenings and weekends for a Hispanic Studies degree in another local university. In particular, he contrasted his approach to learning and communicating through language to what he called the 'British on holidays where there is no engagement with local culture'. He regards learning this language as creating the possibilities of a future life in Spain or Spanish speaking countries.

Revisiting and reworking narratives of responsibility

Narratives by themselves are not enough, however, and there is a need to re-examine them in order to identify the links with wider societal discourses and social structures and so explore the workings of policy. Consequently, further data were collected from the learners and the staff at the institutions where they studied to explore the effects of the wider social field. We carried out further interviews with Jenny's course tutor and course director, to understand how the college provision related to the lifelong learning policy thrust, and with the course tutor and the university departmental manager of Pierre's voluntary undergraduate programme, to understand how this programme was positioned in relation to the 'high skills' policy agenda.

Jenny's struggles with the 'practical logic' of her position

Jenny's initial narrative appeared to revolve around a struggle between her core 'caring' identity and the constraints on its realisation. Her 'reflexive' narrative showed how she recognised the limitations of lifelong learning policy that shifted responsibility for learning onto learners. The narrative conveys a sense of Jenny's life as 'a life constrained', primarily by family obligations, by parental desire for her to go into the 'family business' of catering, by being a 'stay-at-home mum'; and by feeling too old to be a 'responsible learner' who returns to education (i.e. carrying the financial burden of studying at university level to be a social worker). These constraints can be understood in terms of the relation between Jenny's core 'caring' identity and the resources (cultural, social, symbolic and economic) available to her in realising this identity. The initial interview with Jenny only provides us with some intimations of this, which further discussion with Jenny illuminated.

Locating her narrative in the relational and historical context of its production means acknowledging Jenny as a gendered subject. She imagines a particular gendered role for herself: caring as an extension of her 'natural' aptitudes, 'caring' as a symbolic resource available to her as a woman in a gender division of labour. Yet even though she is a mother, and practised caring every day, she almost always imagined this caring identity in terms of paid employment. There is a sense that as part of Jenny's 'practical logic' she assumes that her symbolic and cultural (education/training) capital should be exchanged for economic capital (paid employment). The courses that Jenny has enrolled on become investments in the 'self' as she seemed to embody a veritable 'pure' form of neoliberal responsibility.

Jenny's personal and familial habitus

These investments in the 'self' need explaining since they also provide a way of seeing Jenny's struggle to position herself in particular fields of power. Although she rejected the family business of catering, her attempt to locate herself in a similar position within the caring labour market (e.g. as a care home manager) can be seen as homologous to that of running your own business. Therefore, one reading of Jenny's actions is that participation in formal education could be part of a project of social reproduction and not a break with the family trajectory. Yet, in another way, her moral commitment to particular forms of caring and wanting to make a difference to the lives of the 'cared-for' suggests a break with the family trajectory. She chose to gain qualifications, not merely to fulfil the policy rhetoric of increasing her human capital in order to get a better paid job, but in order to reposition herself within the caring business in more professional and autonomous roles.

Intimation of Pierre's social capital and continuing of familial habitus

For Pierre, personal and family habitus is also presented as a struggle around realising his core identity as a 'cosmopolitan', in contrast to the staidness of French provincial, middle-class life. Yet his familial habitus buffered his choice of a more risky technical pathway from school to higher education, so that he was still able to develop the symbolic and cultural capital needed to position himself well to actively choose at what point he would move out of full-time education and where he would work. While he may not have followed the professional path of his parents, and had rejected for the present the idea of a house for life, he drew on the resources and understandings he had gained from his family in order to live a life with lifestyle choices. These resources included learning from seeing how his father's fluency with languages facilitated a movement across countries and cultures. Thus, although very different from that of his parents, Pierre's life exhibited similarities in valuing communication through languages and in building social networks across cultures and countries. Clearly, his aptitude for language learning and immersion in diverse cultures were investments in his 'communicative' self-identity that enabled him to add value to his existing symbolic and cultural capital and secure employment in England. As Brown, Lauder and Ashton (2011) would argue, this investment in the 'self' gives people positional advantages in the global competition for professional level employment.

A dialogue with policy

The danger with a narrative exploration of policy effects is that an over-reliance on the first-person narrative can produce descriptions and analyses that fail to indicate the way practices might be saturated with social structure. In addition, the danger in the narratives presented here is that they privilege the emblematic figure of the individual who seeks to maximise their potential through investment in education. In this regard they are very likely to produce 'hegemonic tales' that carry the dominant neoliberal ideologies without subjecting them to critical enquiry (Ewick and Silbey, 1995). In other words, by using the narrative method to ask people about their experiences of lifelong learning as adults, the research may actively encourage accounts that illustrate the existence of the policy construct, the 'responsible learner', because they ask people to take narrative responsibility for accounting for learning they have taken up.

However, these two cases provide very different accounts of being 'responsible learners'. Responsibility as a construct is lived out in different fields of power. Critically, differences in the institutional contexts is important to understanding how it is possible for Jenny and Pierre to realise their different identities in particular forms. While both Jenny's and Pierre's practices may appear to mirror the policy construct of the 'responsible learner', that interpretation may disguise the power of social structural factors in constraining and determining their social practices as learners. Looking at their stories again, but this time refracted through the lenses of the interviews with the course tutors and course directors of the settings in which they were studying, and another regional educational broker, a more nuanced understanding emerged.

Different fields of practice and the education policy construct

In this section I will briefly consider two aspects of education policy as it presents itself within the narratives – choice mechanisms within a mixed economy of post-compulsory education and training, and higher education; and institutional position-taking within a field of practice.

For Jenny, enrolling on the part-time course at the FE college is part of the trajectory she is constructing. But we have to be careful in seeing Jenny as being wholly in control of her destiny. She was not an 'active chooser' in the education and training market (Ball *et al.*, 2000), relying on what has been called 'cold knowledge', the formal information provided by the college (Ball and Vincent, 1998). This orientation towards the choice process in education markets is characteristic of working-class and non-traditional participants who often cannot avail of inherited knowledge of how the system works, nor have access to social networks where trusted information about institutions can be gained. Consequently, Jenny's 'choices' are immediately constrained. These constraints are structural in nature; they are partly a product of the location of the FE college within particular circuits of post-16 provision: which students the college seeks to attract, the courses it offers and how it relates to other providers in the area. The second interview with Jenny raised further questions about the effectiveness of enrolling in the part-time course as a means of improving her labour market opportunities: while in the first interview, she echoes the policy rhetoric by presenting her re-entry to formal education as the means to improved employment opportunities, in the second interview, it emerged that it is tacit knowledge gained from previous employment in the care sector that proves more powerful. That is, Jenny's eventual move into employment seemed to rely on her previous working relationship with the employer. It is very unclear whether her success on the part-time course aided her re-entry to the labour market. Instead, it is the wider benefits of learning, the social aspects in terms of improved self-confidence and clarity of purpose that appear to have a transferable quality about them, not the qualification itself. Jenny's second interview narrative resonates strongly with an observation offered by the course tutor, who comments that this course is primarily designed for young early school leavers who are looking for vocational qualifications for progression into employment and that many of the adults on the course may well do better staying in employment and progressing through work-based learning opportunities. Further discussion with the course director elicited that education and training providers' local enactments of policy create different circuits of learning for different types of students. Jenny's second interview, in which she outlines the work-based learning opportunities provided by the private sector social care company she is now employed with, supports this observation. However, she appears unaware of (or at least undeterred by) the churning effect that she will experience, because the only qualification available through this work-based route is at the same level as that she has gained already at the college.

There is a certain tension between the idea of Jenny as the 'responsible learner' maximising her natural caring disposition through an investment in education and the strong sense of serendipity or chance conveyed in the second interview. The failure to achieve an improved employment position or further learning gains from her initial investment in education is not critiqued by Jenny. Instead, the social aspects of formal education, the improved self-confidence and learning how to 'play the game' of the care business, as Bourdieu might put it, are foregrounded in her narrative.

Pierre also discusses both the Master's in Engineering Management and part-time degree in Hispanic Studies as courses that are enabling him to further his life plans. But he was a more 'active chooser'. With knowledge and experience of university level study in France and knowledge of how different study levels fitted within a qualification's framework, Pierre could be said to have 'hot' knowledge in which to contextualise the information provided by educational institutions (Ball and Vincent, 1998). For Pierre, there is a strong sense that he is someone who prefers to combine learning with doing, and he values what he regards as the greater opportunities provided in England for learning alongside employment. His preference is evident in the many ways he contrasted life, learning and education in England and France. This comparative stance enabled him to construct his identity in terms of actively choosing between these different options.

Studying in higher education as an adult has enabled him to pursue his long-held ambitions and identity to learn to use languages to become a 'communicative cosmopolitan'. Investment in the 'self' is regarded as normal; it is part of his familial habitus. However, the bonus for Pierre of working and studying in England in the context of current lifelong learning policy and practices is that his employer is carrying the substantial financial cost of his master's level study and allowing him time off work to attend classes. In contrast, interviews with the course tutor and programme director at the other university, where he is taking a part-time language degree, revealed a policy context that enabled the institution to position this adult learning within the widening participation strategy of that institution; therefore, the fee levels for which Pierre was responsible were set below full cost rates. Consequently, for Pierre, the strategic decision to seek work in England in order to enhance his learning has resulted in many additional and unforeseen benefits. Unlike Jenny, in 'storying' his life to date, there is little or no tension between a narrative of himself as a 'responsible learner' carrying some of the costs of investing in himself, and the underlying realisation of his identity as a 'communicative cosmopolitan'. Rather, the narrative plot presented is one of planned strategic decisions and lucky breaks so that his life plan is being realised through the complementary combining of the resources he brings to different contexts and the opportunities afforded by the policy context in England.

In the city where Jenny and Pierre lived, worked and studied, the tertiary educational providers were connected through formal and informal networks or circuits to widen participation, although these were focused on different learning markets. Arguably, even though widening participation was a core function of the FE college, Jenny was more out of place studying there as an adult, because the majority of programmes were aimed at young adults' initial vocational education and training. In contrast, Pierre was studying his employer-sponsored master's programme at the 'new'[3] university, which engaged significantly in providing part-time opportunities and work-based learning for adults in employment. And in the dedicated adult education department of the research-led university where Pierre was pursuing his language degree, involvement in the circuit for widening participation was understood by the staff to be limited in scope, and, while important to departments such as theirs, was somewhat peripheral to the university's core function of recruiting academically highly qualified students for full-time study.

Increasingly, Jenny does not fit the type of student any of these providers see themselves recruiting. Rather, as her course tutor advised, she should seek employment and follow a work-based learning route, even though the only opportunities in the care sector would mean a repetition of the qualification level she had already achieved. Jenny re-engages with formal education in a context where government policy, using the mechanisms of funding and qualifications' frameworks, is constructing FE colleges as 'last chance saloons', of ensuring a baseline of minimum literacy and numeracy. So, what is the exchange value of Jenny's investment in the self? Is Jenny a 'responsible learner'?

In contrast, Pierre's biography as a higher education diploma graduate working as a production manager in a specialist knowledge-based industry more precisely fitted the policy target for skills investment to increase the prosperity of companies and of individuals. In taking up a course in engineering management and another in languages, this university level study exemplified the policy construct of 'responsible learning' for the high skills economy. Consequently, Pierre's study is likely to carry high exchange value if he continues to work in engineering. Additionally, by learning to be a speaker of three European languages (French, Spanish and English), he will be well positioned for employment in many countries across the world in a range of roles in high tech engineering and beyond. At the same time, his employer, an international company (French owned, with bases in England and suppliers and customers in other countries) is also likely to benefit from the investment in his engineering management degree, Pierre's own personal investment in his Hispanic Studies degree and his informal learning of English.

Comparing the narratives of Pierre and Jenny suggests they both provide accounts of being 'responsible learners' because they take up learning opportunities as adults in order to gain qualifications to enhance their employment opportunities and realise their underlying identities. However, the types of opportunities open to them and the benefits of their investments are somewhat different. For Jenny, the narrative involves a process of continual re-storying to sustain a coherent account of taking responsibility for trying to realise a caring identity in the face of experiences that do not always live up to their promise. Pierre's narrative is less troubled. These differences appear to be related to their different socio-economic positions and habitus, which have afforded different educational opportunities in their chosen fields for realising their investments for employment and how to live their lives. In other words, taking responsibility for one's learning in contexts that are already structured by differences and inequalities means that the benefits and promises of the lifelong learning policy do not necessarily follow for all individuals.

Conclusion

I began this chapter by asking what the policy construct, the 'responsible learner', looks like in practice. The comparison of these two critical cases has shown that individual narratives of responsibility produced in contexts of constraint, and where individual circumstances are very different, are more or less troubled in relation to the expectations of the hegemonic policy discourse. I have also argued that by explicating the relationship of habitus to fields of practice, research can demonstrate how individuals struggle differently and relationally to engage with the effects of policy. Their struggles do not take place in a social vacuum.

I have viewed narrative as a special form of reflexive practice whereby social agents attempt to construct coherent accounts of their lives, where the temporal sequencing of events gives meaning to their storying. While these narratives are personal stories, they rely upon storylines and discourses from within the public realm, and in particular hegemonic stories that connect individual accounts to the operation and circulation of power within the social structure. Therefore, the content, structure and performance of narratives are saturated with social structure. Narratives can provide us with access to how the everydayness of life – or what Bourdieu (2002, 2003) would call 'habitus' – is intimately connected to the dynamic structuring of society and the struggles for symbolic power to account for and guide practices. However, the basis of this understanding requires that narratives be subjected to a process that reveals what Bourdieu calls the 'constructs of the constructs'. By examining the construction of these narratives and connecting first-person narratives to other narratives (interviews, policy texts, statistical data), new reflective stories are produced that seek to better understand the complex relationship between social structure and action in personal lives.

The two cases discussed here reveal that researching empirically the policy modality of 'responsible learners' demonstrates the power of policy constructs to structure learners' narratives as examples of being 'responsible'. Indeed, even in finding that the concept of the 'responsible learner' is as diverse as the positions learners have occupied in the field of education, rather than undermining the construct of the 'responsible learner', this finding shows that the very malleability of the concept could be functional for a political class that is using this to maintain its symbolic power. Differences in notions of 'responsibility' enable the political class, through state policies and practices, to create structuring structures to 'control' diverse practices. Arguably, revealing the reflexive moments and points of serendipity in learners' narratives might be the point when the struggle over 'what works' in policy is most clearly visible to researchers, and perhaps to learners too. I conclude in the hope that if we can put theory to work in these ways, revealing that 'responsible learners' are as diverse as the different ecologies of practice they inhabit, we will reveal that one policy size does not fit all.

Notes

1 The research presented was carried out by the author, Sue Webb, with Dr Simon Warren, University of Sheffield. The ideas initially were developed in an earlier paper presented by both researchers to the ESRC seminar series 'Developing a "How Things Work" Research Agenda in Education', 2009.
2 In England, FE colleges provide qualifications and training post-compulsory education.
3 In the UK, 'new' universities are polytechnics and colleges granted university status after 1992. Broadly, they tend to receive less funding for research and are teaching led, with a greater emphasis on work-based and vocational education. They are less prestigious and have more local students.

Chapter 2

Using theory to understand policy distortions in the context of performativity and marketisation

Geoff Wake

> Doublethink: 'To know and not to know, to be conscious of complete truthfulness while telling carefully-constructed lies, to hold simultaneously two opinions which cancelled out, knowing them to be contradictory and believing in both of them ... To forget whatever it was necessary to forget, then to draw it back into memory again at the moment it was needed, and then promptly forget it again ...'
>
> (Orwell, 1949)

This chapter explores how an innovative programme in mathematics education, which was shown to motivate students through meaningful application of mathematics and hence support a policy aim to widen continuing participation in mathematics education, ultimately does not work and fails in implementation. Understanding why the programme is unsuccessful is unpacked through the lens of Cultural Historical Activity Theory (CHAT) together with Beach's (1999) construct of consequential transitions, as I consider the complexity of the situation from the perspectives of teacher and student. The data arose in the context of a research project[1] investigating participation in the study of advanced mathematics during which the research team increasingly grew aware of how colleges, as institutions, appear to establish expectations of both teachers and learners. These expectations can be all, and often subtly, pervasive, making an impact at multiple levels, from influencing who is recruited and how learning is talked about in classrooms, through to the choices students make in relation to their future progression.

The chapter describes how key actors in one college had to readjust their thinking as the policy intentions of increasing and sustaining participation in mathematics, through the 'Use of Mathematics' (UoM) programme, were squeezed out because of the overriding performativity agenda. Our research concluded that this particular programme has certain features that work in supporting widening participation, particularly for those seeking progression to study in Higher Education where mathematics is used as a tool. Ultimately, however, this college, as an institution, and its leaders, while continuing to speak of inclusion, readjusted their thinking and closed down the programme towards the

end of the research project's lifetime. Through my use of CHAT and consideration of consequential transitions I attempt to understand and illustrate why this
is the case. It is perhaps unfair to suggest that ultimately the key actors practise
Orwellian 'doublethink' as they grapple to rationalise their actions but I leave
the reader to decide. In my analysis I focus on the college[2] as the unit of analysis but also attempt to consider how system-wide tensions, or in CHAT terms,
contradictions, lead to conflict for individual participants, and the consequences
for them as individuals and eventually for the activity system as a whole. In the
account that follows, therefore, I explore the contradictions evident at the institutional level which are lived through the teacher and curriculum manager, Jon,
in terms of his personal and professional development, and a student, David,
in terms of his progression through education and subsequent course choices.
Before considering how theory might provide greater insight into why this particular instance of apparently workable policy did not work, I situate the policy
development in the wider context and tell the story of David and Jon to illustrate
the failure.

Background

Education in the UK, as elsewhere, appears to insiders to be in a constant state
of flux, with managers and teachers having to respond to an increasing number
of initiatives, affecting every aspect of the system at all levels. The important
role that mathematics education has in ensuring the supply of a better educated
population in science, mathematics, technology and engineering, has led to a
UK national agenda and initiatives (for example see Roberts, 2002; Sainsbury,
2007; Smith, 2004) that seek to widen participation in these subjects by students
post-16 when they have a free choice of what to study. One initiative that has
been slowly developing since the turn of the century is a new programme of study
in mathematics that foregrounds applications and use of mathematics with the
aim of supporting students in being better equipped to 'transfer' and use mathematics across subject boundaries. This new programme sits alongside the long
established General Certificate of Education (GCE) AS/A Level programme[3] in
mathematics that is more focused on pure mathematics and which has traditionally been the preparation for university study of mathematics itself as well as all
mathematically demanding subjects, particularly the sciences and engineering.
The new programme leads to a GCE AS UoM qualification after one year of
study. While it is possible to gain such an AS qualification at this halfway stage
in the traditional A Level mathematics (Trad) programme it is the expectation
that the vast majority of students on the Trad course will continue through to
the full A Level, while the UoM did not have an A Level option at the time of
the research.

Our case study classroom observations, and conversations and interviews with
managers, staff and students across colleges, soon alerted us to the all-pervasive
influence of performance measures based on students' examination outcomes.

While it is not surprising that concerns about students' grades have a high profile as they attempt in two years to prepare for university entrance, the fact that these measures were often apparent in classroom discourse and seemed to drive much of the teaching we observed, was noteworthy. It seems that the three interrelated policy technologies of the *market, managerialism* and *performativity* (Ball, 2003) make themselves very much visible and impact directly on teachers' and students' day-to-day classroom experiences. As the account here illustrates, the reform agenda itself, while appearing to deregulate by giving autonomy to the college, in fact leads to re-regulation (ibid., p. 217), as deviation from the norm and risk-taking (and here widening participation has ultimately to be viewed as 'risk-taking') is minimised in pursuit of successful outcome measures (Hayward *et al.*, 2006).

A year in college: into, through and out of mathematics

My story is told primarily through the experiences of one student, David, and a teacher, Jon, who is also Head of the college Mathematics Department over the year of the project. However, to set the scene, I turn to the principal of the college, which is located in an inner-city area of a post-industrial city. She is very proud of the very high league table position the college achieves annually, resulting in it being one of the top schools and colleges in the region in terms of the key performance measures. She is equally keen to emphasise that, unlike other schools and colleges, this high position is achieved while still being open to all: 'We have connections with a wide range of schools. We're a very inclusive college and we value that inclusivity'.

She sums up the institutional culture as 'a culture of achievement and expectation, very close monitoring, very, very close data analysis of how students perform, how staff [perform] really, as well, close scrutiny of data and very much a support culture and investment in students'. This is celebrated widely throughout the college: even as our research team arrived, the car park attendant welcomes us to 'the best college in [city]'.

Into this culture that somehow appears to marry together inclusion and high performance enters David who had always been in the top sets for mathematics, got good grades and enjoyed the subject. However, he felt that he could have been pushed more and ended up in mathematics 'only' achieving an A grade rather than A* in the high-stakes GCSE examinations that he took, aged 16, in the summer just prior to entering college (at the end of compulsory schooling). This grade placed David in the top 15 per cent of his year group in terms of achievement in mathematics and potentially well positioned to carry on to take an advanced course in mathematics at college.

During his AS year, the year of our research project, David had something of a roller-coaster experience in mathematics. This started a short time after his arrival at college: after only a few weeks he was 'moved down' to the UoM programme from the AS Trad course. He attributed his move to mathematics at college being very different and more difficult than at school: 'at [school] you could just blag a few good grades but college is a lot harder'. At this stage David was also studying physics, accountancy and psychology and planned to study radiotherapy at university (combining mathematics and physics) and had a back-up plan of studying accountancy.

At this college the UoM course was seen, almost universally, as being a 'move down', so David's use of the phrase was not surprising. The course was in effect used by the department as a 'safety net' catering for those students who did not appear, even at an early stage, to be coping with the Trad course. Jon's discourse in relation to such a move is very evocative: 'If they're not showing any commitment up here [speaking of Trad maths], then they're not going to show any commitment, because there's no coursework up here, if they have to go down there [speaking of UoM]'.

Jon recognises that ultimately this policy is not very helpful to the long-term sustainability of the UoM course in the prevailing climate of performativity, and indeed during the year of the research the college management decided to close the course down:

> So of course her [Sara the UoM class teacher's] results have looked bad, and in a way it's my fault, because, although I wouldn't say I've used it as exactly a dumping ground, it's like a last chance saloon for some of these people. But really I shouldn't have done that, I don't think, because unless they're [the Trad mathematics students] going to show some commitment, they're never going to do well down there. So, of course, the retention's not been good, the results have not been good, and finally the plug's been pulled on it. And, you know, in a way I feel really bad about that now.

The practice of 'moving down' those who were struggling on the Trad course also proved useful in ensuring the continuing success of the traditional course: those students not likely to cope who might otherwise fail in terms of achievement or retention were 'moved down' and therefore did not adversely affect the Trad mathematics performance data.

At the time of a second round of interviews, about halfway through the year, David talked about his positive experience of the UoM course and how his confidence was increasing, so much so that he planned, after successful completion of the AS, to get back onto the Trad course and complete the whole A level in one year. At this point his aspirations were to continue with physics and accountancy and after completing Trad mathematics to go to a high status university to study physics. His actions at this point, such as sitting on his own in UoM lessons to avoid distractions and his talk of family assistance, including financial help so he could give up his part-time job, all supported his talk of his determination.

However, by the time of a third interview, in the December of the next academic year, David's plans had radically changed: he now intended to revert to his original back-up plan of studying accountancy. The key event that had prompted this change of plan was his failure to achieve a grade A in the AS UoM certification at the end of the year of study. Even though he had been only one mark off, resulting in a grade B (putting him in the top 10 per cent of the population), David was afraid that he might not after all achieve a good grade after a further year of study towards the Trad A Level. In this interview his talk was about maximising his performance across subjects. When he had arrived at college to re-enrol for the A Level year his psychology teacher had advised him to stick with the subjects in which he had already got the best grades:

> I came to re-enrol, you have to re-enrol, I was tempted to do Further Maths,[4] re-enrol and do Further Maths, Maths, Accountancy, and like I came to the day thinking I'm going to do Further Maths and Maths and then I went to see my psychology teacher and my psychology teacher thought it was probably best if I stuck on with Psychology and just do Accounting because I got such a high grade in Accounting. And when I thought about it logically I thought it's probably going to be the same … I enjoy it just as much and I thought maybe I should just stick with something that I've got really good grades in already than put all my eggs in one basket and then fail.

He justified his decision with talk of maximising his potential earnings as an accountant, but there was also talk of regret that he had not stuck with traditional mathematics from the beginning, as with hindsight he felt that this had been the reason why he had not ended up pursuing a career in physics.

David was part of the final cohort to study the UoM course in this particular college. Despite the high grades attained by students such as David, performance measures were such that the course was not perceived to be measuring up: in its quest for continuing dominance in league tables the college withdrew the course from its provision. As the principal pointed out, although the course met its objectives of ensuring increased and continuing participation evidenced by high levels of retention, the relatively low grades of students on the course meant that it did not do well on the performance measures:

> The Use of Maths didn't do it for us. Our data will show you that very clearly. It didn't do it for the students either, because the retention was of a phenomenal, we've never hit a success rate like that in the history of the college and we stuck with it for a few years but the students were missing out, clearly.

In discussion about this Jon explained the two key measures of performance that proved pivotal in the eventual downfall of the UoM course at this particular college: examination results, or 'achievement', and 'retention'. These two measures are combined, 'multiplied together', to give a 'success rate'. These are not part of the performance measures that are reported externally, but are from another layer of the tools of managerial control that are linked to funding. There is a complex funding mechanism for courses run in the college sector which takes account not only of the eventual attainment of students but also makes a very broad attempt to take some account of who eventually makes it through to be counted. In many schools and colleges this leads to careful selection of who is allowed to set out to study mathematics (nationally over 80 per cent of schools and colleges will only allow students gaining a grade B or above at GCSE in mathematics to take A Level, whereas almost all other subjects will allow students who have a grade C at GCSE to study A Level). However, in the same interview in which the principal talks of withdrawing UoM she also continues the rhetoric of inclusion:

> We have not gone down the road of many other colleges and saying you've got to have two Bs, you've got to have two Bs to go on the four AS courses. You've got to have Maths to do Psychology. Because immediately you're selecting out those kids who we know come here and do well. So we have a huge range of, what we do is, we really do want to give every child a chance, but what we do very closely, is monitor how they're progressing, so we don't put them on a course where they're going to fail. We put them on a course where they're going to succeed.

It falls to Jon, as we have seen, to manage the contradictory inclusion and attainment agendas. As he recognises, in the case of mathematics, the UoM programme gave him room for manoeuvre, providing a 'down there' where he could move those not coping with the traditional A Level. His concern at the end of the year is that with the UoM programme withdrawn he will not be able to be inclusive while maintaining high levels of attainment. He tells us, 'If you like, you know, it's just moving the problem somewhere else in a way and I've told the management this.'

As the account here illustrates, individual and organisation (in this case the college) are in a close symbiotic relationship, although, as David found, the relationship is not always mutually advantageous. In a final interview when at university David told us:

> But if I went back and did one thing differently in the whole of college I would have stuck with maths ... I think that was the big, big influence on why I didn't end up doing, pursuing a career in physics, or engineering, or anything.

Our research found many students like David who come to see the learning of mathematics as 'useful' not in terms of their current and/or potential future study but rather in terms of certification/qualification. In other words, mathematics might be considered as having two different values – use value and exchange value (Williams, 2012) – with many students electing to study it for the latter rather than the former. As we have seen, the marketisation of education in the college sector can lead to negative experiences for both students and teachers. In response, doublethink means individuals such as teachers and students can evoke a positive rationalisation, in that students are maximising their potential for progression, even if eventually this progression does not meet their initial aspirations.

Policy distortion: understanding why what works does not work

It appears that a curriculum intervention that does work in terms of its intentions of widening participation can ultimately fail, as in the case here, with not altogether satisfactory outcomes for students such as David. In coming to understand why this is the case I turn now to theoretical tools to unpack the complexity of the case.

Ball (2003) points to the key policy technologies of the market, managerialism and performativity, as being at the core of the apparent deregulation of education instigated in the 1990s under a Conservative government and continued with slight readjustments under New Labour for more than another decade. In the case described here we observed all three policy technologies in operation and impacting on the lives of all in important ways. Crucial to the changes instigated by the Conservative governments of the 1970s and 1980s was the apparent deregulation of the public sector by focusing change on, and in, institutions that were seen to be key in supporting change in social practice at macro and micro levels. In other words, institutions such as colleges were recognised as being the sites of social organisation where individuals and groups interact in meaningful ways with policy intentions. As such, policy was designed to impact upon these key sites, understood to be crucial in bringing about the social reforms desired by the government of the day. Consequently, schools and colleges were given opportunities to become more autonomous in their operation (Seddon, 1997), while at the same time other technologies were put in place that acted to ensure deregulation was in fact re-regulation and autonomous action was compliant with wider policy intentions. These technologies included a range of outcome and target measures that were made public in the interests of freedom of information and 'customer' (in this case students and their parents) choice. Deregulation was the flavour of the age across the public sector, justified by comparison with the private sector where outcome measures and managerialism in the form of technologies such as appraisal or peer review were held as virtuous beacons on the road to increased productivity.

The colleges central to our case study work were removed from local Education Authority control in 1993, becoming independent institutions in an educational marketplace in which students (and their parents) choose where to study. This led to internal upheaval in colleges as new ways of working were established (Burchill, 2001). The competition for students was, and has continued to be, intensified by the introduction of the Parents' Charter (Department for Education and Science, 1991) which required the publication of examination and national curriculum test results. This is required by each institution and, so that comparison is able to be made across schools and colleges, through the publication of ('league') tables of results. For the sake of ease of use, simplistic headlines and figures dominate. Pertinent here are the two key measures used to report the attainment of post-16 students: APS (average points score) and APE (average points per entry). These simply take the final grades attained by students in their post-16 examinations and convert them to a numerical score. As their names imply, the two performance measures give for the college the APS per student in the cohort and the APS per examination entry. Clearly these measures take no account of prior attainment and consequently give no measure of the 'value' added by a student's college experience. While, for such reasons, it is argued that the use of such data is invalid as a means of comparing institutions (Goldstein and Thomas, 1996), in general there is unquestioned acceptance of the validity of what is being measured.

My description of the case and contextual background detail points to a key problem with mathematics for all concerned. We see how an alternative programme can have potential value for both individual students in terms of providing an experience that allows progress towards fulfilling aspirations, and for institutions in meeting aims to be inclusive (at least in terms of engagement in mathematics). However, as the case study documents, the flame of each of these optimistic developments may ultimately be extinguished at the altar of performativity. David readjusts his aspirations while Jon struggles to come to terms with the teacher he has become rather than the teacher he wants to be.

Students, teachers and transitions: an activity theory perspective

It is in the complex activity system of the college that the three individuals of my account, teacher, student and to a lesser extent principal, go about their daily lives: this is clearly very important to each, with principal and teacher engaging with their chosen work and the student David learning mathematics and seeking to make 'progress' into the world of adulthood and independence.

To theorise and better understand these transitions I turn to Beach's (1999) construct of consequential transitions. He develops this construct in an attempt to understand 'transfer' in terms of 'how we experience continuity and transformation in becoming someone or something new' (p. 102). Beach goes to great lengths to distance this approach from the traditional transfer metaphor of moving something from one place and time to another, giving an historical overview and critique of how 'transfer', particularly of knowledge, has traditionally been conceptualised in this way. Beach proposes a sociocultural reconceptualisation developed from the premise that learners and organisations exist in recursive and mutually constitutive relations with one another across time. Thus, he develops the construct of 'consequential transition' which involves a developmental change in the relationship between an individual and one or more social activities, with the change having impetus from either the individual, the activity or both. The transition is considered as consequential when it is consciously reflected upon in such a way that the individual's sense of self and social positioning is changed. As Beach points out, Lave and Wenger's (1991) ethnographic accounts of individuals becoming members of communities of practice tell of just such consequential transitions.

In the case study I have described here, perhaps David's *lateral* transition is the most obvious and expected as he progresses from school, through the first year of college, on his way to Higher Education. However, David's transition, together with those of college principal and teacher as they react to the development of the institution as a social organisation, as it continues to respond to, and work within, the educational marketplace, is more complex than that. As Beach points out: 'In the broadest sense, all social activities are changing, even if only through collective efforts to maintain the constancy of activity through rituals, routines, revivals, and rules' (1999, p. 117).

Such transitions, which take place within the boundaries of a social activity, are classified by Beach as *encompassing transitions*, with these boundaries being considered as neither unchanging nor sealed. Rather, boundaries might be considered to be changeable and adaptable (perhaps particularly in response to the transformation itself). In an encompassing transition, individuals are considered as in a recursive relationship with the social activity, and it is this relationship that is in transition.

This is particularly clear in the case of Jon, teacher and Head of Department: the story I have presented here is one of his struggle to adapt to the realm of performativity, which while not new at the time of the research was, perhaps because of its very lack of novelty, beginning to exert increased pressure as the college attempted to maintain its position as high attaining. However, as all key actors struggle to make sense of how policy impacts on the system as a whole and themselves as individuals, they undergo encompassing transitions that quietly take place and that often remain hidden but that in this case our research unearthed and highlighted.

To better understand the activity system in which this case is situated and in which these encompassing transitions occurred I draw on third-generation CHAT and give some flesh to the activity system of the college by applying the five principles expounded by Engeström (2001): the activity system, multi-voicedness, historicity, the role of contradictions and tensions, and finally expansive transformation.

The activity system: A collective, artefact-mediated and object-orientated activity system, seen in its network relations to other activity systems, is taken as the prime unit of analysis. Here in the case of the college we see, particularly through the interviews with the college principal, how the college has as its desired outcome the maximisation of performance (attainment) measures. What constitutes learning, or more widely education as the expected object of activity (see Figure 2.1), is distorted by the performativity agenda that requires outcomes

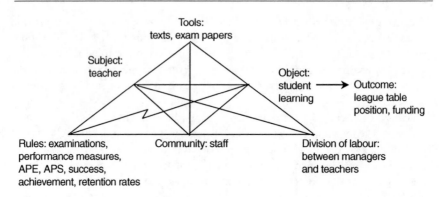

Figure 2.1 The college as an activity system with student learning mediated by not only educational technologies but also those that include crude measures of attainment at an institutional level.

dictated by measurement and inspection regimes. After all, the careers of individuals are on the line, and most at risk are those who are most prominent, particularly the college principal. Our case study touches on how the artefacts of a range of performance measures, such as those of 'achievement' and 'retention', are fundamental in mediating the actions of staff.

Multi-voicedness. An activity system is always a community of multiple points of view, traditions and interests. This we see exemplified clearly in the different perspectives of both workers (principal and teacher) and student. Jon struggles to rationalise what he is 'asked' to do with what he would like to achieve: he illustrates how different participants in the activity system bring to it their diverse backgrounds, histories and aspirations. We can but speculate that other teachers and managers bring their own perspectives to engage with the activity of the system in which they live, work and move onward in their careers and personal histories.

Historicity. Activity systems take shape and get transformed over lengthy periods of time. Important in this regard is how the current activity system reflects its past, how over time it has transformed and adapted to changing objects and tools. In the case presented here that is why I have provided substantial background and contextual detail that situate the current activity of the college in the pervasive climate of performativity that is culturally and historically situated in the wider social setting of education and society more generally. Here I have given by necessity just a glimpse into the complex world of the college and some understanding of how this relates to the wider context in which it operates. To understand this more fully requires considerable immersion in the detail of aspects of educational policy in relation to mathematics education and, more generally, as well as having in-depth understanding of the prevailing politics and ideologies in which these are generated.

Contradictions and tensions. Contradictions have a central role as sources of change and development. Contradictions are viewed as historically accumulating structural tensions within and between activity systems. As Engeström (ibid. p. 137) suggests:

> When an activity system adopts a new element from the outside (for example, a new technology or a new object), it often leads to an aggravated secondary contradiction where some old element (for example, the rules or division of labour) collides with the new one. Such contradictions generate disturbances and conflicts, but also innovate attempts to change the activity.

In the college, the introduction of different performance measures has over time clearly resulted in accumulating tensions within the activity system. Increasingly, measures are introduced that monitor performance both internally (e.g. measures of success that bring together other measures of 'achievement' and 'retention') and externally (e.g. APS and APE). This we detect as leading to a contradiction between the object of the system, that of student learning, and the rules that are used to measure this.

At the individual level such contradictions often give rise to conflict. According to Vasilyuk (1988), conflicts are inner doubts, as experienced by the subject, that paralyse the individual who faces contradictory motives. Conflicts relate to personal and interpersonal crises whereas contradictions are systemic tensions within a collective activity and/or between multiple activities, and have a much longer life cycle with their roots lying in contradictions (Sannino, 2008a, 2008b).

In the case we describe here it is clear to see that Jon struggles with conflicts that result from the contradiction in the activity system between the rules of performance measurement and the object of student learning. These conflicts dominated our interviews with him as he attempted to reconcile the teacher he felt he had been at one point with the teacher he felt he had become. This conflict is illustrated in just one exchange in which the interviewer asked Jon about how he reconciled teaching for procedural rather than relational understanding (Skemp, 1976). Here Jon talked about how in his teaching he sets out for students clearly defined procedures to follow:

> Unless it's set up exactly as the question was that I've shown them, they can't do it, and that's because they haven't got the deep understanding, and that's my fault, that is, in a sense. Because we've not given them the time to really learn how to, you know, when the question's slightly different, they can't cope with it.

Although Jon believes that understanding of mathematics will enhance the potential of students to answer examination questions, he is unwilling to take the risk of focusing on this during lessons as the time might be spent on learning and practising techniques and procedures that, while in the long run may prove less productive, give a feeling of security in the immediacy of the classroom. Thus for teachers such as Jon, following their beliefs rather than conforming to the norms and expectations of colleagues and students, as well as parents and society more widely, is a risk too far.

Expansive transformation: Contradictions in an activity system can be aggravated to such an extent that individuals can begin to question and deviate from established norms, giving rise to a possibility of expansive transformations in which the object and motive of the activity are reconsidered to allow for a richer conceptualisation of the activity of the system. This final principle I see as having optimistic potential for the case I describe, as maybe at a future time in the college's development in relation to mathematics someone, or some group, will be able to creatively reconceptualise key aspects of the activity system in which they operate. Presumably, in this case it will mean redefining rules in relation to what counts as achievement. I suspect that this is already the case for a small number of institutions that perennially fail to find themselves anywhere near the top of the performance tables. Such colleges might be considered to have given up the fight, and instead focus more energetically on supporting the community that they serve by working locally to attempt to meet the needs of all, perhaps broadening provision to include more (pre-) vocational and basic skills' programmes.

While the contradictions and conflicts I describe here are situated in the world of work for Jon and his college principal, who we might expect to exercise agency in relation to the situation, what of David's experience, as a student, or maybe even a customer (to use the terminology of the free-market conceptualisation of education)? David's story in relation to mathematics, as I suggested at the outset, is something of a roller-coaster ride. Not only does he fluctuate from 'up here' to 'down there' to potentially 'up here' again, ultimately he is neither up nor down, but out! This fluctuation of fortunes in relation to mathematics reflects his constantly renegotiated identity in relation to mathematics as he seeks to determine its 'use' to him as he navigates his lateral transition to Higher Education. At various times during the year he appears to view mathematics as not only having value as a qualification but also as having value due to its integral use in his current and potentially future studies and possibly career. David's flirtation with mathematics as having use value in this latter sense is at its most intense as he develops confidence while following the UoM programme. However, ultimately the institution's concern, as voiced by his psychology teacher, to maximise performance, prevails. This is 'sold' to David as being in his best interests. Whether or not this is the case depends, as I have suggested, on how attainment and achievement as well as progress are conceptualised. Even the exchange value of a high grade in one subject (e.g. psychology) compared with another (e.g. mathematics) might be contested when considering individual students as they seek to make progress towards their individual goals. However, for the institution, the value of a grade in one subject is the same as the same grade in another. David we might therefore see as a victim of the climate of performativity where everything that is easy to measure must be measured and used to compare.

Consequences and doublethink

This particular case study suggests that the priority given by senior managers to the exchange value of qualifications in general, and in particular to ensure that they maximise their college's performance measures and league table position, is far more invasive than might be thought, or presumably intended, by policy makers. We find that the institution can neglect the general, educational experience of students and hence the use value of mathematics, and therefore its potential to support them at a programme level, both at the present time and in the future. As Gleeson and Husbands point out, 'Increasing pressures associated with inspection, assessment, attainment, participation, and retention, often linked to funding and pay, acts to maintain the existential tension between what teachers believe in, and what they have to do' (2003, p. 503).

Our case study exposes how this particular institution, in an attempt to meet policy objectives related to inclusion in mathematics education at the same time as being high attaining, has to carry out an Orwellian doublethink. While this is articulated by the college principal it is core to the activity of all at the college as they struggle to allow their values (here symbolised by the rhetoric of inclusivity) to be valued in a climate where the technologies ('rules' in CHAT terms) that dominate ensure that above all it is attainment that is valued. The objectives of inclusivity and high rates of achievement I contend can be mutually compatible, but only if what is taken to represent achievement for both individual learners and the college as an institution in an educational marketplace is redefined in a less narrow manner. The crude performance measures that currently dominate focus only on student attainment in national qualifications, and as Fitzgibbon (2001) usefully distinguishes, we may wish to take account of *achievement* in relation to teaching and learning quality rather than merely *attainment* focused on measured outcomes as at present.

The perhaps unintended consequence of the culture of performativity that persists is a narrowing of participation in mathematics, at both institutional and classroom level, which can be characterised as the domination of use value by exchange value of mathematics in the joint activity of teaching and learning.

For individuals, we have seen how the contradiction that develops at the institutional level between meeting the needs of students and the needs of the college to position itself advantageously in the marketplace, gives rise to conflicts that need to be dealt with. Here, therefore, individual doublethink allows the college principal, teacher and student to readjust their values and identities as they succumb to the view that high attainment is all that matters. This is particularly poignant in the case of David, who in our final interview with him a few months after the end of the AS year talks of his regret at not having stuck with AS Mathematics (Trad) beyond the first few weeks: 'But if I went back and did one thing differently in the whole of college I would have stuck with Maths, instead of taking ...'. At this point, even while still in college he starts to question the pursuit of grades that equip him with neither the exchange value nor use value he would have liked: 'I think that was the big, big influence on why I didn't end up doing, pursuing a career in Physics, or Engineering, or anything…'.

Notes

1 *Keeping Open the Door to Mathematically-Demanding Further and Higher Education Programmes* (RES-139-25-0241); www.transmaths.org.
2 The colleges in the research that were case study sites provide education for students aged 16 and over with most being 16–19 years old and following academic courses.
3 In England students complete compulsory schooling at age 16 taking GCSEs (General Certificates in Secondary Education) in individual subject disciplines and many then take a first year of AS (Advanced Subsidiary) study in four (in some cases, five) subjects and go on to complete three (in some cases, four) of these with a second year of study to full A (Advanced) Level.
4 Further Maths is a second qualification in A Level mathematics that allows students to study more both in terms of breadth and depth in the subject.

Chapter 3

How do mathematics teaching enhancement programmes 'work'?

Rethinking agency in regulative times

Yvonne Barnes, Fiona Cockerham, Una Hanley and Yvette Solomon

Much mathematics education research is based on the identification of presumed shortcomings in current practice which then drive the implementation of a new approach (Brown, Hanley, Darby and Calder, 2007), a view that is frequently accompanied by a conceptualisation of 'progress' as moving towards an 'ideal' or improved state of affairs (Simon and Tzur, 1999; Tzur, Simon, Heinz and Kinzel, 2001). Recent policy in England aimed at educational improvement prioritises the development of high-quality teaching as a means of addressing perceived underperformance in the school system, particularly with respect to science, technology, engineering and mathematics (STEM) area subjects. In this chapter we focus on two contrasting teacher education programmes that aim to intervene in mathematics pedagogy in ways that will enhance teaching and so improve student performance. The first of these is the Mathematics Enhancement Course (hereafter MEC) programme, which recruits non-mathematics graduates who are aiming to train as secondary school (age 11–18) mathematics teachers, often as a second career or change of direction, in order to address a shortfall in well-qualified mathematics teachers. The MEC programme reported here, which is run by a university in north-west England (hereafter given the pseudonym 'NWU'), aims to deepen students' understanding of the concepts underlying their mathematical knowledge and reframe it as knowledge for teaching. It combines university-based study with teaching practice placements and focuses on the development of interactive and student-centred pedagogy. The second case is the Mathematics Specialist Teacher (hereafter MaST) programme, a national initiative instigated by the Williams Review (Williams, 2008), which advocates increasing teacher subject knowledge in order to raise mathematics standards; it also aims to put a 'maths champion' in place in every school, who will raise the profile of mathematics and act as an 'agent of change' in enhancing mathematics teaching in their school. The particular version of the programme we describe here, also run by NWU, focuses on encouraging a more investigative approach to mathematics in teachers' own practice and fostering reflection on managing change in their schools. It targets primary school teachers with varying levels of experience, and involves after-school, university-based teaching sessions emphasising mathematical problem solving and enquiry. Aiming to support teachers in developing new enquiry-based practice, it involves discussion of their experiences in carrying out small 'research projects' in their classrooms in which they experiment with mathematical problem-posing as a vehicle for children's learning. As we will show in this chapter, both programmes challenge traditional, rule-based views of mathematics learning and their associated transmissionist pedagogic practices, seen by many researchers as responsible for disengagement and failure in school mathematics: for MaST participants this highlighted power relationships within education and the tensions between personal pedagogic beliefs and political structures of accountability. MEC students met the same issues as they encountered conflict between 'the school way' in their practice schools and 'the NWU way' that underpins their training. We focus here on how participants on both programmes negotiate their way through these tensions and conflicts, and on how they assert and rework their professional agency as teachers of mathematics. We thus call into question what it means for these programmes and others like them to 'work'.

Evaluating professional development in mathematics education and the complexity of change

The MaST and MEC approaches that we are concerned with are not unusual in their challenge to embedded practices derived from a professional 'habitus' (Nolan, 2012) and from externally imposed practices of accountability and managerialism in schools. There have been many such interventions, some of which have reported positive outcomes. We need, however, to acknowledge the complexity of assessing the impact of continuing professional development (CPD) programmes; a number of typologies have emerged (e.g. Farmer, Gerretson and Lassak, 2003) that chart teacher levels of response to intervention ranging from a perception of CPD as a source of content and classroom activities to sustained change in beliefs and practices. While all 'levels' are positive responses, much CPD success, in terms of sustained change, is judged in terms of its impact on fundamental pedagogic beliefs and practice, which has been shown to be difficult to bring about. For example, Askew, Brown, Rhodes, Wiliam and Johnson's (1997) study of CPD influence on the development of 'connectionist' mathematics pedagogy reported that, in order for change in pedagogical approaches to 'take hold', CPD needed to be extended and/or supported by the school leadership. Similarly, Goulding's (2002) review of the Cognitive Acceleration in Maths Education (CAME) project's aim to disrupt transmission teaching suggests that implementing change at school level does not happen quickly, if at all. This review also underlines the role of the policy context in the impact of CPD, identifying the National Numeracy Strategy (1999) as having a detrimental effect on opportunities for discussion and practice sharing which were essential to the teachers' development of the CAME approach. More generally, policy measures in England around accountability, school inspections, target setting and league tables contribute to the forces of what Troman (2008) calls 'instrumentalism', and have a profound effect on teachers' professional lives, making pedagogic change difficult.

These forces are also visible in pre-service mathematics teachers, as Nolan (2012) reports in her account of the conflict between support for enquiry-based pedagogies at university level and instrumentalism in practice schools (see also Nolan, 2008; Towers, 2010; Van Zoest and Bohl, 2002). Nolan points not just to the role of accountability and assessment in schools, but to the strength of the individual student's educational habitus, which is firmly embedded from a very young age and highly resistant to change. Thus with Bullock and Russell (2010, cited in Nolan 2012), she points to the power of cultural routines associated with teaching such that 'every adult knows what teaching and learning should look like because he or she has spent thousands of hours as a student in school' (Bullock and Russell, 2010, p. 93). Reproduction of these routines is supported by dominant discourses in schools which regulate practices and stifle opportunities for pedagogical change.

Does change mean progress?

A rather different angle on the effectiveness of CPD in changing pedagogic practice is offered by Brown et al. (2007), who contend that it is not easy to achieve a consensus on how 'success' and improvement can be assessed, especially as there is no universal agreement around best practice. Apart from this conceptual consideration, assessing success is also difficult as experiences from earlier initiatives contribute to teachers' understanding of changes and their current practices and identities. Consequently, Brown et al. argue that we cannot assume that when asking teachers to move from one teaching approach to another there will be a straightforward substitution of practice. Drawing on the metaphor of the 'rhizome' which is 'multi directional, a-centred and non-hierarchical', Hanley and Darby (2006, p. 57) also argue that the outcomes of CPD processes are not predictable, and develop differentially among teachers; it is therefore unhelpful to suppose that universal trajectories of 'improvement' will apply to all people in all phases of development. Thus Brown et al. suggest that:

> mathematics education research should seek to recognise difference in teachers' understandings, experiences and contexts of action and assist them in making informed professional judgements about how their practice might be developed in situ, rather than supposing that external evaluative judgements can be based on a movement to a consensually preferred conception of teaching.
>
> (2007, p. 198)

As Troman (2008) notes, the complexity that teachers face in mediating innovation is accompanied by an adeptness in managing commitments and investing in a creative and individual professional identity through which they *mediate* policies, rather than being simply driven by them. Hence we draw here on McNamara and Corbin's development of the notion of 'warranting' as a means of understanding the different ways in which teachers account for what they do by reference to both private and public forms of legitimation of practice. Importantly, and significant for our own analysis, they conclude that 'warranting practices were constructed in a non-unitary sense by different and shifting registers in a complex struggle to interpret and justify individual judgements' (2010, p. 280).

In this chapter, we build on these ideas to argue that 'success' or 'working' needs to be understood differently so that, rather than judging interventions in terms of the reproduction of advocated practices (problematically identified often only through 'outcomes'), it is more useful to look at how teachers *use* development and training in their own sites of practice, focusing on their theorising and construction of their practice as evidenced by the 'different discourses, regimes and registers' that exemplify 'different rationales and warranting appeals' (McNamara and Corbin, 2001, p. 280). Thus we ask: How do they negotiate their way through the constraints of 'the school way' to bring about change in their own practice? What choices do they make? How do they preserve and develop their professional identity and agency as teachers?

Theorising teacher identity and practice

The research reviewed above suggests that one way to understand teachers' and student teachers' responses to mathematics teaching enhancement programmes is in terms of their (self-) positioning within a social context of competing discourses. We take here a theoretical perspective suggested by Holland, Lachicotte, Skinner and Cain (1998) which sees the school as a figured world in which individuals take up positions in 'a socially and culturally constructed realm of interpretation'; in this world, 'particular characters and actors are recognized, significance is assigned to certain acts, and particular outcomes are valued over others' (Holland *et al.*, 1998, p. 52). Thus the concept of a figured world underlines individual roles within social networks and hierarchies. However, this is not a static situation; the context of schooling that we are dealing with here is one that is perpetually re-forming: building on Bakhtin's (1981) emphasis on dialogism, Holland *et al.* argue that our activity is always 'dialogized, figured against other possible positions, other possible worlds' (1998, p. 238). It is this dialogic authoring of self that is the key to continually developing identities as we draw on the multiple discourses that surround us:

> In authoring the world ... the 'I' draws upon the languages, the dialects, the words of others to which she has been exposed. One is more or less condemned, in the work of expression, to choices because 'heteroglossia', the simultaneity of different languages and of their associated values and presuppositions, is the rule in social life.
>
> (Holland *et al.*, 1998, p. 170)

Thus, as Hanley and Darby suggest, the practitioner participating in multiple, sometimes conflicting, discourses may well exhibit many different manifestations of practice that do not resolve into one coherent approach – 'rather, they jostle together in ways that appear more fluid' (2006, p. 56). However, reflection on the nature of the figured worlds they inhabit may drive particular choices, even resistance, in their self-authoring. So, as Skinner, Valsiner and Holland (2001, para. 10) put it:

> The author of a narrative generates novelty by taking a position from which meaning is made – a position that enters a dialogue and takes a particular stance in addressing and answering others and the world ... In weaving a narrative, the speaker places herself, her listeners, and those who populate the narrative in certain positions and relations that are figured by larger cultural meanings or worlds. Narrative acts may reinforce or challenge these figured worlds.

Applying these ideas to our data, we focus here on the practitioner positions that primary mathematics specialist teachers and pre-service secondary mathematics teachers take up and their storying of those positions as a manifestation of the multi-layeredness and multi-voicedness of their teacher identities. In particular, we are interested to explore how teachers develop and maintain professional identities and learning trajectories within the power hierarchies of the school and its wider context – how do they position themselves, and how are they positioned by the discourses that circulate in schools and in education policy? We thus investigate how practitioners must 'choose a language ... consciousness must actively orient itself amidst heteroglossia, it must move in and occupy a position for itself within it, it chooses, in other words, a "language"' (Bakhtin, 1981, p. 295). In doing so, we will argue that while we can see multiple, often conflicting, discourses in what teachers say, they are not completely constrained by the current regulative context. As they self-author as teachers of mathematics, our participants draw on visions of teaching, emotional investments and personal experiences to reflect on their situation. They can be seen as making active choices about what they take from the course, and as theorising their own practice in ways that recognise and meet challenge and conflict, rather than necessarily being determined by it. Thus we will argue that a CPD course's 'success' lies in its contributions to teachers' reflective practices, rather than in their take-up of 'blueprint' ways of teaching.

This study

Our data are drawn from two sources that target contrasting mathematics enhancement audiences. First, ten teachers attending the MaST programme were recruited to participate in a semi-structured interview focusing on: their usual teaching practices, and any changes in their practice as a result of participating in MaST; their general feelings about teaching mathematics; obstacles and support in relation to their mathematics teaching; and how they enact the role of 'maths champion'. Second, the MEC programme sample focused on a group of 80 students who completed the course in 2009/10, closely followed by a PGCE course for one year during 2010/11. This group had the opportunity to try out some of the MEC-supported pedagogical approaches in their practice situations. At the end of their MEC year, students were asked to participate in this research by providing written free text responses to seven questions, and to a further five questions at the end of their PGCE year. The questions invited them to reflect on the influence of MEC on their thinking about mathematics teaching and on their actual practice and sense of progress. Four of the students also volunteered to participate in an interview.

All interview data were fully transcribed and were analysed alongside the free text written answers to identify recurring themes. We looked in particular for a range of professional voices, for references to dominant discourses, including those that characterised their practice environments, and for narratives of reflection and resistance.

Analysis

It might be assumed that students on a secondary mathematics course for mathematics specialists would have little in common with experienced primary teachers for whom mathematics is just one of a number of subject areas covered and who in general have not pursued mathematics subject knowledge beyond GCSE level. However, each group expressed both positive and negative feelings about their experiences with mathematics in the classroom as both pupils and teachers, framed by the tensions between 'how things ought to be' and 'how they are'. Both groups provided illustrations of the multi-voicedness noted by McNamara and Corbin (2001), and the complex identities described by Troman (2008) as a marker of teachers caught in accountability discourses alongside professional pedagogic visions. Our analysis records these shared aspects, while following Hanley and Darby's (2006) and Brown et al.'s (2007) approach of identifying how teachers theorise their own practice in navigating their way through conflicting discourses and demands. Our application of the concept of self-authoring within a figured world provides a means of understanding how, despite the contradictions, these teachers and students develop what are nevertheless meaningful narratives of professional agency. The themes identified in our analysis illustrate five 'warranting appeals' which were proffered by our interviewees in relation to their respective contexts and constraints. The first focused on struggle.

One: Struggling with dominant discourses

Classrooms and schools are cultural systems in which neoliberal discourses supported by government legislation and policy position both teachers and pupils as needing to meet objectives, and 'tick the boxes' of assessment and accountability.

Professionally persuaded by the MaST emphasis on enquiry learning rather than transmissionist teaching-to-the-test, teachers described how putting the programme ideas into practice meant that they must run counter to the demands of internal and external stakeholders. They reflected on this conflict in terms of taking a risk, feeling under pressure and 'fear' that the MaST approach would fail to 'work' in terms of meeting pupil targets. Charlie, a deputy head teacher, was typical in his liking for the MaST approach while being simultaneously concerned about meeting objectives:

> Now I've got this MAST course and I feel torn between on the one hand I get these wonderful ideas from MAST … but I'm aware that yes I've got all these objectives to cover … the clock's ticking. I'm behind where I should be. I need to keep those objectives …

David, a Year 6 teacher, also emphasised the tension between MaST connectionist teaching and demands for speed and coverage:

> It doesn't feel like there is this time to let things evolve or to have the opportunity where there is a more holistic view on the maths … there is that need for speed in schools, isn't there? I have spoken endlessly about this, speed is bad for teachers, it is bad for pupils.

The discourse of measurement by results is a recurring background for David's struggle. He fantasised about asserting his pedagogic principles, but felt that this was risky:

> I suppose I'd love to have that confidence to go, 'listen, back off, leave me with it for two terms and let's see where they are at'. But for one, do I have the confidence that my approach would have [worked] … That may not happen, and then I want to be [i.e. would be] shot down.

Even though they had spent far less time in the classroom than the primary teachers, MEC students also reported that the pressure to privilege results was a constraining feature during their teaching practice, preventing them from trying out their own activities. As one student put it: 'They [MEC sessions] did have the impact I'd hoped, but were not appreciated by my … school as it did not fit in with their results – first mantra'. MEC students recognised that the relationship with their teaching practice mentors meant that compromises needed to be made with regard to what was dubbed the 'NWU style' of connectionist teaching; although the style itself was not necessarily unwelcome in principle, the different approaches that students and mentors employed jostled together with varying degrees of discomfort. As secondary school teachers, they also experienced an additional challenge in the form of pupils' reluctance to move away from their 'comfort zone' preferences. Helen noted the difficulties that pupils experienced in reconciling old and new ways:

Encouraging more investigative work, pupils discovering rules and patterns for themselves. I definitely tried to apply this ... even though I found that especially younger pupils were reluctant to follow this approach and wanted to be spoon fed answers.

Two: Multiple voices and complex identities

Despite these critical reflections, the tension between MaST and MEC discourses and those of accountability frequently resulted in a situation where teachers and students appeared to hold on to traditional pedagogic discourses at the very same time that they criticised the system. Charlie provides a good example of these multiple voices: despite his advocacy of the 'wonderful ideas' and emphasis on 'coming through the problem' from the MaST programme, he struggled to hold on to a stance that values understanding over speed, returning to a discourse of teaching as delivery and coverage of a syllabus, and of teachers as potentially 'sloppy' if they fail to do this job:

> I think there's been a rigour introduced by the demand for all these objec- tives to be taught and all this constant emphasis on age-related expectations ... without it I think there was a lot of children in classes where teachers used to teach their favourite ... parts of maths, bits would be neglected ... there's always the tension between moving on and making sure they've understood what really should be necessary. Um, without the demand that teachers cover these objectives I think there'd be too much sloppy neglect of what should be going on and a slow pace.

Complexity and contradiction was also discernible among the MEC students' accounts. Here, Peter explains how he had tried to employ MEC concepts – to which he, like other MEC students, expressed a kind of 'allegiance' – but had felt some 'loss of faith' in the face of perceived pupil needs for traditional teaching practices:

> I felt that I had to bring in as many different activities as possible, and try to bring in things I was taught in MEC 9. Whether I wasn't comfortable with them, or whether I thought they would go ... I did think they would go better than they did, and they didn't ... I felt that I had to sort of in a way justify what I'd been taught because it went well at university, but that would be because, in hindsight, we knew what was expected of us, they [the pupils] didn't, so if they're not comfortable with it, they don't understand it, they don't get it, then they won't do it, so then you ... you are stuck.

Three: Emotional investments and personal experiences

Although the constraints of the school system dominate their accounts, it is also possible to see, as noted by Troman, that teachers and student teachers have emotional responses to teaching and personal experiences, which are important drivers in how they self-author and which enable them to invest in new ways forward in their use of CPD. Charlie and Jean both referred to wanting to inspire children. Jean always liked mathematics and was good at it, and she talked about the 'light-bulb' moment that teaching, especially MaST-type teaching, can uniquely bring:

> I love all the problems, I like the problem solving stuff myself, because it's quite a challenge teaching it to children who don't get that sort of stuff. I like it when the children suddenly get that light-bulb moment ... You know because it is that sort of subject where they can go from nothing to suddenly having their eyes open ... those moments of understanding ...

Most teachers talked about their own experience at school, wanting to either pass on their love of mathematics, as Jean did, or to help children avoid the fear they themselves experienced. So, for example, Cathy didn't like mathematics at all when she was at school and wanted things to be different for her class:

> I like seeing the children get it. It was a subject that I never liked at school ... teaching the children ... and seeing why things worked has instilled an enjoyment of teaching maths in me and the fact that I don't want the children to have the experiences that I had when I was at school.

The MEC data also illustrated how students drew on their own school experiences of 'very traditional lessons' as a driver for their desire to both understand learners and inspire them. Many responses focused upon their delight in the MEC repertoire which marked a considerable shift away from tradition and had the potential for creating a different classroom ethos. Echoing the MaST responses, they expressed a strong sense of identity with the 'new' pedagogy and an emotional investment that went beyond just an appreciation of new teaching styles and approaches. Joanna explained:

> My ambition was to make maths accessible to all children by taking out the 'fear factor' from lessons. I believe that the 'realistic' style of teaching mathematics and the fun learning activities are the way to do this. It comes across to me as being modern, cosmopolitan and progressive ... something I feel [resonates] with the liberal in me as I am always looking to make the future better by changing the present.

Four: Posing resistance

If we take up the view of a school as a figured world, with established roles, positions and values, we can see the importance for teachers to reflect on these values as a means of 'figuring it otherwise' (Holland *et al.*, 1998, p. 143). As we have seen, the MaST and MEC participants are well aware of the constraints that abound in schooling, but they cannot always disentangle themselves from dominant discourses – they can be seen as 'ventriloquated' (ibid., p. 185) by the dominant ideologies of objectives, measurement and accusations of poor subject knowledge. But reflections on ideologies, spurred on by emotional investments and experience, can lead to resistance: David tells us how he has been putting his ideas into action, and that, despite his fear that his results may not meet the school's senior management demands, he believes in what he is doing:

> I have been teaching maths to Year 6 and it's been a more holistic more investigational kind of approach all about the understanding of what they are doing and it has been a slow process ... the assistant heads at the school have been asking about data ... It's not looking like there's an amazing amount of progress from my teaching at the minute, and although I am saying 'it will come' ... you do start to feel that pressure, of 'well, I can just teach them' ... 'this is how you do equivalent fractions' ... and they will be able to answer it on a test. I can feel myself getting that pressure now of slipping back into it a bit ... I don't really believe in it, but it is there.

He resources his resistance by articulating the contrasting emotions that he experiences in MaST-inspired teaching, versus teaching in the test-driven 'comfort zone':

> It's not that enjoyable, I don't think, that style where it's constant ... that half an hour of intensity and 'I'm doing this' and 'right what's next', 'show the whiteboard', 'do this, open this, right OK I've done that!' I know within those [MAST] lessons I've had lovely times where I've just sat and just listened to a group: 'yes this is happening without me doing anything and that feels nice' ... rather than sitting with that group waiting until they say something and you go, 'why do you think that?' 'What is this?' 'What is that?' 'How did you work it out?' 'What about this one?'

In their responses, MEC students showed a very strong affiliation to the course and their understanding of its purposes. However, this attitude was difficult to sustain in school for many, particularly where the ethos of the school was dominated by an emphasis on pace and coverage of schemes of work. Peter described his discomfort:

> I used to think that ... if fractions was six lessons ... in each lesson I felt I had to achieve a certain thing in that lesson, I had to, no matter what, that

'you will ALL get to that point', and it did take a while to realise that they are not all going to get to that point ... and it took a while to think 'no, it's not [failure], sometimes they won't get it, but you have to move on'. I still can't get it straight in my mind that how can they move on if they don't get it at that point.

Later in his interview, Peter described how he developed his own way of teaching which did not 'toe the line' in this way. Referring to the school scheme of work, he says: 'Yes later on in the placement I did change it [the scheme] and I didn't always use it'; significantly perhaps, this particular resistance involved managing adjustments in the privacy of unobserved lessons.

Five: Finding a way forward: maintaining agency

Both the MaST teachers and MEC students had made an investment in approaches to teaching that did not sit easily in a school environment dominated by the need for learning measured in the shorter term. However, both groups were called upon to initiate change in their respective environments: MaST teachers were expected to take on the role of 'expert' embodied in the figure of the 'Maths Champion', while MEC students were expected to assume the role of novices with valuable specialist training that could be disseminated in their future teacher roles. For both groups, the figured world of the school presented a value system premised on conflicting calls for both 'change' and 'more of the same' which allowed for restricted manoeuvrability in the gaps and spaces that were created.

For MEC students, their affiliation to the programme ideals provided a new language and set of concepts that enabled them to navigate their way between these conflicting demands while developing their own practice. Here, Alan discusses the 'NWU style', in contrast to his original traditional vision of mathematics teaching:

> I really like ... what keeps being called the NWU style, whenever I'm in schools they say 'yeah it's NWU's type stuff' ... I don't think that [i.e. NWU-style connectionist teaching] was something I would have necessarily done on my own. If you'd said to me, 'you're going to be a maths teacher and you're going to teach this' I'd have probably just thought 'OK how can I explain how to do that. What questions could I then ask to see if they've understood the explanation'. And I'm not saying there's no place for that, but I don't use it very much myself ... I may use it more ... I don't know.

Thus the 'NWU style' provided a warrant for this MEC student to try out innovative practices, even in a context of constraints. For MaST teachers, though, the specific mandate to become 'Maths Champions' with the brief of changing practice in their own schools presented additional conflicts and challenges. Well aware of the problems inherent in the role both for themselves and their colleagues, they provide strong examples of the 'different rationales and warranting appeals' observed by McNamara and Corbin (2001, p. 280), as they describe how they have sought to navigate the diverse discourses 'at play' or different 'calls' to practise. So, for example, Charlie uses current power systems to make MaST changes happen. He has, he says, a good chance to change things because he is the deputy head, which means that he can exert a certain amount of leverage:

> I felt I'd done two or three staff meetings and it [i.e. the training he was passing on in the meetings] wasn't having an impact ... So they had an extra staff meeting where they had to show the impact [laughs] and they understand now ... There are ways and means ... there's the staff meetings, there's the checking up on them to check that they're doing what they've been asked to do ... I found I've had to chase them up.

In contrast to Charlie's hints at a possibly rather cynical use of power to achieve change, Cathy describes her role as a member of the senior management team as one that enables her to involve other teachers in generating pedagogic change:

> I've worked ... to try and improve the teaching and move the teaching from 'Satisfactory' to 'Good'. So I've used ... a coaching process ... to try and change people, so rather than me going in and saying 'This is how we do it' it's getting it coming from them so that they can see it. And I think ... that's had an impact.

As part of his more general reflections on the power hierarchies in his school, David theorises in elaborate terms how practices change, and his potential role in that change. He begins by arguing that just holding staff meetings can never be enough:

> I don't think it can be just through that kind of staff meeting, sure they know what a good maths lesson looks like and they all go and repeat it but when it comes to their planning, they don't know what it is they are really doing.

He recognises the influence of individual experiences of school, together with a sort of 'training habitus', which gets in the way of bringing about the changes he would like to see:

> I think people feel comfortable now in that delivery of, 'I will teach you, I will give you, I am the source of all knowledge, I will give you that knowledge and then you will show me that you know that knowledge', and that feels comfortable to teachers. I think that is ingrained not only in their training but it could be ingrained in their own education that they've had, so you are kind of battling against a long time.

Conclusions

As the analysis shows, there are common threads in the way our two samples experience CPD designed to change perceptions and practice in mathematics pedagogy, and in the case of the MaST teachers, changing others' perceptions and practice too. Our analysis shows how teachers and student teachers negotiate positions within classroom workplace cultures that indicate the assertion of agency and choice among competing discourses. What resources do they draw on to make it happen? Holland *et al.*'s (1998) idea of reflective agency is useful in alerting us to the role of reflection in identity development, and we use David as a final example here. When we first spoke to David we offered the concept of conflicting 'voices' in teaching, and he instantly warmed to the idea, returning frequently to it as he explained his teaching style and choices. His explicit reference to conflicting voices brings to mind Bakhtin's (1981) dialogic self: at the very beginning of the interview, he says 'I don't know which voice to listen to in my own head though'. It is David's recognition of voices and his reflection on how he needs to juggle them that enables him to theorise his own practice, and to make choices that resist the powerful discourses of which he becomes aware. He talks here about listening to his internal voice, using the MaST programme as a source of 'renewed energy':

> It's really made me question some things I am doing. I suppose it upset me when I started doing the MaST thing, looking back on some of my more recent practice, and 'I didn't used to do that, what has happened?' It [MAST] did provide me with a kind of renewed energy and a freshness again and 'yes my internal voice is right' ... 'yes ... I remember I used to be alright at this'.

So in response to our overall question 'how do mathematics enhancement programmes "work"?', our answer is that the programmes provide ways of affirming visions of teaching and reactions to previous experience. They also provide a language and conceptual tools that add to teachers' stock of warranting appeals, enabling them to navigate their way through conflicting discourses and so 'choose a language' through which they self-author in relation to innovation, personal history and power hierarchies which call for both change and continuity. As Brown *et al.* (2007) suggest, we have tried here to show how teachers develop and theorise their practice *in situ*, rather than judging them in terms of their proximity to a supposed ideal. Evaluating CPD programmes purely on 'blue-printed' outcomes may not only miss the full picture of how things are working in complex, conflicting and sometimes contradictory ways in practice, but the assessment regimes needed for such outcomes-based judgements may disrupt 'ideal' practices from being implemented at all. As Watson and De Geest (2005, p. 231) conclude, 'the search for a "holy grail" of successful methods, organisations and structures for improving mathematics is a misguided quest'. More important is teachers' own theorising and development of practice to meet the needs of local contexts within the constraints of existing performative discourses.

Chapter 4

How do you make doctors?

Emma Pearson, Janine Carroll and Tim Dornan

This chapter introduces, explores and contrasts two answers to the question that titles it. One, described by Dornan (2010) as a 'Fordist' answer, mirrors the way quality was improved in the early twentieth-century automotive industry. Doctors, it is argued, are made by quality assuring the component parts of their professional practice in medical schools, which have analogies with production lines. Fordism cost-effectively produces a car that is able to drive away from the showroom – or, it is argued, a doctor who will practise safely. While Fordism was a step forward in producing products that were affordable and identical to one another, it threatened the quality of the finished product by focusing on parts rather than the whole. Teachers reading this allegory of contemporary education may not be surprised to hear that another shortcoming of Fordism was to demotivate production line workers, again threatening quality. Thus, Dornan (2010) contrasts the Fordist approach with a craftsmanlike one that, although it might be seen as more risky and unpredictable, appeals to an enduring, basic human impulse – of doing a job well for its own sake. Thus, the pragmatist philosopher Richard Sennett (2008) would frame the task of teaching not as the task of an assembly worker, but as that of the craftsman. For him, doctors are people who treat patients in the round rather than just broken bones and who are equally craftsmanlike in how they teach the next generation of doctors. Doctors, from a craft perspective, have attributes that are very individual and not, therefore, developed by reductionist, assembly line approaches. Thus craftsmanlike education and practice tends to focus on relationships (Sennett, 2008); the 'craftsmanship' answer to our question, then, is that practitioners make future doctors by forming craftsmanlike relationships with their students, just as they do with their patients.

In this chapter, we first explain how medicine championed the 'what works' agenda by means of the evidence-based medicine movement. We argue that the current vogue for competency-based medical education is an extension of that agenda into the process of making doctors. We outline the curricula within which doctors are currently made and then trouble Fordist simplicity by presenting two vignettes describing how trainees in medicine actually experience their learning. We introduce the craftsmanship agenda by considering medical training as a process of identity formation. We align ourselves with Sinclair (1997), whose participant–observer research into basic medical education framed it as an essentially social process, and report on how medical educators are moving away from a naïve Fordist approach. We end by suggesting that putting practice at the centre of practice-based learning and making identity formation an explicit educational process could resolve some of the tensions we have described.

The 'what works' agenda

A major reason for medicine's role in driving the 'what works' agenda is that its ontology and epistemology are firmly rooted in the natural sciences, and the use of controlled experiments to test causal associations. In the 1970s, a highly regarded epidemiologist berated doctors for using ineffective or frankly harmful treatments (Cochrane, 1973). Cochrane urged doctors to find which treatments did and did not work by carrying out randomised controlled trials. The evidence-based medicine movement gained momentum slowly over the next two decades until two more or less coincident events. A clinical trial was published, showing that 'clot-busting' treatment (streptokinase) and aspirin could, together, save the lives of people after heart attacks (ISIS-2, 1988), and a statistical meta-analysis was also published, showing that evidence for the effectiveness of streptokinase had existed in fragmentary form for a long time but had simply not been assembled (Antman, Lau, Kupelnick, Mosteller and Chalmers, 1992). The inference was that conducting systematic reviews and meta-analyses was the answer to Cochrane's criticism. An international collaboration, The Cochrane Collaboration, was therefore formed to promote the scholarship of evidence synthesis (Cochrane Collaboration, n.d.). Meanwhile, a group based in McMaster University, Canada, developed Evidence-Based Medicine (EBM) as a discipline that could bring such evidence to bear on clinical practice. Heuristics for appraising and applying evidence were developed and promoted (Sackett, Richardson, Rosenberg and Haynes, 1997) to support EBM.

A central concept of EBM is the 'evidence hierarchy', which prioritises various research methodologies and evaluates the strength of evidence according to its level in the hierarchy. Statistical meta-analysis of randomised controlled trials is at the top of the hierarchy and any other methodology is considered inferior. EBM therefore aims to take uncertainty out of clinical practice by showing 'what works' and using methods that weight probabilities in favour of one course of action over another. This approach resonates with doctors, who have to demonstrate proficiency in science to enter medical education, and whose learning of medicine is dominated by the experimental paradigm of the natural sciences; it has also influenced medical education research and the processes involved in educating medical students.

Medical education and the competency movement

Medical training programmes

Students enter medical school directly from secondary education, or as graduates with a bachelor's degree. A grounding in physical sciences, particularly chemistry, was formerly regarded as a prerequisite, although that requirement has been relaxed to some degree as views on the ontology of medicine – notably the place of humanities and social sciences in learning medicine – have broadened over recent years (Kuper and D'Eon, 2011). Despite that, medical schools are, above all else, dedicated to biomedical science, whose discourse dominates at least the early years of medical education (Weatherall, 2011). It was traditional for the study of anatomy, physiology, biochemistry and, perhaps, pharmacology to occupy all of a student's study time for two or even three years, without any learning taking place in clinical settings. Recently, workplace experience has been provided in the early curriculum years (Dornan and Smithson, 2009; Hopayian, Howe and Dagley, 2007) to provide a more practically focused education. After two to three years of university-based learning, students make the transition into practice-based learning.

This next phase of medical education, 'clerkships', involves rotating through different medical specialties that can resource students' learning (Holmboe, Ginsburg and Bernabeo, 2011). Clerkships last from three to four years, during which time the mode of learning is best described as 'clinical apprenticeship'. As their education progresses, medical students are increasingly brought face to face with their future role as doctors, a process referred to as proto-professionalisation (Hilton and Slotnick, 2005). They are expected to dress and behave like professionals and learn from contact with patients under the tutelage of experienced practitioners. This privileged access to patients exposes students to both opportunities and risks. They have positive experiences when doctors and other health professionals (notably nurses) behave supportively towards them and they perform the duties of doctors to the benefit of patients. They also have negative experiences when they are abused by doctors, excluded from practice and observe insensitive behaviour towards patients. In many countries, medical students have defined roles in clinical teams, though less so in the UK. Box 4.1 presents a medical student's narrative account, which describes an experience during clerkship and which will be explored in detail later.

Having succeeded in an exit examination, medical students become residents, when they take on the role of patient care providers, but still in the capacity of learners, developing the skill set of their chosen branch of medicine. Box 4.2 presents a narrative from a resident to give a flavour of their learning, which will, again, be explored later. Even after the progression from resident to independent practitioner, doctors participate in mandatory programmes of continuing professional development, whose purpose is more a regulatory one than a stimulus to personal development (Dornan, 2008) so medical education is a process of lifelong learning, but under quite close scrutiny by regulatory bodies. Most people who study medicine go on to practise medicine, often for their whole working lives. There is scope within the profession for diversification, but people who 'become' doctors tend to remain doctors. The transition from school student to university student, from university student to proto-professional, from learning how to practise in workplaces to learning from practice in workplaces, and from apprentice to master, are milestones along a trajectory of personal development. Consequently, learning, teaching and practice remain tightly integrated and ongoing.

Box 4.1 A medical student's narrative

It sounds really bad but ... you're glad something's happened ... I wasn't glad that it had happened to the patient, but it was good because it was ... a really good learning experience ... your first cardiac arrest is always gonna be a big thing ... we heard about it and we thought, we'll go and follow this because, when you're a medical student, anything that's slightly interesting you just hook onto immediately and go because you've got to like really search for these opportunities ... while I was sad that the patient hadn't survived, I was also ... quite pleased that I'd just witnessed that event and that I'd actually had that learning opportunity ... cos medicine's so opportunistic when you're ... in your clinical years that anything that happens you're grateful that you've seen it cos ... it doesn't come along everyday ... one of the junior doctors who was there was saying to us, 'Oh come and, you know, come in and do some chest compressions' ... we didn't end up doing it because I think we were too scared to do it, because we ... thought we'd do it wrong or thought we'd be in the way, and I was like, I don't feel comfortable ... I think I'd feel a bit more confident next time I see, I saw one.

(Pearson, 2011)

Box 4.2 A qualified doctor-in-training's narrative

I don't feel I learned a massive amount in clinic today I must say, although there were probably a few minor learning points. Much of that's probably because I don't discuss much with the consultant so you don't know what you don't know, if you see what I mean ... I did ask the consultant about two patients. One was just a logistical thing really ... The other patient, I had an idea in my head of the plan and that's kind of what the consultant agreed with. I'm not sure I learned anything kind of knowledge-wise, but it did reinforce to me the fact that this particular consultant I do the clinic with always looks at his own scan images and I am really bad at doing that and I'm not very good at interpreting things like MRI scans and so on and I did look at some MRI images with him today, which probably helped a little bit actually and it's just reinforced to me that I should be doing this more and more.

(Shah, Smithies, Dexter, Snowden and Dornan, in preparation)

A new emphasis on learning outcomes

Hodge (2007) describes how the successful launch of Sputnik in 1957 gave Russia a competitive edge in the space race and caused deep soul searching in America, where the education system was perceived to have let its citizens down. Massive resources were invested in defining and measuring outcomes. So, outcome-based (or competency-based) education came to dominate education thinking. Mørcke, Eika and Dornan (2012) trace the equivalent movement in medicine, which was propelled into centre stage four decades later by an article, grounded neither in theory nor empirical evidence, that presented outcome-based education as 'a powerful and appealing way of reforming and managing education' (Harden, Crosby and Davis, 1999). Coincident with or consequent on this publication, undergraduate and postgraduate curricula have been reorientated towards outcome-based education. A landmark report from the USA, for example, has called for wholesale reform of medical education towards standardised learning outcomes or competencies (Cooke, Irby and O'Brien, 2010). Proponents argue that this new movement is a real advance from the Fordism of earlier years if desired learning outcomes are framed at a rather general level rather than the myriad components that make up a car. Critics argue that such a general outcome specification is useless and outcome-based education can only work if it does, indeed, break professional proficiency down into automotive components (Norman, 2006).

Mørcke et al. (2012) argue that the outcome discourse is closely linked to a regulatory purpose of holding the medical profession accountable to society. From a 'what works' perspective, it is more appealing to think of medical proficiency as a sum of component parts, quality assurance of which assures the quality of the whole, than an organic process of developing learners as (future) doctors. Hodges (2010) echoed this accountability critique of outcome-based education when he argued that the notion of standardising learning outcomes is based on a production (i.e. Fordist) discourse of greater efficiency. Reviewing the rather limited empirical evidence available, Mørcke et al. (2012) find that the positive evidence of benefit was limited and there was also negative evidence that students who made the greatest use of predetermined learning outcomes were the weakest ones, as judged by their examination performance. Perhaps more concerning is that humane attributes, which define doctors as 'good' ones, defy formalisation as standardised learning outcomes. We conclude that present evidence does not show outcome-based education to 'work' any better than other approaches when it comes to making doctors. But it would be patently absurd to suggest that curricula should give no indication of what they set out to achieve. The real question is whether curricula should focus primarily on processes, primarily on outcomes, primarily on 'time served' in appropriate experiences, or a balance between them all. Dornan (2010), invoking complexity theory, considers how rather broadly framed learning outcomes could act as 'fuzzy boundaries', within which learning might emerge as a result of social processes. Outcomes, according to that conceptualisation, exist to foster craftsmanship rather than production. It is an emancipatory more than a regulatory discourse of curriculum, which brings us to a question posed by our critique of outcome-based education: if a 'what works' agenda of assembling micro-components of medical proficiency is not a promising avenue, what else should be considered? The next section takes an affective turn and proposes that identity, which defies expression as a standardised learning outcome, should be a focus of attention.

Identity

The narratives in Boxes 4.1 and 4.2 illustrate just how complicated the education of doctors really is, in terms of both learning outcomes and the impact of learning experiences on how medical learners 'fit' into clinical contexts. The first box tells how a cardiac arrest, which was 'always going to be a big thing', created a tension between strong positive learning opportunities, and the gravity of the situation, the student's reaction to being present at such a moment, her low level of self-confidence and the sadness of the patient's death. The second box describes how a resident explores the place of MRI scan interpretation in the identity of a rheumatologist. Relatedly, Monrouxe writes that 'medical education is as much about learning to talk and act like a doctor as it is about learning the content of the medical curriculum' (2010, p. 47). You make doctors, then, by helping people develop the *identity* of a doctor. Sfard (1998) distinguishes between two metaphors of learning: as acquisition or participation. Demonstrating that one has attained competence according to a pre-specified standard is plainly within the acquisition metaphor. Developing the identity of a doctor, we argue, is better framed within the participation metaphor, which considers the learning of young doctors, the craftsmanship of their experienced supervisors and the social processes that draw them together within the social milieus of workplaces. Identity is lived within a craft world.

Understanding identity development

Vignoles and colleagues (Vignoles, Schwartz and Luyckx, 2011) emphasise the multilevel nature of identity as a construct, and identify four different levels at which it can be conceptualised: *individual*, whereby identity is viewed as 'internal' and involves self-definition; *relational*, whereby identity includes definition and interpretation of interpersonal 'roles'; *collective*, whereby identity refers to identification within social groups and categories; and *material*, whereby material artefacts are treated as part of a person's identity. Identities and the process of identification are dynamic and ongoing (Monrouxe, 2010). Professional identity formation occurs as part of a process of socialisation into the roles of doctors-in-training and links an individual with their community of practice (Jarvis-Selinger, Pratt and Regehr, 2012). At the individual level, Jarvis-Selinger *et al.* (2012) highlight the shortcomings of 'behavioural competency checklists' in representing learning from experience and individual development. Educators need to be aware of moments of identity instability, which occur when new information is introduced that challenges an individual's sense of identity, in order to provide necessary support as professional identity evolves. At a collective level, they emphasise the relationship between identity formation and social navigation within a community to develop complex roles and relationships (Jarvis-Selinger *et al.*, 2012). Linking with Vagan's (2011) argument that learners' positions within communities of practice fluctuate, as does their power to articulate their positions, Hilton and Slotnick (2005) describe differences in the work undertaken and relationships formed between medical students, junior doctors and independent clinicians, which emphasise how approaches to learning that are acquired early in medical education have an important impact on the development of doctors' identities.

There are ways of addressing identity development formally within curricula; for example, by swearing affirmations at graduation. However, as Monrouxe (2010) argues, informal rituals associated with the medical profession are also important to acknowledge. Students develop their professional identities as 'participating professionals' within the interactional, emotional and contextual aspects of workplaces (van der Zwet, Zwietering, Teunissen, van der Vleuten and Scherpbier, 2011), and learning environments exert more or less positive influences (Kasman, Fryer-Edwards and Braddock, 2003). Affects are intimately tied to identity development in that confidence, motivation and sense of reward both result from and influence students' development of clinical proficiency (Dornan, Boshuizen, King and Scherpbier, 2007). Interaction with medical staff and opportunities to contribute to patient care facilitate identity development and boost confidence as medical students progress through their training (Dornan *et al.*, 2007).

Competence and caring

Macleod (2011) emphasises the need for students to balance professional identities that are associated with two contrasting discourses: of competence and of caring. She argues that medical education centres more on the biomedical and clinical skills necessary for professional competence, while developing and maintaining a caring identity is emphasised less, perhaps influenced more by what Hafferty and Franks (1994) termed the 'hidden curriculum' than by the formal curriculum. Enculturation proceeds rapidly from the time of application to medical school, and the hidden curriculum has a strong shaping effect on students' identity development (Boudreau, Cruess and Cruess, 2011; Gaufberg, Batalden, Sands and Bell, 2010). Coulehan and Williams (2001) discuss how explicit teachings of empathy, trust and good communication can conflict with messages of detachment, objectivity and distrust delivered tacitly. Allen and colleagues (Allen, Wainwright, Mount and Hutchinson, 2008) report that students may struggle to marry caring competencies with professional behaviours; the development of cynicism and the objectification of patients is thought to be an inevitable part of professional life by some students as they perceive themselves to be relatively powerless in the hierarchy of the clinical environment, and so incorporate this into their professional identity. Griffith and Wilson (2001) similarly discuss identity development in relation to the transformation of altruistic, idealistic students into hardened, cynical doctors. Since medical students may struggle to unite conflicting explicit messages of caring with tacit messages of detachment and cynicism (Testerman, Moreton, Loo, Worthley and Lamberton, 1996), medical educators need to be aware of these discourses and their impact on professional identity development. MacLeod (2011) suggests that becoming a doctor means learning to negotiate a balance between professional identities consistent with competence and those consistent with caring. Understanding that this is an ongoing, dynamic process involving interaction with the environment and the experiences that one gains has important implications for medical education (Monrouxe, 2010).

The 'what works' agenda, acquisition metaphor and regulatory discourse of outcome-based education create rather clear roles for medical teachers as instructors and assessors of clinical proficiency. But how, we consider in the next section, can the role of a teacher be framed within the participation metaphor?

Craftsmanlike identity formation

Lave and Wenger's (1991) theory of legitimate peripheral participation (LPP) drew sociocultural theory to wide attention among medical educationalists and was taken up so avidly that it is now the most quoted learning theory in the field (Dornan, Mann, Scherpbier and Spencer, 2010). The notion of entering a community of practice (COP) as a legitimate peripheral participant resonates strongly with the time-honoured way medical students and interns learn. 'Arenas of mature practice', described by Lave and Wenger (1991), are easily identified in the multi-professional communities that deliver clinical care. Popular as Lave and Wenger's theory is, the way learners define themselves by participating in the practices of various communities (Wenger, 1998) has received much less attention in the medical education literature than their concepts of COP and LPP. Boxes 4.1 and 4.2 clearly illustrate the situated nature of medical learning and the degree to which it is embedded in the social processes of workplaces, and the importance of identity within this complex environment. From an identity development perspective, both vignettes are at Vignoles and colleagues' (2011) relational and collective levels because both learners are interacting with people who are members of relatively homogeneous professional groups.

Taking Box 4.1, the cardiac arrest was an educationally salient instance of practice. The junior doctor's invitation to join in resuscitating the patient placed the medical student within the boundary of practice, as McLachlan, King, Wenger and Dornan (2012) have described in relation to patients' involvement in medical student education. Being a supported participant rather than a lay observer of a tragic situation allowed the student to reflect on the meaning of the situation to her proto-professional identity. Her peripheral position within the practice allowed her to explore her conflicting emotions and learn from them without being responsible for the outcome. Positive and negative emotions of the sort described here are typical of early career medical learners who feel unsure of themselves and how they fit within medical teams due to their inexperience, and they report stress and fear alongside motivation and excitement as they enter clinical training (Dornan and Bundy, 2004). The resident described in Box 4.2 was already a well-established member of a COP. Whereas a 'what works' agenda would have focused on her ability to interpret MRI scans and promoted formal training and testing of her proficiency in the skill, what was salient to her was the place of interpreting them (rather than reading a radiologist's report of them) in the professional identity of a rheumatologist.

The emphasis given by COP theory to learning as an essentially communal phenomenon has attracted criticism. Billett (see, for example, Billett, 2011) sees learning as resulting from interdependence between the agency of learners and the affordances of workplaces. Vagan (2011), likewise, criticised COP theory for over-emphasising the impact of communities (structure) on learners' identity formation, and paying insufficient attention to how actors relate themse lves to their social surroundings (agency). Learners, he argued, adopt positions within communities that fluctuate over time, and different individuals articulate their positions differently. Not every learner, Vagan's argument might go, would arrive at the decision to put more effort into learning the skill of MRI scan inter-pretation as modelled by the supervisor. Billett's emphasis on affordances is also relevant to this case, because learning MRI scan interpretation solely by trial and error is not the best way of doing it. Another affordance of workplaces is the expertise of radiologists, who the resident could seek out to help her develop applied expertise in the skill.

Vagan (2011) advocated Figured Worlds (Holland, Lachicotte, Skinner and Cain, 1998) as a more informative sociocultural approach to identity. Following the approach of Holland and colleagues (1998), we may say that the medical student in Box 4.1 is constructing her identity in a world figured by doctors whose chest compressions make the difference between life and death. The world of medicine is one that is socially and culturally constructed, and in which the ability to respond to life-threatening emergencies, and to respond kindly and considerately to younger colleagues, is highly valued. For the qualified doctor in Box 4.2, the world of rheumatology practice is figured by people who do not simply examine MRI scans, but are able to interpret the abnormalities they see on them and make diagnoses. Rheumatologists plan out courses of action that address the rheumatological diagnoses MRI scans allow them to make.

These two vignettes show medical education to be a series of lived experiences by whole people in dynamic transaction with sociocultural environments. Students and residents constantly negotiate and renegotiate their identities within a nexus of activities, knowledge, skills, attitudes, emotions, actions and relationships. There is a stark contrast between nurturing those complex learning processes and a Fordist approach to ensuring doctors accrete a 'what works' set of competencies.

Conclusion: Not 'what works' but 'how does it work?'

The medical education community is collectively shifting the 'what works' agenda towards a 'how can we make it work better' one. The Best Evidence Medical Education (BEME) collaborative (Thistlethwaite and Hammick, 2010) came into existence in 2000, and with it evidence-based medical education was born. Unlike Cochrane, which was founded around a clear epistemological assumption of 'proof', BEME took no explicit epistemological position, though its adoption of a subtly modified version of Kirkpatrick's 'levels' (renamed the Kirkpatrick 'hierarchy' (Yardley and Dornan, 2012)) implied that the design of studies determined the 'value' of the evidence they produced and that patient outcomes were the 'best' test of educational quality. In the relative epistemological void that followed BEME's foundation, assumptions from the medical domain led people to look for randomised controlled trials of educational interventions, and to be disappointed when they found none. The evidence on which medical education was based, therefore, appeared relatively weak. The *British Medical Journal* epitomised this stance by publishing an article commenting on the paucity of randomised controlled trials in medical education under a banner headline announcing a 'state of stagnation' in medical education research (Todres, Stephenson and Jones, 2007).

Perhaps because practitioners of medical education are from a broader disciplinary background than practitioners of medicine, there has been strong resistance to giving controlled experiments the same primacy as in medicine, and resistance to orientating education research solely towards 'decision support' (Pope, Mays and Popay, 2007). An important milestone was when Schmidt reviewed the literature that had followed his seminal work on the cognitive psychology of problem based learning (PBL), classifying publications into three types: description ('this is what we did'); justification ('is PBL better than traditional education?'); and clarification ('how does PBL work for whom, how and under what circumstances?'). The conclusion of his analysis was that researchers too often asked the justification question 'does it work?' and could invest their energy more productively in high-quality clarification research (Cook, Bordage and Schmidt, 2008). A subsequent publication explained the value of examining medical education from the perspective of complexity theory (Mennin, 2010) and qualitative evidence has gained increasing currency. Consequently, medical education is moving progressively beyond naïve 'what works' questions to richer questions that allow educational theory and a wealth of research findings to provide solutions that can inform practice. This stance was strongly supported at a symposium in 2011, where one speaker after another gave a personal view of evidence as something much more complex than 'what works', summarised in a published report as: 'Evidence has multiple meanings depending on context and use, and this reflects the complex and often chaotic world in which we work and research' (Thistlethwaite *et al.*, 2012).

We have argued that making doctors is much more complex than is suggested by contemporary notions of professional learning as the acquisition of a set of competencies. Recognising this, the field is starting to distance itself from its parent discipline, medicine, which championed the 'what works' agenda in the guise of evidence-based medicine. We offer medical education to scholars in other fields as an arena of professional practice where learning by participation remains strong. The personhood of practitioners and their identity development, we propose, lies at the heart of vocational education.

Chapter 5

Participative learning in online contexts

Focusing on 'participation'

Erica McAteer, Mary Thorpe and Cormac Lawler

Models of participation and interaction considered effective for learning have been informed by a cluster of research-informed theoretical frameworks building on the concept of socio-cognitive conflict through peer group discussion, drawn from Piagetian theories of child development, as well as those highlighting 'expert guidance' between new learners and experienced others, developed from Vygotsky's work. These are often extended to adult learning contexts, where the different levels, and different types, of subject experience that learners bring to their learning encounters are particularly noticeable. Considerable attention is also given to sociocultural dimensions of collaborative group learning development (e.g. McConnell, 2000; Steeples and Jones, 2002), important corollaries being group size and composition, tutor management and maintenance of 'effective' participation (Dillenbourg, 2002). Critical aspects have been: *dialogue* between learners, as well as between learners and teachers, and the extent to which this is resourced and supported; *structure*, that is, the extent to which the learner is guided, encouraged (or, through assessment requirements, perhaps driven) towards the learning goal; and *autonomy*, that is, the extent to which the participant is free to take responsibility for his or her own learning (Moore and Kearsley, 1996).

In this chapter, we argue that while such models are useful in designing online learning environments, they do not sufficiently account for the wider contextual factors that co-construct these e-learning opportunities. The intersections of multiple learning contexts (and individual identities) become evident when participation is purposefully investigated. Our claim is that online learning goes beyond the e-learning environment itself to include the learners' social and work lives, and that, by engaging in these other aspects of the learner's identity and practice, e-learning opportunities can be enhanced. In developing this argument, we refer to Lave and Wenger's (1991) construct of legitimate peripheral participation which highlights ways in which individuals engage in structured forms of participation that enable learning in contexts of practice (e.g. professional practice). The individual learner is provided with opportunities to participate that are judged appropriate for their novice status, and that provide a basis from which they can progress into more demanding kinds of participation and opportunities to develop expertise. In this way, learning is possible through participation, and participation is structured by the demands of the practice and practitioners. Wenger's (1998) elaboration of this to a 'community of practice' framework emphasises participative learning as a process of identity development as well as a gaining of expertise. Engagement in shared tasks and mutual dependence for achievement of those tasks lead to interactions that develop specialist knowledge and discourse.

What is clear from recent research is that users bring expectations from their own learning and work practice contexts (Thorpe, 2009), and that these expectations influence the nature of their online participation. Inexperienced users of online educational forums can find it difficult to 'read' the purpose and task demands of their forum contribution, as well as the stance and intent of fellow participants, tutors and subject experts. Bayne (2010) has widened this concern to issues of familiarity, comfort and mutual trust, where online access to a wide range of resources (human as well as material) creates uncertainty about who can be trusted and what counts as valid information and reliable knowledge: 'in working online as teachers and learners, we are working in "destabilised" classrooms, engaging in spaces and practices which are disquieting, disorienting, strange, anxiety-inducing and uncanny' (Bayne 2010, p. 6).

To illustrate the importance of wider contexts, cultures and communities already familiar to individual participants interacting within an online learning community, we present three case analyses of adult, voluntary learning groups. Participative goals, participatory activities and participation procedures differ between each example, as to how, by whom, or indeed whether, any learning outcomes of their participation are assessed. Each case features participants who are positioned from their own personal biographies and situated within their own everyday working communities, presently engaging online as participants within specific scholarly communities of enquiry (Garrison, Anderson and Archer, 2001). Figure 5.1 represents the key pedagogical features of the three cases.

For case one ('Partners in Learning'), participative interaction between learners within the online environment had a dual goal of developing group as well as individual scholarship and, grounded by that experience, contributing to learners' development within their diverse communities of workplace practice (i.e. as school teaching assistants). The second case (a Master of Engineering (M.Eng.) module) provides an example of online participation designed to take advantage of the interaction between online learning and external communities of practice in order to build an online community and to support learning. A common feature for both was the role of assessment through multiple strategies which targeted development of collaborative and individual skills and knowledge. The third (Wikiversity) presents a case in which productive participation may be compromised by conflict, centred on decisions relating to who may participate and how, as well as what their individual contribution might be to a collaborative academic outcome.

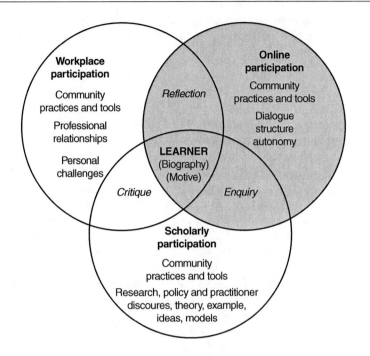

Workplace
participation

Community
practices and tools

Professional
relationships

Personal
challenges

Reflection

Online
participation

Community
practices and tools

Dialogue
structure
autonomy

LEARNER
(Biography)
(Motive)

Critique

Enquiry

Scholarly
participation

Community
practices and tools

Research, policy and practitioner
discoures, theory, example,
ideas, models

Figure 5.1 Participation within and across learning communities.

In presenting these examples, we illustrate how theoretical frameworks might usefully inform pedagogical design and resource provision for online participative learning. We also identify critical issues for their successful engagement within learning communities which are comprised of multiple identities, serve a range of learning goals and index diverse contexts of workplace practice.

While early research into online learning sought to establish the degree to which there was evidence of learning processes (social, cognitive or affective), reflecting the expectations of learning in place-based communities of practice, there is a need for a better understanding of the ways in which participation, in its wider conceptualisation, can be fully harnessed for online learning development. In focusing upon online learning participation through our three illustrative case examples, we extend current theoretical frameworks to envelop the more encompassing conceptualisations of participation outlined by Lave and Wenger (1991).

Case one: Attempting to situate participative learning at the interface of workplace practice and online course communities

Our first case[1] draws upon the pilot implementation of a core module in a Vocational Level 3 course for teaching assistants working with children with visual impairment (VI) in mainstream schools, following conversion from traditional face-to-face to online distance delivery (Wall, McAteer and Miller, 2008). In line with current UK government policy agendas, the course sought to inform and develop participants' workplace practice, extending and enhancing the quality of 'inclusive' educational provision.

Delivered through an 'open source' virtual learning environment (VLE), supported by two tutors and piloted with 46 students, the module provided three themed units. Each accessed web portals providing information, activities and resources for individual learning interaction, reference texts, discussion fora, one–one or one–many emailing, and an assignment task for individual submission. For each participant, the hub of the VLE was their unit discussion forum, which accessed all course resources. The course aimed to facilitate development of knowledge within small forum groups, through individual and collaborative engagement with course materials and learning tasks, sharing reflections on potential applications of that knowledge to their particular workplace contexts.

'Tutor presence' (Garrison et al., 2001) within each forum was in general provided summatively, as each collaborative work-task closed. Participants worked in small groups of six or seven, sequentially through the three themed discussion tasks set by the module units. Forum contributions counted for individual assessment, in broad terms of their clarity and language expression, relevance to topic and (with an emphasis on quality rather than quantity) level of contribution to the learning group. 'Participation' was thus accounted for and measured from a course management perspective and given equal weight with unit assignment grades.

Despite the anxieties that many professed upon returning to study, feedback from students over the period of familiarisation and early use of the forum was reassuring, with some voicing initial uncertainties on 'how to begin' or indeed 'when to stop'. However, these uncertainties did settle down and all students steadily contributed to their individual small-group forum. Evaluation responses from the pilot student cohort gave high ratings to this aspect of online provision, with comments indicating its value for social as well as learning development:

> I am employed as a peripatetic teacher, and simply don't know what is coming next, could be a special school, a mainstream primary ... That's how the course can help, because you get an insight into how other people, other contexts, work and you learn from that.

Subsequent reflection upon structural and dialogic support for *participatory* learning through post-pilot study of forum archives, discussions with VLE designers, tutor interviews and student focus meetings enabled a nuanced analysis of the extent to which this aspect of the course design had 'worked'.

Focusing on participants' social and cognitive presence (Lombard and Ditton, 1997; Rourke, Anderson and Garrison, 1999) within their forum spaces, *interaction* as evidenced by initiation of ideas, task contribution and responsive feedback was consistent throughout the units, with many students clearly providing *transactional* input to their forum, indexing additional reading, reflection and analysis of the forum task itself as it developed, summarising joint input and widening debate. Taking an analytical step further, tracking group forum task development to individual assignment text gave no clear indications of *transformational* learning, learning that developmentally changes the learner (Mezirow, 1991, 1997). In other words, little evidence was found to confirm that knowledge, understandings and, potentially, practice developed as a direct outcome of participation within the forum groups.

It must be acknowledged that, aside from occasional 'aha' moments that might occur during interaction or immediate reflection, transformational learning as a process culminating in perceptible change to person and practice may manifest outwith the learning engagement itself, and is therefore not necessarily evidenced through textual analysis. Objective measures to test the value of participation for learning against the range of social, cognitive and behavioural learning outcomes anticipated by this course design would be hard to devise and implement – certainly within the period of its pilot implementation.

The subject tutors, themselves well versed in learning content and familiar with teaching similar groups of students on the traditionally taught version of the course, commented that the quality of learning generally shown by the pilot cohort was consistently satisfactory or, in many cases, higher than expected. Some students actually gave cause for concern lest they be 'doing too much' beyond what was needed to achieve the qualification, reflected in these tutor comments:

> It goes way beyond Level 3 standard … more Level 5 or even 6 and I am just sorry we can't give credit for that.

> Should we say 'do much less' or should we leave it flexible? A minimum amount they have to do, but the maximum is their own choice.

The 'Partners in Learning' course targets a very wide and diverse student community, and the extent to which course structure and dialogue affordances foster development of student autonomy, individual learning strategies and outcomes will depend on personal life biographies, professional roles, career trajectories and the course objectives of individual students. A key objective of the required forum participation, from a learning design perspective, was the integration of group learning with individual workplace experience, with the hope of developing work practice. Lack of opportunity for, and support for, voluntary cross-community interaction may have curtailed or compromised the extension of online community 'presence' to enable learning transfer, and potentially transaction, with students' workplace communities of practice. Evaluative analyses of feedback from students on this aspect indicated that the impact of the course within workplace contexts was experienced very differently between participants. Some felt a real benefit from the coverage of topic areas with which they were not familiar and reported that they had brought their course experience back to line management, where it had been appreciated and in some cases had resulted in developmental change to workplace practice. Others, however, several of whom had specialist roles in their professional settings and were, in a sense, peripheral to the main business of the classroom, felt a lack of support in terms of an interface between course and workplace.

Explanations for this lack of integration cannot solely index the online learning design and curriculum. Our analysis points to aspects of the workplace context that need to be considered, and ways of opening windows between the virtual course community and their professional contexts. Student study time allocation at work, course team support for workplace mentors and accessibility of course resources within the workplace could be negotiated – though this would necessarily have to be within the constraints of this relatively low-cost course provided to a number of schools by a voluntary sector organisation with limited resources. Within the online communities themselves, there could be potential for wider access across the course learning cohort. Allowing read-only access of all fora at the close of each unit task would provide for reflection upon others' participatory activity against that of one's own group, and also upon further workplace contexts and practice issues raised and shared within task discussions; and the possibility of greater 'social presence' afforded by voluntary informal chat-spaces or special interest groups would increase the level of dialogic support beyond the immediate, task-focused forum.

So far as provision for participative learning for educative purposes is concerned, this case analysis confirms that simply 'being as much like face to face as possible' is not the solution. Text-based, asynchronous communication resources can flexibly adapt to learning purpose and learner need. Continuing development issues relate to course structure and dialogue opportunities within that structure, in order to flexibly encompass a diversity of learner contexts and learning needs. Nevertheless, choices of web-based communication technologies are important within course design, as our next case makes clear, for realisation of the particular kinds of 'participatory presence' that are needed to support specific learning outcomes.

Case two: Online participation enables successful teamwork: online functionality and community of practice elements combined

Our second case shows how the design of learning and its assessment shapes online participation and can lead to positive learning outcomes. Distributed teams had to use online tools to complete their shared task, and group assessment fostered development of a community of practice approach within each team. In this example, participation through use of an audio-visual conferencing environment and Skype afforded synchronous discussion and messaging for small project teams of five to seven students studying part time, at a distance, for their final M.Eng. module. Each team also used a jointly constructed wiki to deliver their final project report for assessment. All professionally accredited engineering degrees in the UK require students to demonstrate ability to contribute effectively as team members, achieving complex outcomes through working together. As a course requirement therefore, M.Eng. students had to design, develop and report on a group project of their choice, demonstrating and reflecting upon effective team practice, including their individual contributions to the team, made during regular video conferencing meetings and through their contributions to the project wiki. Without online tools enabling easy and regular communication, discussion and contribution, the learning outcomes would not have been achievable. The benefits of online participation here derive from the fit between the core learning outcomes, their assessment and the essential role of online communication for achievement of the group's tasks.

Use of Information and Communications Technology (ICT) on this module was researched as part of a JISC-funded project,[2] involving interviews of the module chair and a sample of students at the beginning, middle and end of module study (Thorpe and Edmunds, 2011). The aim of the research was to explore students' experience of ICT across a range of work-related modules, and the M.Eng. was one of our case studies.

In the M.Eng., students were able to choose the project they worked on during this module after attending a residential meeting where they met other students and formed the groups that worked together online for the rest of the module. Students used video-conferencing and messaging software to meet virtually at least once every week in order to agree their role and task in delivering the group project, to report progress and to agree contributions to their group project wiki. Their pass or fail grade for the group project report was shared – either all passed or none passed. Individual assignments were also submitted in order to enable each student to be graded individually on their reflection on the team processes and their own contributions to the development of the group's project.

This form of participation echoes the mutual obligation and shared tasks characteristic of Wenger's community of practice model, and there is evidence that the often intense weekly online interactions did generate a group identity around the shared task of submitting the final project report. Students also drew on their workplace expertise, where skills of chairing, note-taking and contribution to team meetings were familiar, and were explicitly used to support effective conduct in the online weekly meetings. Teams for example rotated the chair between meetings, and members took responsibility for notes and progress chasing. Students who lacked prior experience of this kind might not have been as able to adapt so quickly to the online environment, and more structured support for participation might be necessary in such circumstances.

Students commented positively on the impact of being able to see and talk with their colleagues through audio-visual conferencing, and the way this built the familiarity and mutual trust that enabled teams to edit each other's work on a shared wiki:

> It was an awful lot of work, a very hard course ... but it was quite strange towards the end of the last Flashmeeting [audio-visual conferencing software] – it was almost quite sad ... being able to see people was brilliant 'cause you can see their expressions ... and emotions and also the recordings were useful for the assignments ... it was interesting to see how the group changed as we started off working on our own bits but towards the end we were much more of a team and were editing as we did our final project report on the wiki ... I don't know whether it was just a team of old [meaning the team had worked together over several months] or we gained people's trust, they knew people wouldn't be offended ... I think you're always worried to begin with you're going to change something and someone's going to be upset and change it back but no it worked well for us.

This interview extract makes clear that participation generated trust, enabling the difficult task of editing the work of others. However this was not purely a product of successful online participation, but reflected the wider course structure, where individual assessment included a group mark so that each member had a vested interest in all members of the team contributing effectively. Identification with each other, fostered by the software, enabling students to see each other as well as communicate, therefore enabled the team to demonstrate that they could collaborate in the complex task of drafting and editing, without animosity. To this extent therefore we see online participation leading into growth, if only in embryo, of an online community of practice.

As the virtual meetings were recorded, individuals could watch archives and reflect on the process of interaction, using this reflection to support assignments that required them to comment on their effectiveness as a team and their individual contributions to the project. This afforded a two-stage process of participation, during and after the event, going beyond the possibilities of face-to-face meetings which normally are not recorded. The practical and learning benefits of this functionality were made clear by students in interview:

> I like the fact it's recorded and you can go back and ... preview the meeting. 'Cause I was late for one of them, got stuck coming home from work and then I went back and watched probably about 45 minutes of the team meeting before I actually joined. It was fascinating to actually sit back and watch it rather than play a part.

This comment highlights a new perspective on participation in online environments allowing not just a single participatory process, but post-hoc reflection on the participation of others and even of one's own performance. Participation therefore can be multilayered, and our appreciation of it needs to take into account not only the visible contributions but the invisible activities of observation and reading (in the case of text messages and forums), with its potential for vicarious learning (Cox, McKendree, Tobin, Lee and Mayes, 1999) and of reflection on process, made possible through a recorded archive. The module chair highlighted in an interview that the archiving and re-run function of the software supported 'vital learning processes in that team members can reflect on the collaborative process. Technology has enhanced learning here through supporting the kind of practices that the course requires'.

We argued earlier that online participation may not necessarily facilitate learning, let alone the formation of a community of practice among participants in an e-learning course. In this case, however, students came to identify with each other as carriers of shared responsibility within a shared task – individuals in other words became aligned with the group. This arises not only from participation per se, which included affective as well as communicative elements, but from the relationship between participation and the wider course context. Learners' motivation to pass the course and thus achieve their degree required them to work as a team on a project where a large proportion of the final mark was the group mark for their project report. The reasons for online participation – its benefit for each student – were therefore clear. Students also used their own work experience where chairing and managing face-to-face meetings had developed skills they could draw upon to help make the online participation work effectively.

Participation in this context therefore had something of a hybrid quality, reflecting both offline participation in work environments as well as online interaction. Here we see new possibilities for combining individual and group learning, and for reflection on the process of interaction that can enhance both conceptual understanding and practical skills engagement. Working as an individual but with evidence of the contributions of a group to hand can offer a unique opportunity for growth and personal identity development. It is feasible now to use participation in audio-visual interaction to build team competences, hitherto assumed impossible to achieve at a distance. Indeed, online participation in virtual teams can offer new possibilities for reflection that are not normally available for face-to-face meetings. Our case here shows how students valued online participation and used it effectively. However, it also illustrates that this was not an 'easy win'. Highly motivated and skilled groups of students worked within a module designed in ways that meant they had to work as a team in order to pass their module and sophisticated online tools were available to enable them to do that. Software tools can deliver particular functionality but not guarantee effective participation. It is the fit between learning outcomes, the functionality of the online tools and environment, and the design of student activity and assessment that supports the achievement of effective participation and apprenticeship into an engineering 'community of practice'. This synergy between task design, assessment and learning environment enabled students to engage with the group task and to make active connections between their learning environment online and the practices and demands of engineering in the (physical) workplace.

Case three: Participation, inclusion and exclusion in a networked 'open learning' community

Our third case considers online participation in a broader and more open educational context, within which multiple purposes can become cross purposes, evoking conflict and blocking participation. Wikiversity, a 'sister' project of Wikipedia, has attempted since its founding in 2006 to create both editable open educational resources (OER) and a space for 'learning in the wiki way'.

Wikis are intentionally participatory spaces – indeed, they require community work to build and to maintain them. Bruns and Humphreys (2005, p. 3) lay out several aspects of wiki-based learning, some of which were seen in the previous cases:

> [L]earning in a wiki environment is learning technical literacy, content creation in a digital environment, the art of collaboration, consensus building, creating explicit knowledge from tacit understanding, and effectively communicating ideas to other people through networked knowledge environments.

But, useful though this list is, its positive framing might conceal the fact that these activities are fraught with tension. The Wikiversity community, in its activity to collaboratively develop educational materials and a wiki-based space for learning, has grappled with many issues and tensions that we believe have significant implications for educational practice and research – particularly around how collaborative development works in an online environment that networks members from different scholarly and other communities with a variety of subject discipline knowledge, teaching expertise, higher educational practice community experience and, indeed, expectations and conceptions of education. This varied background will, necessarily, influence participants' motives for participation in the shared Wikiversity enterprise, which is further complicated by the fact that the scope of the project – as well as how it works – is in continual negotiation. In a sense, this project is the antithesis of the 'what works' agenda in that decisions on how to structure the learning environment are not based on evidence of 'best practice' but are left to the community to collectively decide.

A good example of an issue around networked and participatory knowledge with which the Wikiversity community grappled can be seen in a conflict around the proposed deletion of a number of Wikiversity pages, on the basis that they were redundant, of poor quality and/or lacking in visible utility. One such page was one set up purportedly as a 'student union', or a portal for Wikiversity learners, which stated: 'Wikiversity is devoted to the joy and adventure of active learning. Explore what is of most interest to you. Ask for help. Create and join Learning Projects. Have fun'. The page was barely edited or used over an

18-month period, at which point it was nominated for deletion with the justification: 'This page is an ancient relic from a time when it looked like a good idea. It's unlikely this page will ever be developed, and it might encourage silliness'.

In response to this proposed deletion, the 'Student union' page was then significantly reframed by one participant as itself a 'learning project', questioning how deleting this page would fit with Wikiversity's claim to be open to participation, and with the assertion: 'Right now, the Wikiversity Student union is under attack by deletionists who cannot stand the idea that students might participate at Wikiversity'. This pattern was repeated: pages proposed for deletion were reframed as learning projects enquiring into the practice of deleting pages and the philosophy of 'deletionism'. However, many Wikiversity participants were unhappy with recognising these as 'learning projects'; with some participants instead calling them 'attack pages' (directed towards the people proposing to delete the pages). At issue here was whether there should be standards of quality underpinning the community and, furthermore, principles around what is or isn't a legitimate learning project; and whether these could constitute mechanisms for defining legitimate and illegitimate participation (and hence, inclusion and exclusion), and by what principles such reifications could be defined.

Considering this issue from a learning theory perspective, for Lave and Wenger (1991), learning involves a person gaining and claiming competence within a community, and being recognised as competent by the community. A person entering a project such as Wikiversity will need to negotiate what it means to be a participant in that community, and how to become a competent member of it (Bryant, Forte and Bruckman, 2005). Conversely, a community will need to define, or have a sense of, what kinds or standards of participation it values (MacIntyre, 1981), and to encourage and facilitate the kinds of 'competent' or 'valuable' participation it needs to sustain itself (Wenger, 1998). But this implies that some participants (and their participation) may be deemed incompetent by community standards – a conclusion that was resisted by some participants on account of its exclusionary implications. This tension between legitimate peripheral participation and community standards, therefore, cuts to the heart of the aspiration of Wikiversity and, by extension, other similar open learning communities wishing to be inclusive of diverse individuals' learning goals and to allow individuals to learn and gain competence through participation.

There is also cause for reflection here around an assertion often made: that a wiki will improve over time, through diverse input. A page on a wiki may often be created with placeholder text – with the expectation or promise that the page will be improved iteratively in the future. Indeed, unfinishedness is a model for inviting participation – many wiki participants will attest that fixing an error or expanding something when they noted some information was missing from the wiki was how they got involved in the wiki in the first place (Bryant *et al.*, 2005; Schmidt and Glott, 2009). But, of course, communities of practice need to define a sense of common value – for example, the development of 'good' or 'high-quality' materials – and to galvanise collective activity around that end. In this sense, the ambiguity of 'eventualism' versus 'quality' can cause social tension – pitching the perspective of 'this is not good enough' against that of 'give it time to be improved'.

Here the community's desire for quality comes into conflict with the ability for a newcomer to contribute to the project and thereby align themselves to the learning potential of participation. On the one hand, it was argued that newcomers should be welcomed so as to enrich the community and to enable them to become competent practitioners; and that deleting a resource – or perhaps even nominating it for deletion – may curb potential learning, thereby representing a loss, or even an act of hostility, to the community. On the other hand, a resource's nomination for deletion was seen to serve as a mechanism for the development of that resource – drawing people into its development – as well as a means for clarifying the community's shared activity by virtue of collectively defining value or quality. Of course, this latter point begs questions about who defines quality, to which criteria and how these criteria are defined. The community was divided over setting standards by which some resources could legitimately be described, as they were at one point, as 'garbage' – on the basis that deleting such resources, or even using labels such as 'garbage', may put off the people who created them from participating further. The argument by some in the community – though disputed by others – was less for an absence of standards, but rather that an 'agenda of quality' could lead to an impoverished version of Wikiversity if standards were too strictly defined and/or applied. Underpinning this controversy, of course, was the question of who has the legitimacy to make such decisions; in other words, what modes of authority and accountability are in use by the community in its decision-making processes?

The conflict around 'deletionism' exposes a central tension for Wikiversity and similar projects, raising questions as to how the community decides what is appropriate or legitimate and, indeed, as to the legitimacy of the process by which legitimacy is defined. Furthermore, the question arises of whether a person is free to learn what they like, in whatever way they wish, or whether the community overrides the will of the individual, and, if the latter, how space is provided for individual participants' learning. If the individual's agency is contingent upon the cohesiveness of a shared space and activity, and thereby accountable to the community, what should be the nature and utility of a community-based learning space? Could multiple spaces provide opportunities for legitimate peripheral participation? Outside of the 'content development' workspace itself, what manner of space or spaces should be made available for personal and social, as well as intellectual, learning development? Would the pattern of conflict around deletionism that caused such fragmentation within the Wikiversity community have been so damaging had it been conducted even partly face to face, or using more sociable online tools than asynchronous text? Clearly, these questions point to the tensions – both social and technical – that underpin online collaborative learning environments, and that communities need to resolve *in practice* in response to their own dynamics and aspirations.

Concluding thoughts

Theoretical models of social learning, drawing on 'communities of practice' models of development, provide useful tools for conceptualising supportive environments and pedagogies for effective participation in online learning contexts. Our three case analyses provide useful perspectives on participative learning that can inform design and practice of online provision.

Importantly, they show that looking at measurable and visible evidence of interaction between members of online communities only addresses one dimension of participation for learning. Particularly in cases where the online, interactive learning course is intended to feed into and perhaps change workplace practice, any evaluation of participation for learning must look further, into the ongoing development of the learners themselves in their day-to-day contexts of practice. Connecting online study and professional workplace communities could be accomplished by identifying common practices or tasks that serve purposes in each community, or actually building in opportunities for shared engagement between communities to bridge and scaffold development of both. Online team tasks that are essential and assessed components of key skills development may enable students to see how their own workplace collaborations might work together better, through use of similar communication tools across multi-located project teams. Where, as in the case of the Wikiversity, the online environment is itself the context for participative development as a community of practice within its own right, structure and dialogic support should include debate space, procedural maturation and reflection time for forging rules of engagement that reflect values and preferences not yet enshrined, rather than seeking legitimation through more historical authorisation.

In using theory to think through 'participation' in these cases and considering implications of these analyses for 'virtual community' design and support, we are not claiming any neat correspondence between specific aspects of theory and their practical application in the virtual world. The design options for *dialogue*, *structure* and *autonomy* as well as their actual uptake differ markedly across different participative contexts in terms of learning development purpose, personal biographies and motivations of the participant groups; research advances our educational knowledge and practice only if it continues to study, *in situ*, how people participate (or do not participate) and why. We can use this experiential and developmental knowledge, and our empirical investigations of participation across diverse contexts, to refine and strengthen our understanding about how to organise and structure those environments to best use web-based technologies (themselves continually developing in response to user needs and practice) to support participative learning for purpose. We can also gain a wider understanding of the diverse and complex nature of e-learning (and learning) which begs the question of a 'one size fits all' pedagogical design that 'works'.

Notes

1 Case one draws on evaluative research, funded by the Royal National Institute of Blind People, into their online provision of vocational education and professional training.
2 Case two draws on research funded by the Higher Education Funding Council Joint Information Systems Committee, within its Learners' Experience of eLearning Programme, Phase 2, 2007–9.

Dialogue II

Engaging with theory to make things happen

This next dialogue moves from using theory to *think* differently about educational policies and practices to using theory to *do* things differently. The researchers here describe two projects that uniquely positioned them in ways that enabled them to both initiate and understand systemic changes. Both authors illustrate the ways in which goal-oriented activity and systems-based perspectives support changes in practice, but they apply different theoretical lenses to do so.

For Mel Ainscow it was his role as the advisor to a £50 million initiative to improve educational outcomes for all young people in his region that provided him with this opportunity to combine research and practice. The 'practice' in this case was the allocation and coordination of resources, in a region with approximately 1,150 schools and colleges, to bring about improvements in educational practice and hence educational outcomes. He describes how he drew on his knowledge of theory and practice in networks and cross-school collaborations in order to make better use of available expertise. He offers us a way of rejecting the anomaly of 'best practice' while still acknowledging that there could be better practices.

For Harry Daniels, the opportunity to enable 'expansive learning' (Engeström, 2007) was provided by his involvement in a project involving three local authorities in England and the operational staff and operational managers who were working in different areas of children's services. These professionals took part in a series of workshops where activity theory provided a shared analytical framework with which they could systematically reflect on their current working practices, with the goal of developing innovative, multi-agency working practices.

These two chapters together take up the question of how research can be an integral element of educational reform. They address a second assumption underpinning the 'what works' agenda and also voiced by potential users of educational research, that theory will not help with what to do on Monday morning. These two chapters directly address this assumption by using theory in their analyses and by employing interventionist methodologies. In reflecting on how things worked (or did not) in their respective projects, they draw out lessons that may be relevant to other contexts. They thus provide existence proofs of theory and practice intersecting in productive ways while simultaneously offering methodological and practical considerations relevant to the development of a new research agenda.

Chapter 6

Developing more equitable education systems

Reflections on a three-year improvement initiative[1]

Mel Ainscow

As countries make efforts to improve their national education systems, equity continues to be a major challenge. Put simply, how can schools ensure that every child is treated fairly, particularly those from less advantaged backgrounds? England is a useful context to consider when thinking about this issue, as noted in a 2007 OECD study which reported that the impact of socio-economic circumstances on young people's attainment was more marked in the UK than in any other of the 52 countries considered.

Recent years have seen intensive efforts by successive British governments to address such concerns. These efforts have been part of an intensification of political interest in education, especially regarding standards and the management of the state system (Whitty, 2010). Competition between schools is seen to be the key to 'driving up standards', while also further reducing the control of the local authority over provision. All of this is intended to 'liberate' schools from the bureaucracy of local government and establish a form of marketplace. In this way, it is intended that families will have greater choice as to which school their youngsters will attend. At the same time, there has been a huge number of specific policy initiatives aimed at addressing the equity agenda (Ainscow, Dyson, Goldrick and West, 2012).

Predictably, government statements point to improvements in test and examination scores, arguing that the impact of the various interventions has been significant. Within the research community, however, there are a variety of views, including some who argue that there has been very little impact, particularly among learners from disadvantaged backgrounds, and that the apparent improvements in measured performance are not supported by detailed analysis of national data (Meadows, Herrick and Feiler, 2007; Sammons, 2008; Tymms, 2004). Concern has also been expressed that improvements in test and examination scores may have been achieved by the use of particular tactics – some of which are, to say the least, dubious – such as orchestrated changes in school populations, the exclusion of some students and the careful selection of the courses students follow. All of this casts doubt on both the authenticity of improvement claims and the sustainability of whatever progress is made (Gray, 2010). There is also a worry that the various national strategies, whatever their benefits, have tended to reduce the flexibility with which schools can respond to the diverse characteristics of their students (Ainscow and West, 2006).

Meanwhile, it has been argued that the development of the educational marketplace, coupled with the recent emphasis on policies fostering greater diversity of schools, has created a quasi-selective system in which the poorest children, by and large, attend the lowest-performing schools (Ainscow et al., 2012). Consequently, the low achieving and, many would argue, the least advantaged schools, fall progressively further and further behind their high-performing counterparts. In terms of these effects, through selective advantaging and disadvantaging of schools, those policies that have generally led to increased standards have also increased rather than decreased disparities in education quality and opportunity between advantaged and less privileged groups. The policy priority, therefore, is to find ways of continuing to improve the education system but in a way that fosters equity.

A city challenge

Between 2007 and 2011, I led a large-scale initiative that set out to address this important policy agenda across ten local authorities[2] in England (Ainscow, 2012). Known as the Greater Manchester Challenge, the project involved a partnership between national government, local authorities, schools and other stakeholders, and had a government investment of around £50 million. The decision to invest such a large budget reflected a concern regarding educational standards in the region, particularly among children and young people from disadvantaged backgrounds. The approach adopted was influenced by an earlier initiative in London (Brighouse, 2007).

The Greater Manchester city region is home to a population of 2.5 million people, and has over 600,000 children and young people. Across the region, there are approximately 1,150 schools and colleges. The area is diverse in a number of ways, with very high levels of poverty. Children and young people come from a range of ethnic and cultural backgrounds, with a high proportion whose families have Asian heritage. Nearly 16 per cent have a first language other than English.

A detailed study of patterns of school attendance in Greater Manchester confirms the concerns noted earlier about the impact of national policies on the educational experiences of young people from disadvantaged backgrounds (Robson, Deas and Lymperopoulou, 2009). In particular, it shows that deprived students who attend low-performing schools do worse than deprived students who attend higher-performing schools. And, since such students go disproportionately to poor-performing schools, this exacerbates the gulf between the results of deprived and non-deprived students, thereby acting as a significant driver of social polarisation.

The overall aims of the Challenge project were related to these concerns. They were to raise the educational achievement of all children and young people, and to narrow the gap in educational achievement between learners from disadvantaged backgrounds and their peers. A vision document, developed through extensive consultation between the national and local partners, led to a worrying proliferation of what were described as 'pledges', as the various stakeholders – nationally and locally – attempted to promote their own areas of interest.

In an attempt to create a sense of common purpose within this over ambitious agenda, it was eventually agreed that the focus of Challenge activities would be on 'three As'. These were that all children and young people: should have high *Aspirations* for their own learning and life chances; are ensured *Access* to high-quality educational experiences; and *Achieve* the highest possible standards in learning. It was immediately obvious that these goals would necessitate reforms at all levels of the education service. This being the case, the aim was to encourage experimentation and innovation, rather than simply doing more of the same. Significantly, there was government approval for taking this approach, including the active involvement of a minister.

The Challenge also set out to take advantage of new opportunities provided as a result of adopting an approach that drew on the strengths that existed in different parts of the city region. These included possibilities for: tackling educational issues that cut across local authority boundaries (such as declining school performance at the secondary school stage, the development of personalised learning pathways for older students); linking educational issues to broader social and economic agendas (such as population mobility, employment, transport, housing, community safety, health); and the freer exchange of expertise, resources, and lessons from innovations.

After three years the impact was significant in respect to overall improvements in test and examination results and, indeed, the way the education system carries out its business. So, for example, Greater Manchester primary schools now outperform national averages on the tests taken by all children in England. And, in the public examinations taken by all young people at 16, in 2011 secondary schools in Greater Manchester improved faster than schools nationally, with the schools serving the most disadvantaged communities making three times more improvement than schools across the country. During the same period, the number of schools below the Government's floor standard[3] decreased more than it did in other areas of the country. In addition, the proportion of 'good' and 'outstanding' schools, as determined by the national inspection system, increased, despite the introduction of a more challenging framework (see Hutchings, Hollingworth, Mansaray, Rose and Greenwood, 2012 for a detailed independent evaluation of the impact of City Challenge).

Within such a large-scale and socially complex project it is, of course, difficult to make causal claims in respect to the factors that led to these improvements, particularly within an initiative that incorporated such a wide range of strategies. It is also the case that I walk a delicate line here in using these measures to describe the success of the intervention, given that I have already expressed concerns about their reliability and impact. And, of course, my ambiguous role

– both the leader of the project and a researcher trying to make sense of what was going on – has to be borne in mind when considering the conclusions I present.

Keeping these caveats in mind, in what follows I reflect on statistical data compiled as part of the formal monitoring of the impact of the project and qualitative evidence collected through numerous informal observations and conversations, plus more occasional formal interviews with stakeholders, in order to draw out some lessons. This leads me to indicate some of the social and political complexities involved.

A framework for analysis

The approach used by the Challenge emerged from a detailed analysis of the local context, using both statistical data and local intelligence provided by stakeholders. This drew attention to areas of concern and also helped to pinpoint a range of human resources that could be mobilised in order to support improvement efforts. Recognising the potential of these resources, it was decided that networking and collaboration should be the key strategies for strengthening the overall improvement capacity of the system.

In trying to make sense of the complex processes involved I have found it useful to see them in relation to what my colleagues and I have recently described as an *ecology of equity* (Ainscow *et al.*, 2012). By this we mean that the extent to which students' experiences and outcomes are equitable is not dependent only on the educational practices of their teachers, or even their schools. Instead, it depends on a whole range of interacting processes that reach into the school from outside. These include the demographics of the areas served by schools, the histories and cultures of the populations who send (or fail to send) their children to the school and the economic realities faced by those populations. Beyond this, they involve the underlying socio-economic processes that make some areas poor and others affluent, and that draw migrant groups into some places rather than others. They are also influenced by the wider politics of the teaching profession, of local authority decision-making and of national policy making, and the impacts of schools on one another over issues such as exclusion and parental 'choice'. In addition, they reflect new models of school governance, the ways in which local school hierarchies are established and maintained, and the ways in which school actions are constrained and enabled by their positions in those hierarchies.

It is helpful, therefore, to think of three interlinked arenas within which equity issues arise. These relate to: *within school* factors that arise from existing policies and practices; *between school* factors that arise from the characteristics of local school systems; and *beyond school* factors, including the wider policy context, family processes and resources, and the demographics, economics, cultures and histories of local areas. In what follows I examine the work of the Greater Manchester Challenge in relation to each of these sets of factors, remembering that, in practice, they interact.

Within school factors

Our earlier research had thrown light on the sorts of strategies needed in order to foster improvements in schools facing challenging circumstances (Ainscow and West, 2006; West, Ainscow and Stanford, 2005). Inevitably such research attempts to identify common elements, as it seeks to determine the ingredients that combine into success. However, useful as it is to know what these ingredients are, it is equally important to recognise that they do not readily come together into any one 'recipe' that will transform a school. Therefore, a note of caution is necessary. Yes, there do seem to be common ingredients, but these need to be mixed in different proportions and added in a different order according to the school's circumstances. This suggests that possibly the most important attribute of leaders in a school facing challenging circumstances is the ability to analyse the context as quickly as possible, as suggested by Harris and Chapman (2002).

So, for example, it is clear that focusing on teaching and focusing on learning are both important, and that once a school is into a cycle of improvement, both are kept under regular evaluation and review. However, whether to start from teaching and progress to its impact on learning, or to begin by looking at learning and then explore the implications for teaching, needs to be considered in context. A school with a static and exhausted teaching force is unlikely to respond to having current practices placed under the microscope, but may be engaged by looking at the learning needs and problems of the pupils. Conversely, in a school with relatively inexperienced teachers but poor subject leadership, staff may respond very positively to measures that focus on teaching approaches that reduce the number of classroom problems they are encountering.

Our earlier research had shown how the use of evidence to study teaching can help to foster the development of more inclusive practices (Ainscow *et al.*, 2006). Specifically, it can help to create space for reappraisal and rethinking by interrupting existing discourses, and by focusing attention on overlooked possibilities for moving practice forward. Particularly powerful techniques in this respect involve the use of mutual observation, sometimes through video recordings (Ainscow, 1999, 2003), and evidence collected from students about teaching and learning arrangements within a school (Ainscow and Kaplan, 2006; Messiou, 2006; Miles and Kaplan, 2005). Under certain conditions such approaches provide 'interruptions' that help to make the familiar unfamiliar in ways that stimulate self-questioning, creativity and action. In so doing they can sometimes lead to a reframing of perceived problems that, in turn, draws the teacher's attention to overlooked possibilities for addressing barriers to participation and learning.

However, such enquiry-based approaches to the development of practice are far from straightforward. An interruption to thinking that is created as a group of teachers engage with evidence may not necessarily lead to a consideration of new ways of working. Indeed, we had documented examples of how deeply held beliefs within a school may prevent the experimentation that is necessary in order to foster the development of more inclusive ways of working (Ainscow and

Kaplan, 2006; Howes and Ainscow, 2006). This reminds us that it is easy for educational difficulties to be pathologised as difficulties inherent within students. This is true not only of students with disabilities and those defined as having special educational needs, but also of those whose socio-economic status, race, language and gender renders them problematic to particular teachers in particular schools. Consequently, it is necessary to explore ways of developing the capacity of those within schools to reveal and challenge deeply entrenched, deficit views of 'difference', which define certain types of students as 'lacking something' (Trent, Artiles and Englert, 1998). This involves being vigilant in scrutinising how deficit assumptions may be influencing perceptions of certain students.

Bearing these ideas in mind, the Challenge placed particular emphasis on supporting within-school efforts to improve practice. Most notably, what we referred to as the 'Keys to Success' programme led to striking improvements in the performance of some 200 schools serving the most disadvantaged communities. There was also evidence that the progress that these schools made helped to trigger improvements across the system.

The approach used in each of the Keys to Success schools was particular, based on a detailed analysis of the local context and the development of an improvement strategy that fitted the circumstances. A team of expert advisers had a central role here, working alongside senior school staff in carrying out the initial analysis and, where necessary, mobilising external support. A common feature of almost all of these interventions, however, was that progress was achieved through carefully matched pairings of schools that cut across social 'boundaries' of various kinds, including those that separate schools in different local authorities. In this way, expertise that was previously trapped in particular contexts was made more widely available.

Crossing boundaries sometimes involved what seemed like unlikely partnerships. For example, a highly successful school that caters for children from Jewish Orthodox families worked with an inner city primary school – the largest primary school in the city region – to develop more effective use of assessment data and boost the quality of teaching and learning. This school had a high percentage of Muslim children, many of whom learn English as an additional language. Over a period of 18 months, the partnership contributed to significant improvements in test results, and throughout the school the majority of students reached nationally determined expectations for their ethnic groups. It also led to a series of activities around wider school issues, such as the creative arts and the use of student voice, where the two schools shared their expertise.

Another partnership involved a primary school that had developed considerable expertise in teaching children to read, supporting a secondary school in another local authority where low levels of literacy have acted as a barrier to student progress. And in another example, involving an outstanding grammar school[4] partnering with a low-performing inner city comprehensive school in another local authority, the impact on attendance, behaviour and examination results was remarkable.

Through such examples we saw how boundaries to do with cultures, religion, age group of students and selection could be crossed in order to facilitate the exchange of expertise. Significantly, these examples also indicated that such arrangements can have a positive impact on the learning of students in both of the partner schools. This is an important finding in that it draws attention to a way of strengthening relatively low-performing schools that can, at the same time, help to foster wider improvements in the system. It also offers a convincing argument as to why a relatively strong school should support other schools. Put simply, the evidence is that by helping others you help yourself.

While increased collaboration of this sort is vital as a strategy for developing more effective ways of working, the experience of Greater Manchester shows that it is not enough. The essential additional ingredient is an engagement with evidence that can bring an element of mutual challenge to such collaborative processes. We found that this is particularly essential in the partnering of schools, since collaboration is at its most powerful when partner schools are carefully matched and know what they are trying to achieve. Evidence also matters in order that schools go beyond cosy relationships that have no impact on outcomes. Consequently, schools need to base their relationships on evidence about each other's strengths and weaknesses, so that they can challenge each other to improve.

In order to facilitate this kind of contextual analysis, various strategies and frameworks were devised to help schools to support one another in carrying out reviews. In the primary sector, this involved colleagues from another school acting as critical friends to internally driven review processes; while in secondary schools, subject departments were involved in 'deep dives', where skilled subject specialists from another school visit to observe and analyse practice in order to promote focused improvement activities. The power of these approaches is in the way they provide teachers with opportunities to have strategic conversations with colleagues from another school.

Between school factors

Our earlier research had suggested that collaboration between differently performing schools can reduce polarisation within education systems, to the particular benefit of learners who are performing relatively poorly (Ainscow, 2010; Ainscow and Howes, 2007; Ainscow, Muijs and West, 2006; Ainscow and West, 2006). It does this by both transferring existing knowledge and, more importantly, generating context-specific new knowledge.

With this in mind, an attempt to engage all schools in the city region in processes of networking and collaboration was made through the creation of so-called 'Families of Schools'. This involved the use of a data system that grouped schools on the basis of the prior attainment of their students and their socio-economic home backgrounds. There were 58 primary Families and 11 secondary, each of which had between 12 and 20 schools from different local authorities.

The strength of this approach is that it groups together schools that serve similar populations while, at the same time, encouraging partnerships among schools that are not in direct competition with one another because they do not serve the same neighbourhoods.

Varied performance among Family members offered possibilities for using differences as a resource to stimulate the sharing of expertise and joint efforts to innovate in order to: improve the performance of every school; increase the numbers of outstanding schools; reduce the gap between high- and low-performing groups of learners; and improve outcomes for particular vulnerable groups of students. We found, however, that for this to happen schools had to dig more deeply into the comparative data in order to expose areas of strength that could be used to influence performance across their Family, while also identifying areas for improvement in every school.

With this in mind, the average performance for each Family – both in terms of overall attainment and recent improvement trends – provided a benchmark against which overall goals for each of the partner schools could be set. At the same time, the analysis of data with regard to sub-groups of students (e.g. boys and girls; those eligible for free school meals; minority groups) and different subject areas also enabled a Family to work on the issue of within-school variations. The collective goal, then, was to move all of the Family members forward in respect to an agreed improvement agenda.

In thinking about how to make this happen, we found that it is important to be sensitive to the limitations of statistical information. What brings such data to life is when 'insiders' start to scrutinise and ask questions as to their significance, bringing their detailed experiences and knowledge to bear on the process of interpretation. The occasional involvement of colleagues from partner schools can deepen such processes, not least because of the ways in which they may notice things or ask questions that those within a school may be overlooking.

Even then there remain other limitations that have to be kept in mind. Statistics provide patterns of what exists: they tell us what things are like but give little understanding as to why things are as they are, or how they came to be like that. This is why qualitative evidence is needed to supplement statistical data. As I have indicated, mutual observation among colleagues and listening to the views of learners can be a powerful means of challenging thinking and provoking experimentation. Again, here, there is potential for schools to support one another in collecting and engaging with such evidence in a way that has the potential to make the familiar unfamiliar. Of course, all of this necessitates a commitment of time in order to take advantage of such opportunities, a factor that, unfortunately, some head teachers found difficult to accept.

Led by head teachers, the Families of Schools proved to be successful in strengthening collaborative processes within the city region. So, for example, primary schools in one Family worked together to strengthen leadership in each school. This included head teachers visiting one another to carry out 'learning walks', during which colleagues had opportunities to reflect upon and debate noticeable differences in practices. Eight schools in another primary Family identified a shared desire to build stronger relationships with the children's homes – for example, parents of children with English as an additional language where there were communication issues, or groups of students with lower attendance. And in the secondary sector, schools within one of the Families used a web-based system where students could showcase their work via podcasts, videos and blogs, allowing teachers, parents and students from their own and other schools to view and comment on their efforts.

However, involvement of schools in the Families remained patchy and there were concerns that too often those that might most benefit chose not to do so. Our monitoring of what went on suggests certain conditions that led to higher involvement and a greater impact on student achievement. These included a collective commitment to: improve the learning of every student, in every school in the group; analyse statistical data, using professional insights in order to identify areas that need addressing; and pinpoint expertise within the schools that could be used to address these concerns. It also required collaborative activities involving people at different levels, including, in some instances, children and young people; and a small number of head teachers taking on the role of leading these collaborative activities.

In moving collaboration forward in a way that supports development within a Family of Schools, we found that shared leadership was a central driver. This requires the development of leadership practices that involve many stakeholders in collectively sharing responsibility. Often this necessitates significant changes in beliefs and attitude, and new relationships, as well as improvements in practice. The goal is to ensure that collaboration is between school communities, and not restricted to head teachers, since arrangements that rely on one person are unlikely to survive the departure of those individuals who brokered them.

Beyond school factors

In developing the strategy for the Challenge, I was conscious of the danger of separating strategies for school improvement from a consideration of the impact of wider context factors. This danger is referred to by those writers who recommend more holistic reforms that connect schools, communities, and external political and economic institutions (e.g. Anyon, 1997; Crowther, Cummings, Dyson and Milward, 2003; Levin, 2005; Lipman, 2004). These authors conclude that it is insufficient to focus solely on the improvement of schools. Rather, such efforts must be part of a larger overarching plan for system-wide reform that must include all stakeholders, at the national, district, institutional and community levels.

In pursuing the goals of the Challenge we introduced a series of strategies in order to inject further innovation and pace into the system. Each of these initiatives was led by one of the local authority partners and focused on educational issues facing all local authorities, linking improvement efforts to broader social and economic agendas. Importantly, this led to the involvement of local busi-nesses, professional sports clubs, universities, and arts and media organisations. For example, the four universities in Greater Manchester worked together on an initiative known as 'Higher Futures for You', the aim of which was to raise self-belief and aspirations among primary school children from disadvantaged backgrounds. Through carefully orchestrated visits to local places of employment, 10- and 11-year-old students were helped to understand the career opportunities that could be available to them. During a final workshop, the children shared their knowledge with their parents. This initiative, which worked with some 200 primary schools, was originally developed by the head teacher of one school. Through the Challenge, this creative project reached many more children and families.

Another initiative set out to explore the use of learner voice as a strategy for rethinking what schools offer to their students. In carrying out this work a part-nership was developed with an independent charity that promotes democratic citizenship and life skills. This led to an additional focus on the experience of young people outside of school. As a result, schools across Greater Manchester collaborated in addressing the question: *In developing children as participative citizens in designing the way things are in school, can we achieve greater civic par-ticipation beyond school?* The schools involved were enthused by the opportunity provided, and in some instances became committed to widen and deepen the involvement of students (and parents).

In another experimental initiative – known as 'Better Futures' – 16 students from disadvantaged backgrounds shared jobs in three major companies. Each student attended their internship one day per week throughout the year and caught up with missed schoolwork during the rest of the week. The evidence sug-gests that parents were very positive once they saw the impact on children's social skills in their home environment. Meanwhile, within school, aspirations changed, so did attitudes to catch up on missed school work, as the students made links between a good career and attaining targets at school. There was evidence, too, of shifts in aspirations – for example, from mechanic to engineer, childcare to business, and 'don't knows' to IT and law. The approach was subsequently devel-oped in many more schools, involving other business organisations.

Reflections

Central to the strategies I have described were attempts to develop new, more fruitful working relationships: within and between schools; between schools and their wider communities; and between local and national government. A helpful theoretical interpretation that can be made of these strategies is that, together, they help to strengthen *social capital*. In other words, they create pathways through which expertise and lessons from innovations can spread.

In recent years, the work of Robert Putnam (2000) has been influential in making the idea of social capital a focus for research and policy discussion.

Interestingly, he notes that the term was first used in 1916 by a supervisor of schools in West Virginia. Writing about the more recent situation in the United States, Putnam states that 'what many high-achieving school districts have in abundance is social capital, which is educationally more important than financial capital' (2000, p. 306). He also suggests that this can help to mitigate the insidious effects of socio-economic disadvantage.

Reflecting on his work with schools serving disadvantaged communities – also in the United States – Payne comes to a similar conclusion. Thinking specifically about school contexts that are characterised by low levels of social capital, he argues:

> Weak social infrastructure means that conservatives are right when they say that financial resources are likely to mean little in such environments. It means that expertise inside the building is likely to be underutilized, and expertise coming from outside is likely to be rejected on its face. It means that well-thought-out programs can be undermined by the factionalized character of teacher life or by strong norms that militate against teacher collaboration.
>
> (2008, p. 39)

Mulford (2007) suggests that by treating social relationships as a form of capital, they can be seen as a resource, which can then be drawn on to achieve organisational goals. There are, he explains, three types of social capital, each of which throws further light on the processes that could be developed within an education system. The first of these is 'bonding social capital' – this relates to what can happen among work colleagues within a school. 'Bridging social capital' is what can occur between schools through various forms of networking and collaboration. And finally, 'linking social capital' relates to stronger relationships between a school and wider community resources.

As I have explained, the work of the Greater Manchester Challenge involved a series of interconnected strategies that appeared to foster stronger social capital of all three types. These strategies helped to break down social barriers within schools, between schools, and between schools and other stakeholders, in order to facilitate the sorts of mutual benefit that I have described. However, it is important to recognise that, within the context of changing and, at times, contradictory national policies, the gains made through such approaches were hard won, and remained fragile and easily lost. Here, continuing tensions regarding priorities and preferred ways of working between national and local policy makers, and, indeed, between schools and local authorities, were factors that continued to create barriers to progress. So, for example, those near to central government remained pre-occupied with achieving short-term gains in test and examination scores in ways that can create barriers to efforts for promoting sustainable improvements. Coupled with this was a mistrust of local authorities – the staff of which were sometimes seen as part of the problem, rather than part of the solution – and doubts about the need to have separate strategies that fit particular contexts.

Certainly, the creation of education systems where improvement is driven by schools themselves, and that involves cooperation between schools, and between schools and other community organisations, begs questions regarding the roles of local authorities. Indeed, it raises the possibility that the involvement of a middle-level administrative structure may not even be necessary. The authors of an influential McKinsey report, having analysed 'how the world's most improved school systems keep getting better', express their surprise at the critical role that what they call the 'mediating layer' plays between school delivery and central government (Mourshed, Chijioke and Barber, 2010). This leads them to conclude that sustaining improvements in the longer term requires 'integration and intermediation' across each level of the system, 'from the classroom to the superintendent or minister's office'.

The authors of the report go on to suggest that the specific functions the mediating layer plays are: providing targeted support to schools; acting as a buffer between central government and the schools, while interpreting and communicating the improvement objectives in order to manage any resistance to change; and enhancing the collaborative exchange between schools, by facilitating the sharing of best practices, helping them to support each other, share learning and standardise practices.

Our experience in Greater Manchester suggests that local authority staff can have an important role to play, not least in acting as the conscience of the system – making sure that all children and young people are getting a fair deal within an increasingly diverse system of education. In order to do this, they need to know the big picture about what is happening in their communities, identifying priorities for action and brokering collaboration. This requires significant structural and cultural change, with local authorities moving away from a command and control perspective, towards one of enabling and facilitating collaborative action. I experienced many situations where local authority colleagues found these changes challenging, particularly during a time of reducing budgets. Nevertheless, I remain committed to the view that local coordination – the presence of an effective 'mediating layer' – is vital.

Concluding thoughts

The argument I have developed in this chapter does not take the form of a simple 'what works' formula. Rather it offers a way of thinking about system level improvement that involves an analysis of particular contexts in order to develop strategies that make better use of available energy and expertise. My suggestion is that this 'way of thinking' offers more promise than suggestions that seek to impose externally generated, one-size-fits-all improvement mechanisms.

There are, however, some rather obvious questions that can be asked about my analysis, not least in relation to my status within the Challenge initiative. As a researcher, I was provided with a remarkable opportunity to put into practice ideas that had emerged from years of investigating ways of developing more effective, equitable schools and education systems. At the same time it placed me in a position of having privileged access to information regarding the way decisions are made within an education system, from the levels of government ministers and senior civil servants, through to that of teachers in the classroom. All of this provided frequent reminders of the social complexity involved when trying to bring about changes in the way that a system does its business.

On the other hand, as the person charged with the task of championing the Challenge, how far can my interpretations be trusted, not least because my efforts to collect data about the processes involved were largely carried out in an incidental way? My response to this concern is that, while readers must take it into account in determining the weight of my argument, they should recognise that my 'insider' stance enabled me to experience things in ways that researchers rarely do. It is also worth adding that, throughout the three years, a small group of my academic colleagues acted as critical friends, reading the frequent discussion papers I prepared in order to stimulate debate with stakeholders within the project and offering their more detached views.[5] In particular, I invited them to challenge the interpretations I was making and to draw my attention to any evidence that I was falling into the trap of becoming an agent of central government.

Another obvious question relates to the large amount of funding involved. Put simply, how far were the successes of the Challenge the result of the investment of additional money into the system? And, therefore, how viable are the approaches I am recommending without extra resources? This remains an area of debate within my mind. Certainly, the project involved a lot of additional finance. On the other hand, over the previous decade or so, far more money had been invested in the system through a plethora of national improvement strategies that had led to very little improvement in the performance of schools across the city region.

Notes

1 The work described in this chapter is the product of the efforts and creativity of many colleagues in the schools, local authorities and communities of Greater Manchester. Particular thanks must go to the splendid team of advisers and civil servants who worked with me on the project. Their efforts were in themselves a demonstration of the power of collaboration.
2 There are 152 English local authorities. They are democratically accountable for providing a range of services for their local communities, including education. The ten local authorities in Greater Manchester are: Bolton, Bury, Oldham, Manchester, Rochdale, Salford, Stockport, Tameside, Trafford and Wigan.
3 This is the minimum standard set by the Government, below which schools are subject to some form of intervention.
4 Grammar schools select students academically at the age of 11. In general they do not tend to cater for young people from economically disadvantaged backgrounds.
5 Chris Chapman, Alan Dyson, Peter Farrell, Denis Mongon and Mel West acted as critical friends throughout the project and, in so doing, contributed many ideas to the analysis presented in this chapter.

Chapter 7

Researching complex systems
Developing a language of description

Harry Daniels

This chapter[1] is concerned with the way which we understand and investigate the relationship between human functioning and social setting. It deploys post-Vygotskian theory, which attempts to account for the social formation of mind mediated by artefacts understood as cultural–historical products, and Bernsteinian theory (e.g. Bernstein, 2000), which seeks to forge analytical linkages between structure, communication and consciousness. As I have noted elsewhere much of the sociocultural or activity theory research that claims a Vygotskian root fails to fully articulate an appropriate theory of social structure and an account of how it directs and deflects the attention of the individuals it constrains and enables (Daniels, 2001, 2008). Sawyer (2002) argues that the way forward is to be found in an approach that 'must include postulates about the two-way causal relationship between individual and social properties, including the internalization processes associated with development and the externalization processes whereby individuals affect social structure' (p. 300). In this way he rejects the individualism that is the hallmark of much cognitive psychology and the deterministic internalisation that Bernstein suggests is to be found in some approaches to macro-sociology:

> A crucial problem of theoretical Marxism is the inability of the theory to provide descriptions of micro level processes, except by projecting macro level concepts on to the micro level unmediated by intervening concepts through which the micro can be both uniquely described and related to the macro level.
>
> (Bernstein, 1993, p. xv)

The central thrust of this chapter is that this theoretical perspective draws attention to aspects of practice that are sometimes overlooked by policy makers and practitioners who are, albeit tacitly, operating with more traditional theoretical models. In this sense the chapter seeks to provide one illustration of the way in which theory can come to deflect and direct research and the attention of policy and practice.

There is a growing interest in what has become known as 'sociocultural theory' and its near relative 'activity theory'. Both traditions are historically linked to the work of L. S. Vygotsky and both attempt to provide an account of learning and development as mediated processes. In sociocultural theory the emphasis is on semiotic mediation with a particular emphasis on speech (e.g. Wertsch, 1991). In activity theory it is activity itself that takes the centre stage in the analysis (e.g. Engeström, 1993). Both approaches attempt to theorise and provide methodological tools for investigating the processes by which social, cultural and historical factors shape human functioning. Neither account resorts to determinism in that they both acknowledge that in the course of their own development human beings also actively shape the very forces that are active in shaping them. This mediational model (as shown in Figure 7.1), which entails the mutual influence of individual and supra-individual factors, lies at the heart of many attempts to develop our understanding of the possibilities for interventions in processes of human learning and development. For many educators the model provides important tools for the development of an understanding of pedagogy. Importantly, this body of theoretical work opens up, or rather insists upon, a pedagogic imagination that reflects on the processes of teaching and learning as much more than face-to-face interaction or the simple transmission of prescribed knowledge and skill. My suggestion is that given that human beings have the capacity to influence their own development through their use of the artefacts, including discourses that they and others create or have created, then we need a language of description that allows us to identify and investigate:

- the circumstances in which particular discourses are produced;
- the modalities of such forms of cultural production;
- the implications of the availability of specific forms of such production for the shaping of learning and development.

I will use the term 'language of description' here because I wish to suggest that there is a need to connect theory with the descriptions that are used in the activity of research.

I will outline the methodology that was deployed in the course of a study of the emergence of new forms of professional learning in rapidly changing workplaces and then discuss the method of data analysis that was developed in the course of this study. I will present an account of an approach to the analysis of data collected over an extended period of time as professionals, who provide services for children, participated in a series of workshops in which they discuss data that mirror their professional action and try to bring about change in their own institutional settings which themselves have been subject to radical change. The data trace the emergence of new ideas that were formed as tools with which individuals and groups may act to change their professional work practices as the demands of such work change.

In order to establish the context in which these data were gathered and analysed I will summarise a recent report of an investigation of the relationship between human functioning and the social relations of institutional settings (Daniels, 2010). The Learning in and for Interagency Working project (LIW)[2] was concerned with the learning of professionals in the creation of new forms of practice that provide joined-up solutions to complex and diverse client needs. Working with other professionals involves engaging with many configurations of diverse social practices. It also requires the development of new forms of hybrid practice. The call for 'joined-up' responses from professionals places emphasis on the need for new, qualitatively different forms of multi-agency practice, in which providers operate across traditional service and team boundaries.

This was a study that examined the challenges involved in doing what Victor and Boynton (1998) describe as *co-configuration* work. In the context of professional collaboration for social inclusion, co-configuration involves an ongoing partnership between professionals and service users to support young people's pathways out of social exclusion. This work demands capacity to recognise and access expertise distributed across local systems and to negotiate the boundaries of responsible professional action with other professionals and with clients. These are the key features of multi-agency working that focused our attention.

One of the project aims was to investigate the mutual shaping of human action and institutional settings. In order to fulfil this aim the project required theoretical tools that would generate a methodology (design) and methods that facilitated the examination of reciprocal transformation of institutional structure and individual agency. In Daniels (2010) an account of institutional structures as cultural–historical products (artefacts) which play a part in the implicit (Werstch, 2007) or invisible (Bernstein, 2000) mediation of human functioning and which are in turn transformed into tools through human action was developed. Invisible semiotic mediation is concerned with the ways in which unself-conscious, everyday discourse mediates mental dispositions, tendencies to respond to situations in certain ways and how it puts in place beliefs about the world one lives in, including beliefs about both phenomena that are supposedly in nature and those that are said to be in our culture (Hasan, 2002). Invisible semiotic mediation occurs in discourse embedded in everyday, ordinary activities of a social subject's life. Institutional structures themselves are cultural products that serve as mediators. When we talk in institutions, history enters the flow of communication through the invisible or implicit mediation of the institutional structures (Makitalo and Saljo, 2002). In the context of the research reported here we were interested in the meditational effects of different modalities of organisational structure in Children's Services on the actions of professionals in those services. Conversely, we were also interested in the ways in which these same professionals learned to act in new ways and in so doing brought about change in the institutions in which they worked. This research focus demands an appropriate theoretical stance on the challenge of macro–micro relations that can gain access to data on the processes of invisible semiotic mediation which are in play in rapidly changing workplaces.

Post-Vygotskian theory, which attempts to account for the social formation of mind mediated by artefacts, understood as cultural–historical products, and Bernsteinian sociological theory (e.g. Bernstein, 2000), which seeks to forge analytical linkages between structure, communication and consciousness, were both deployed (see Daniels, 2010 for details). The theoretical move attempted in the work reported here was to show how Bernstein (2000) provides a language of description that allows Vygotsky's (1987) account of social formation of mind to be extended and enhanced through an understanding of the sociological processes that form specific modalities of pedagogic practice and their specialised professional concepts. The two approaches engage with a common theme, namely the social shaping of consciousness, from different perspectives and yet, as Bernstein (1993) acknowledges, both develop many of their core assumptions from the work of Marx and the French school of early twentieth-century sociology.

Vygotsky was concerned to study human functioning as it developed rather than considering functions that had developed. The essence of his 'dual stimulation' method is that subjects are placed in a situation in which a problem is identified and they are also provided with tools with which to solve the problem or means by which they can construct tools to solve the problem. When applied to the study of professional learning, the notion of dual stimulation directs attention to the ways in which professionals solve problems with the aid of tools that may be in circulation in their workplace or may be provided by interventionist researchers.

We studied professional learning in workshops that were broadly derived from the 'Change Laboratory' intervention sessions, developed by Engeström and his colleagues in Helsinki on the basis of their work in the development of Cultural Historical Activity Theory (CHAT) (Engeström, 2007), which incorporates a Vygotskian dual stimulation method. They seek to analyse the development of consciousness within practical social activity settings. Their emphasis is on the psychological impacts of organised activity and the social conditions and systems that are produced in and through such activity.

CHAT helped us explore the interrelated changes over time of the *subject* (the practitioners), the *tools*, material and conceptual, that they used, their conception of the *object* (what they were working on and trying to change), the *division of labour* (roles and power relations), the *rules* (procedures and protocols) and the *community* (all the people involved).

Engeström (1999a) sees joint activity or practice as the unit of analysis for activity theory, not individual activity. He is interested in the process of social transformation and includes the structure of the social world in analysis, taking into account the conflictual nature of social practice. He sees instability (internal tensions) and contradiction as the 'motive force of change and development' (Engeström, 1999a, p. 9) and the transitions and reorganisations within and between activity systems as part of evolution; it is not only the subject, but the environment, that is modified through mediated activity. He views the 'reflective appropriation of advanced models and tools' as 'ways out of internal contradictions' that result in new activity systems (Cole and Engeström, 1993, p. 40). Much of Engeström's work involves developmental, intervention-based research. He argues that research has a dialectical, dialogic relationship with activity and he focuses on contradictions as causative and disturbances as indicators of potential.

He sees interventions as enabling the construction of new instrumentalities, and bringing about, through externalisation, the 'transformative construction of new instruments and forms of activity at collective and individual levels' (Engeström, 1999a, p. 11).

In this way Engeström studies transformations in work and organisations, combining micro-level analysis of discourse and interaction with historical analysis and the macro-modelling of organisations as activity systems working through developmental contradictions. CHAT underpinned the Developmental Work Research (DWR) sessions that provided the main data source for our examination of conceptual change.

DWR is used to help practitioners reveal understandings that are embedded in their accounts of their practices and the systemic tensions and contradictions they encountered when developing new ways of working. In DWR, 'second series stimuli' are used with the participants to achieve this. In DWR sessions these stimuli are the conceptual tools of activity theory. The research team shared these conceptual tools with the practitioners to enable them to analyse and make sense of their everyday practices, the things that they were working on and trying to change during those practices and the organisational features that shaped them. In the sessions, evidence of the practices of the participants, gathered in previous interviews, workshops or compiled with practitioners as case study examples, were presented by the facilitators. As they worked on the evidence using activity theory, practitioners revealed the conceptual tools they were using as they engaged in or hoped to develop their work. This methodology enabled the research team to see what practitioners were learning in order to undertake inter-professional collaborations, and what adjustments they were making to existing practices and their own positions as professionals within those practices.

Bernstein's (2000) general model is one that is designed to relate macro-institutional forms to micro-interactional levels and the underlying rules of communicative competence. This is something that CHAT struggles to achieve. Bernstein focuses upon two levels: a structural level and an interactional level. The structural level is analysed in terms of the social division of labour it creates (e.g. the degree of specialisation, and thus strength of boundary between professional groupings) and the interactional with the form of social relation it creates (e.g. the degree of control that a manager may exert over a team members' work plan). The social division is analysed in terms of strength of the boundary of its divisions, that is, with respect to the degree of specialisation (e.g. how strong is the boundary between professions such as teaching and social work). Thus the key concept at the structural level is the concept of boundary, and structures are distinguished in terms of their relations between categories. The interactional level emerges as the regulation of the transmission/acquisition relation between teacher and taught (or the manager and the managed), that is, the interactional level comes to refer to the pedagogic context and the social relations of the workplace or classroom or its equivalent. Bernstein's work has not placed particular emphasis on the study of change (see

Bernstein, 2000) and thus, as it stands, has not been applied to the study of the cultural–historical formation of specific forms of activity.

The interventionist methodology

In each of three local authorities, our research interventions were organised around a sequence of six workshops involving operational staff and operational managers working in different areas of children's services. The workshops enabled the LIW research team to examine practitioners' 'everyday' interpretations of the professional learning emerging in the shift towards multi-agency working and the organisational conditions that support such learning. Using activity theory as a shared analytical framework, the workshops were designed to support reflective systemic analysis by confronting 'everyday' understandings with critical analysis of the ways in which current working practices/activities either enabled or constrained the development of innovative, multi-agency working.

In each workshop analyses of professional learning in and for multi-agency working were developed collaboratively between the research team and children's services professionals. These focused upon:

- present practice: identifying structural tensions (or 'contradictions') in current working practices;
- past practice: encouraging professionals to consider the historical development of their working practices;
- future practice: working with professionals to suggest new forms of practice that might effectively support innovations in multi-agency working.

The aim of the workshops was to address the challenges of multi-agency professional learning by encouraging the recognition of areas in which there is a need for change in working practices and suggesting possibilities for change through reconceptualising the 'objects' that professionals are working on, the 'tools' that professionals use in their multi-agency work and the 'rules' in which professional practices are embedded.

The workshops were conducted over a period of 12 months at intervals of around six weeks. Each session ran for two hours and was, on most occasions, conducted by a team of four or five researchers. Sessions were organised around the presentation of 'mirror data': that is, data derived from analysis of individual interviews with staff and from previous workshops. Professionals and researchers discussed the mirror data, using activity theory as an analytical framework with which to identify structural tensions (or 'contradictions') in their practice. The key elements of this analysis were: a historical analysis of the development of professional practices (i.e. how had current practice developed out of older ways of working, what changes might enable current practice to evolve) and identification of the constituent parts of present, past and future multi-agency practice (what objects, rules, divisions of labour etc. did participants identify (Figure 7.1).

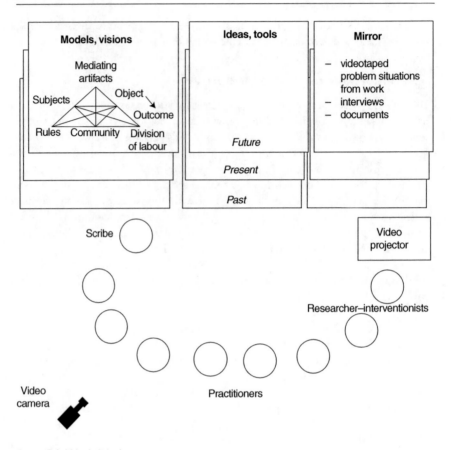

Figure 7.1 Workshop layout.

In this way, critical incidents and examples from the ethnographic material were brought into workshop sessions to stimulate analysis and negotiation between the participants. The crucial element in a Vygotskian dual stimulation event is the co-occurrence of both the problem and the tools with which to engage with that problem.

A Bernsteinian analysis revealed the professional boundaries where communicative action in each site was engaged and how that action was regulated. In a situation where boundary crossing was required in the general drive for 'joined-up' approaches, we inferred that the weakest boundaries would be those that were most likely to be crossed and transformed. Analysis revealed how a focus on institutional boundaries and relations of control provided important tools for understanding the shaping of transformative learning in specific settings.

This approach gives some insight into the shaping effect of institutions as well as the ways in which they are transformed through the agency of participants. We modelled the structural relations of power and control in institutional settings, theorised as cultural–historical artefacts, which invisibly or implicitly mediate the relations of participants in practices in which communicative action takes place. The Bernsteinian analysis was indicative of the points at which change was most likely to take place in specific institutional modalities as pressure for change was invoked from outside those settings.

Methods of data analysis

There were two approaches to the analysis of data. First, a top-down selective 'structural' analysis, using CHAT and cognate concepts to provide mirror data that would stimulate discussion of past, present and future work in the dual stimulation scenarios that constituted the workshops.

A second approach was developed to analyse the audio-visual recordings of the six, two-hour workshops that took place at each of three sites over one year with the practitioners who were working in multi-professional settings or were moving towards inter-professional work. The data were collected by three teams of researchers from three English universities.

The rest of this chapter will consist of a discussion[3] of the analysis of:

- communicative accomplishment in the facilitation of the workshops;
- accomplishment and organisation of participant contributions and emergent engagement;
- the emergence of what it is to learn as an analytic object across the workshops.

In order to identify evidence trails of professional learning in multi-agency settings in this multi-site and multi-centred study over time, a 'bottom-up' comprehensive analysis of audio-visual recordings of workshops was needed. David Middleton proposed an approach to analysis that focused on the forms of social action that are accomplished in talk and text and the sorts of communicative devices that are used (Middleton et al., 2008). This was termed the 'D-analysis'. It was designed to focus the analytic attention of the research team on emergent distinctions that were argued by participants. This involved the examination of the shift from the 'given' to the 'to-be-established'. We emphasised that addressing such issues required a focus on the sequential and contingent organisation of session communicative action. That is, how people's contributions to the sessions are contingently related to each other in terms of the sequential organisation of their talk (Middleton et al., 2008). Its cyclical application enabled: reading, reviewing, interrogating, collating and comparing all the audio-visual evidence from the intervention sessions in order to identify the emergent strands of learning and proposals for change.

The approach was developed as a means of identifying strands of communicative action that witnessed the sequential and contingent development of concepts over the course of the year in which the six workshops were organised at each site. In drawing analytical attention to the significance of claims to experience we were also able to highlight the temporal organisation of communicative action. We also used forms of discursive analysis to trace the emergence of what can be taken as the collective and distributed knowledge of people who are charged with the task of working together. We aimed to track the emergence of practical epistemologies (c.f. Wickman and Ostman, 2002) that come and need to be taken-as-given in order to take account of hitherto unaddressed gaps in the realisation of multi-agency practice. Such gaps were identified and worked on through participation in the DWR sessions at each research site.

In the first instance we approached the data with what could be termed a minimal operationalisation of what-it-is-to-learn from a participant's perspective. We examined the data for ways participants signalled some forms of awareness that theirs or another's knowledge state is at issue. Such 'noticings' provide the resource that engages the participants in their definition, delineation and deliberation of the nature of the practices that make up their multidisciplinary work. In the data we could identify many such strands of noting and noticing such distinctions that differentiate between old and new orders of understanding. Indeed, this sort of analysis provided us with a basis for defining a protocol for guiding interrogation and analysis of the data in terms of the sequential organisation of such strands. The analysis was therefore initially guided in terms of the following protocol:

- Deixis: identify when there is some nomination or 'pointing' to a particular issue in terms of drawing attention to a distinction that is then worked up to make a difference in subsequent turns.
- Definition and delineation: look for how that issue is elaborated in the uptake of others in terms of how the following are warranted and made relevant through: (i) qualifications identifying further distinctions; (ii) orderabilities in the organisation and delivery of past, present and future practice; (iii) expansive elaborations of the problematics of practice.
- Deliberation: identify how a working consensus on the case under discussion emerges.

The analysis then turned to examining in what ways such sequences mattered. If we identified strands of deixis, definition/delineation and deliberation, what were their contingent consequences for participants? Did they make visible distinctions that made the difference in ways that participants could be identified as attending to what was necessary to attend to in order to learn to do multi-agency working? In other words, did they lead to some form of departure or development in claims concerning the practice of the participants? Thus enabling us to complete the definition of the protocol with:

- Departure: identify shifts towards qualitatively different positions in practices in relation to the formulation of emergent distinctions.
- Development: identify when participants specify new ways of working that provide the basis for becoming part of, or have become part of, what they take to be and warrant as a significant reformulation of their practices.

Sequences of communicative action were analysed in the transcripts of the workshops and the development of these sequences was collated in strands that stretched across the series of workshops. Related sequences were identified and these were grouped into strands of talk that wove their way through the progress of each series of workshops. These strands are given in Box 7.1.

Box 7.1 Strands across workshops

- Focusing on the whole child in the wider context.
- Being responsive to others: both professionals and clients.
- Clarifying the purpose of work and being open to alternatives.
- Knowing how to know who (can help).
- Rule-bending and risk-taking.
- Creating and developing better (material and discursive) tools.
- Developing processes for knowledge sharing and pathways for practice.
- Understanding oneself and one's professional values.
- Taking a pedagogic stance at work, particularly the need to enable operational staff to communicate the implications of emergent practices with strategists.

Some sequences progressed to departures while others remained at other stages within the model. Each Local Authority workshop witnessed distinctive patterns of development as shown in Table 7.1.

Table 7.1 The distribution of emergent strands across research sites

Concept	Local Authority 1	Local Authority 2	Local Authority 3
1 To know how to know others	Delineation	Departure Delineation	Delineation
2 Rule-bending and risk-taking	Delineation Development	Departure Delineation	
3 Pedagogic and developmental stance at work	Delineation Development	Delineation Development	
4 Creation and development of better tools	Delineation	Delineation Departure Development	Departure Development
5 Work on understanding oneself and professional values	Development Delineation	Delineation Departure Development	Departure
6 To be clear what they work on and to be open to alternatives	Development Delineation	Departure Development	Departure Development
7 To organise to be able to be responsive to clients and other professionals	Delineation Departure	Delineation	Departure Development
8 To focus on the whole child in a wider context	Delineation Departure	Departure Delineation	Delineation Departure
9 To develop processes for knowledge sharing e.g. two-way flows, new pathways for practice		Delineation Departure Development	Delineation Development
10 To negotiate their institutional strategies			Departure Development
11 To recognise different assessment regimes and practices within different services and agencies			Delineation Departure Development

Conclusion

The data suggested that while relationships between their organisations were reconfigured around them, practitioners remained focused on what they saw as the needs of children and adjusted their ways of working accordingly. In many ways their practices raced ahead of both local and national strategies as the practitioners worked creatively for children in shifting systems. Our research suggests that in some instances professional practices have moved to *co-configuration* with an attempt to adapt practices to respond to the changing needs of clients and to involve clients in co-designing the services they receive. We also identified the challenges to the learning that was needed to move to this new way of working. These challenges arise from contradictions in working practices when different professionals collaborate. Management structures, for example, could inhibit the development of collaborative working, not least because supporting the use of expertise distributed among different professionals made line-management hard to maintain. The professional identity of practitioners working in this way became destabilised, and this subverted established patterns of authority and accountability. Working with professionals we discovered and developed what, using the terminology of CHAT, can be described as new *tools* and *rules* for co-configuration working. These included a professional approach to rule-bending and risk-taking to enable joined-up service provision working around systems that were not changing as fast as the child-focused, inter-professional practices being developed. The current chapter is limited to a partial demonstration of this analysis in order to present the use of theory and methodology in this project.

The overall challenge of the project was to show how institutionally established categories, such as those established in the division of labour, and ways of arguing could be reformulated and transformed into new strategies and activities as part of learning what it is to become engaged with and in multi-agency work. In Daniels (2010) it was shown how Middleton's D analysis, taken together with an application of Bernstein's sociology of pedagogy, provided empirical evidence of the mutual shaping of communicative action by organisational structures and relations and the formation of new professional identities. However, without the comprehensive analysis of the communicative action within the sessions across all the research sites, we would not have been able to progress to the final analysis of those transformations (Daniels, 2006). The D analysis provided a means of tracking the sequential and contingent emergence of new concepts. It permits analysis of interaction as mediated by/in the institutional context and the identification of the ways in which attention and action was directed and deflected by histories of professional cultures. This form of analysis of communicative action provides evidence of the ways in which the institution itself is shaped as well as shapes the possibilities for action.

In order to refine an understanding of organisation and discursive practices in such situations, new theories of concept formation that emphasise the complex nature of concepts will need to be deployed. There is a need to develop current work on the predictive relationships between macro structures and micro processes. Research in this field requires a unified theory that can give rise to a coherent and internally consistent methodology rather than a collection of compartmentalised accounts of activity, discourse and social positioning which have disparate and often contradictory assumptions.

This approach to modelling the structural relations of power and control in institutional settings theorised as cultural–historical artefacts that invisibly or implicitly mediate the relations of participants in practices in which communicative action may be analysed in terms of the strands of evidence of learning in and for new ways of working gives some insight into the shaping effect of institutions as well as the ways in which they are transformed through the agency of participants. The workshops provide an arena in which the often tacit or implicit, everyday understandings that circulate in practices may be made explicit and open for conscious reflection. This reflection enables these everyday understandings to be brought into relation with the more general explicit meanings or scientific concepts that have been developed more widely. This approach also opens up the possibility of developing increasingly delicate descriptions of the rules and division of labour that obtain within and between settings and thus a more sophisticated account of the forms of regulation that structure practices.

Notes

1 This chapter builds on work published in Daniels, H. (2008). *Vygotsky and research*. London: Routledge.
2 TLRP-ESRC study ESRC RES-139-25-0100 'Learning in and for Interagency Working' was co-directed by Harry Daniels and Anne Edwards. The research team included Paul Warmington, Deirdre Martin, Jane Leadbetter, David Middleton and Steve Brown.
3 I am grateful to David Middleton for permission to draw on project notes for this section.

Dialogue III

Developing a practice-based research agenda in education

Having addressed a number of problematic assumptions about the 'what works' research agenda that have been unpacked through practice-based, theoretically informed research across a range of contexts, we now move to consider the possibilities of an alternative research agenda. Rather than 'evidence-based practice', we have identified a need for practice-based evidence and theoretical perspectives that account for the complex historical, institutional and political contexts that mediate the practices and decisions of those engaged in teaching and learning. This shift in the dialogue places the spotlight on researchers rather than on educational practitioners expected to implement 'best practice'.

The chapters in this dialogue consider a range of theoretical perspectives, methods and researcher orientations in an effort to drive home the idea that diversity is a valuable commodity when it comes to addressing the complexities of educational problems and the multiplicity of personal and professional investments and objectives. Etienne Wenger-Trayner addresses this opportunity from the perspective of a theorist, reminding us of the rich theoretical field at our disposal. His 'confession' comes from over ten years of consulting with practitioners interested in developing practice within their organisations, using the 'communities of practice' framework. Although he does not identify as an 'educationalist', his reflections have wide-reaching applications for educational research, not least because they relate to a question asked by all researchers at some point: which theory is most appropriate given my data, my research methodology and the story I am telling? A common follow-up question would query whether we may choose more than one theory. Etienne outlines a 'plug-and-play' approach that says you can. He offers a set of principles and guidelines for this approach to running one theory through another, using his own theory as an example. Tim Deignan continues the theme of respecting diversity in perspectives by describing a unique combination of theory and method which he proposes can be used to develop systems that are multi-voiced and values-respecting. Using the example of dyslexia support in a UK university to demonstrate his approach to modelling the interplay of activity and subjectivity at a range of levels, his theorisation offers a way towards more effective and more democratic policy and practice – a conceptual tool for a variety of contexts.

Anna Sfard moves then to discuss the strengths and challenges of discursive methodologies, arguing that these provide a worthy alternative to the politician's demand for 'scientific evidence' produced through randomised experiments. A particular challenge of staying true to this methodology, in its radical form, is avoiding claims and interpretations that slip into dualistic and deterministic epistemological frames. Using a study in mathematics teaching and learning as an illustrative example, she elaborates upon a number of principles that discursivists must follow when employing the radical approach she describes. Her account reminds us that, regardless of our methodological approaches, all methods are underpinned by theories that, in turn, are contingent upon particular epistemologies. If we are to develop a theoretically informed, practice-based research agenda as an alternative to 'what works', we will need to keep this at the forefront of our discussions.

Rounding off this discussion of the intersections of theory and method, Valerie Farnsworth combines different perspectives on identity to explore the relationship between learning and curriculum, and between the learner and cultural models. Her chapter suggests that useful concepts and conceptualisations can emerge from an analysis that brings different theoretical perspectives in dialogue with each other. This suggests that one way in which research can inform practice, as an alternative to identifying 'what works' or defining 'best practice', is to offer conceptual tools that can support theoretically informed decision making in education.

However, as Seth Chaiklin argues in his chapter, it is not enough to 'offer' new ways of thinking if our goal is for the knowledge we produce to be useful and relevant for policy and practice in education. Seth addresses this issue by starting with the fundamental question: What is the relation between educational research and educational practice? He draws on a theory of activity to examine this relationship, and so proposes a research pathway that holds possibilities for strengthening the relationship between research and practice. The onus is placed on the researcher to be strategic from the beginning to the end of their research projects.

Chapter 8

The practice of theory
Confessions of a social learning theorist

Etienne Wenger-Trayner

This is an essay on the craft of producing and using social theory. I argue that social theory contributes to knowledge by producing perspectives that can be used to make sense of the world. This sense-making purpose entails a complex relation between theory and practice. The two can inform each other, change each other, but do not determine each other. Moreover, because perspectives can coexist, social theory does not progress in a linear fashion, with one theory replacing another, but by assembling a puzzle of interacting pieces. I propose that theories contribute to this progress by clarifying their location in this puzzle and thus enabling a 'plug-and-play' approach to the combination of related theories.

I like to think of myself as a practitioner in social learning theory in the sense that I produce theory. I am also a practitioner in the sense that I often act as a learning consultant in various settings where my theory has relevance. This essay is a personal reflection anchored in this experience. I will use my own theorising as a basis for these reflections and relate my theory to those of a few other theorists.[1] I will assume familiarity with my work and the work of these authors.

The nature of theorising in social theory

Let me start with a reflection of the nature of theorising in the social sciences. Social theory aims to organise a perspective on the world rather than generate statements that can be true or false. This focus on perspective making produces more complex relations between theories, and between theory and practice, than in disciplines where the purpose of theory is to create and debate empirically verifiable statements about the world.

Two ways to create knowledge

To reflect productively on the nature of theorising in social theory it is useful to distinguish between two ways of producing knowledge.

New knowledge through methodology

One way to generate knowledge is to produce statements about the world that are not possible to make through daily experience, that is, telling people something they do not know. For instance, saying that the universe is 15 billion years old is not something we can induce from personal experience. Scientific communities have methodologies and instrumentation that allow them to produce such statements and claim a high degree of reliability for them. In the social domain too, statisticians can make pronouncements about the world that are not achievable through experience, such as the number of students who graduate from college in various countries around the world or the probability that a person with a given profile will have a car accident. Such methodological claims to knowledge are achieved within communities where they are contestable and under scrutiny. These communities can enforce adherence to practices that have become established as reliable (through processes such as peer reviews or doctoral supervision). This allows people to build on each other's work in a process of accumulation of knowledge. Once a theory has become established others can build on it to create new statements about the world. If a theory proves inadequate, people can replace it. My characterisation is a seriously oversimplified view of the process,[2] but the point is that this social and methodological apparatus allows members of these communities to produce statements about the world that can be considered reliable even though such statements usually cannot be verified through personal experience.[3]

New knowledge through perspective

I remember being at a meeting to talk about my theoretical work and a graduate student remarked: 'Is there something I am missing here? This all seems completely commonsense to me.' His assumption was that if I was contributing to knowledge, I should provide him with some information he did not have. My response was that he had not missed anything. My work is commonsense in that I produce knowledge not by telling people things they do not know, but by providing tools to make sense of what they already know through personal experience – and hence know it anew. I would say that the characteristic of a good social theory is this ability to experience the familiar in a new way or to articulate our experience in a new way. A theory in the social sciences is not a statement of truth that can be verified or falsified. The notion of community of practice, for instance, is not true or false. It is a way of thinking about the social nature of the negotiation of competence. A theory in this sense is a framework that provides more or less useful ways of seeing the world. It allows one to tell certain stories. It enables one to know the world anew by focusing on new aspects, asking new questions, and seeking new observations and interpretations. Whether this counts as producing knowledge is a matter of definition; but it certainly contributes to our ability to make sense of the world.

Creating technical languages

Social theory is not the only endeavour that can result in new ways of looking at the world. A good novel or a moving speech can do this. The difference between social theory and literature or oratory lies in the systematic creation of a technical language.

Technical terms and vernacular language

In forging a language of concepts and metaphors, a theory makes certain terms technical. These are often words borrowed from vernacular language (e.g. identity, boundary, trajectory) or phrases made up of common terms (e.g. community of practice, negotiation of meaning). Once a term has been technicised this way, it is lifted from vernacular language and given a formal role in the theory.

Note that it becomes tricky to use a technical term in a vernacular way when one uses the framework of a theory. For instance, if I use the term 'identity' in my writing, I usually have to restrict myself to the role of this term in my theory; or if I want to use the term in a more vernacular way, I have to give a caveat or make my use obvious.[4]

Conversely, accounts crafted on the basis of a theory will use lots of terms and concepts that are simply left as vernacular language. Let me illustrate this with an example. I am often asked where motivation is in my learning theory, on the reasonable assumption that a learning theory should address the issue of motivation. It is not in the theory as a technical term. But it can still be part of accounts based on the theory, as a vernacular term. When I write I can make use of the term motivation, I can say that strong identification with a community provides a motivation to learn its practice, but it is used here as a vernacular term (at least for now, as a theory evolves and new terms become appropriated by the theory). The theory has technical terms such as identification, trajectory, paradigmatic trajectory or non-participation, which can be used to do this work. This distinction between technical and vernacular terms requires discipline in using language.

Qualities of technical languages

Through technical language, a social theory reifies aspects of the world. This system of reification brings certain aspects and elements of the world into focus. It forces accounts to be organised around its technical terms, concepts, models and metaphors. The process can be more or less productive. The usefulness of a technical language depends on several qualities:

- *Generative.* The theory enables the creation of interesting stories, suggests probing questions and generates good insights.
- *Evocative.* The theory expands our perspective. It stimulates the imagination and encourages us to see things in new ways.

- *Recognisable.* The language resonates with our experience in ways that make it easy to appropriate. Because social theory is about us, the more we can 'live' it, the more we can 'use' it. A theory that allows personal identification with its perspective also allows appropriation of it for sense making.[5]
- *Systematic.* The system of concepts is rigorously constructed, with an economy of technical terms. Concepts do not overlap, but complement each other tightly. They form a systematic whole, which results in a coherent perspective.

There can be tensions between these qualities. Clarity and precision in definitions of terms are an important part of their transition to technical status in a system of concepts. Such formalisation is necessary to free terms from unwanted baggage of their vernacular origin. For instance, I always have to fight the connotations of harmony or homogeneity that come with the term community (which I only use in a technical sense in the expression 'community of practice'). Yet overly restrictive definitions can reduce the evocative power provided by the vernacular origin of terms. A tightly systematic theory can sometimes lose evocative power. A theory needs to strike a balance. It can be more or less directive about the use of the language, with precise definitions or process templates that proceduralise the use of the language. For instance, the triangles of Engeström's version of activity theory (1987) are rather directive in proposing a model of human activity and a tool for locating potential contradictions. This is one reason many people really like the theory while some others do not.

The art of theorising has to do with choosing a collection of technical terms that are both precise and evocative and form a coherent whole. I know I spend a lot of time sweating over the addition of a new technical term: Is it needed? What specific conceptual work will it do that a combination of existing terms would not do? Is it overlapping with or orthogonal to other concepts and dimensions of the theory and how does it articulate with them to enrich the potential accounts to be derived? What word or phrase would fit best to convey the idea?[6] The value of a theory as a perspective is rooted in a systematic discipline of language.

The 'plug-and-play' principle

The nature of theorising I have just described creates a problem for the evolution of social theory. Social theories do not compete in terms of being true or false; they compete in terms of the usefulness of their perspective in enabling certain types of accounts about the human world: they are created for different purposes, from different perspectives and therefore with different languages. As a result, it is not easy for theorists to build on each other's work. Competing on usefulness leads to a proliferation of theories without simple criteria to weed them out. As the saying goes, social theorists walk on each other's toes rather than stand on each other's shoulders.

Rather than lamenting this state of affairs or aspiring to imitate the natural sciences, I would like to propose a more constructive alternative, which celebrates the diversity of theories in light of the complexity of human experience, but without giving up on a discipline of progress. This is what I call the 'plug-and-play' principle.[7]

Again, I'll start with my own work as an example. Its focus is to produce a social learning theory. It does not theorise what is being learned, or whether it is good for the learner. It just shines a social perspective on the process of learning. But the social context of learning is complex. For instance, I am often asked why there is no social class, gender, ethnicity, institutionalised power or similar key sociological concern in my theory. Surely those are important to a social view of learning in practice. And indeed it would be tempting to expand the technical language of the theory to cover these.

I have always resisted this temptation so far. I can think of a number of reasons. First, countless issues and dimensions would be good candidates for inclusion. It is also important not to build into the theory things that one wants to be able to use the theory to explain. Finally, for most potential dimensions, there already exist numerous well-established theories. The 'plug-and-play' principle suggests another approach: rather than expanding the learning theory itself, find theories with an existing apparatus and run them through the learning theory. There exist many theories covering class, gender, institutions and other relevant topics. Rather than burdening the learning theory, why not see whether the theories can be run through each other in a plug-and-play fashion?

If social class is a significant concern, for instance, a variety of Marxist and conflict theories provide ample theorising about the nature of economic dominance in class relationships. But one could apply social learning theory to investigate the learning processes by which people become members of a social class in practice. This was the approach taken by Paul Willis in his wonderful study of *Learning to Labour* (1977). He accepted the Marxian premise of the reproduction of social classes; but he wanted to know in practice why working-class boys ended up with working-class jobs even though they heard their father complain about their work all the time. And the result of his ethnographic investigation is a very complicated story involving, among other things, resistance in school and the development of a male ('lad') identity. He was running Marxist theory through cultural-practice theory (which is very closely related to social learning theory) and the result was very insightful.

Running a theory through another

Not all theories are equally easy to combine through plug-and-play, especially if they cover the same territory but use different languages reflecting different perspectives. In some cases they may be incompatible and one may need to choose. But I suspect that it is often a productive approach to see whether two theories can run through each other. To this end, it is necessary to understand the perspective of each theory in the context of its historical roots, its location in the theoretical landscape and the intentions of its authors: the focus of the theory, the commitments it represents and the terms that are chosen as technical.

Focus

Because of the multidimensionality of human experience and the infinite variety of possible accounts of that experience, social theory always serves a specific purpose. The ability of a manageable technical language to produce useful accounts about the human world requires focus: aspect of human experience, level of scale and intended use. My own theory aims to produce a learning theory based on the assumption that learning takes place in the relation between the person and the world. The concept of community of practice is an example of a key technical term that localises this relation in the social world. This social perspective situates learning in a social geography of competence that defines localities and boundaries in the social landscape. As a journey through this landscape, learning shapes an identity, which reflects the experience of the landscape over time.

Plug-and-play between theories is useful if the focus of each theory contributes to the focus of the other by enriching and expanding the perspective. For instance, the work of Willis mentioned earlier enriches the theory of class with the local focus of practice theory; and, in turn, articulating the class-reproducing effects of practice embeds it in a broader context that gives historical significance to apparently anodyne actions. Similarly, a theory of the firm is enriched by a theory of practice while practice is enriched by an articulation of its embeddedness in an organisational context.

Stance

A social theory also represents a stance – explicit or implicit commitments to historical and intellectual roots, as well as theoretical and ethical positions.[8] Critical theory, for instance, starts by recognising the existence of power imbalances in society and this leads to a commitment that theory should help expose and redress these imbalances. Such a stance not only gives coherence to the choice of technical terms; it is something one needs to honour when engaging in plug-and-play.

Let me illustrate this by briefly articulating some commitments typical of the stance of my theory. Its focus on learning as a relation between the person and the world, typical of its anthropological roots, rejects a dichotomy between individual and social, but insists on their mutual constitution. In this mutual constitution, the theory affirms agency through engagement in the negotiation of meaning in two ways. At a collective level it theorises a local definition of competence negotiated by the community through participation. Practice is, in the last analysis, the production of a community, no matter how many external constraints influence this production (Wenger, 1998). At a personal level, the theory embodies agency in processes of identification. While identification with a community entails accountability to its competence, identification is a relationship that can be modulated (Wenger-Trayner and Wenger-Trayner, in preparation). Because of this local definition of competence, there can be no relation of subsumption between one practice and another: each practice has its own home-grown logic. While my theory is not critical in the traditional sense since it does not theorise the value of what is learned for the learner or for society, it does have an underlying ethical commitment to agency and to social learning capability as a social good. This commitment to agency and to learning capability as essential characteristics of social systems can be used as a stance for critiquing social arrangements (Wenger-Trayner and Wenger-Trayner, 2012).

Language

Plug-and-play between theories entails integrating some aspects of their respective technical languages. When two theories are brought into interplay, their technical terms can be in various relationships:

- *Vernacular in one theory, technical in the other.* This is the more common case, and the one that makes it relatively easy to plug-and-play. It is a matter of making the vernacular term technical by adopting the conceptual apparatus related to that term. Any theory can use the term community of practice as a technical term and inherit related concepts such as regime of competence, boundary and identity.
- *Two terms, similar technical usage.* When two terms refer to the same phenomenon, plug-and-play requires processes of translation that can be tricky because terms have connotations rooted in different traditions as well as vernacular usage. For instance, Gee (1999) adopts a language rooted in linguistics to describe phenomena close to my focus. He uses the term 'Discourse' (with capital D) in ways that I find indistinguishable from my notion of practice. He also talks about 'grammar' in a community to refer to what I call 'regime of competence' (Gee, 2003). I think that my theory could be enriched by plug-and-play with theories of discourse because it does not address the use of language and its power in very sophisticated ways (Barton and Tusting, 2005). In Gee's case, the common technical term provides a pivot between the theories, but the plug-and-play process will involve choosing the terms that best fit the specific purpose.
- *Same term, different technical usages.* For instance, the term practice is used in different ways in various theories (see Bourdieu's usage below). This makes it more difficult to plug-and-play because the use of the same term can lead to confusions. It is then necessary to specify in which sense one uses the term and be consistent.

As can be seen from these three dimensions, the difficulty of the plug-and-play approach is that it requires a deep understanding of the theories involved – their respective focus, stance and technical language.

Examples of plug-and-play

It is useful to illustrate these three aspects of the plug-and-play principle with a few examples. For this purpose I have chosen some theories that are close neighbours to mine and explore the potential for plug-and-play.[9]

Structuration theory

Anthony Giddens' structuration theory is an attempt to transcend some of the fundamental dichotomies of traditional social theory (agency/structure, micro/macro) by seeing social structure as both the input and output of action (Giddens, 1984). This perspective is highly compatible with my theory where practice is both the input and the output of the engagement of community members in social learning. The two theories have rather different purposes, but they can enhance each other. While the notion of structuration runs from the macro to the micro level, it is useful to create mid-level categories such as practice and identity. Such mid-level concepts refer to a context where structuration is experienced concretely by people. A community of practice is a locus of structuration. It is a social history of learning that has become a social structure (Wenger, 1998). But it is a locus of structuration where learning involves a direct interaction between the structure and the people whose experience is shaped by it and which shapes it in turn. The learning theory provides a concrete context in which people negotiate what counts as competence, and become 'structurators' as it were, through these specific competences (Wenger, 2006). This contributes a learning theory to structuration theory; and in turn the learning theory can adopt concepts from structuration theory, such as the unintended consequences of action. The purposes are complementary, the perspectives are fully compatible and the languages are quite distinct, so it is easy to plug-and-play terms of one theory into the other.

Activity theory

Activity theory has its roots in attempts to create a social theory of development rooted in the Marxist view of productive activity as the source of consciousness. This was certainly the intent of Vygotsky (1978), whose work is a foundation of activity theory. It is also true of the more recent version of Engeström (1987), which addresses the historical development (continuity and change) of sociocultural forms through activity structures. Focusing on development in terms of activity structures, activity theory does not place much emphasis on how people become able to participate in activities as acting subjects. Nor does it focus on how learning takes place across activities for specific people through the communities of practice to which they belong. Both theories adopt a sociocultural perspective, but they have produced distinct, though closely related, sets of technical terms referring to activity and practice as two different aspects of human engagement in the world. Table 8.1 gives a brief overview of the complementarity between the two perspectives by comparing a few related aspects of the theories.

Table 8.1 Related aspects of activity theory and practice theory

Aspects of theory	Activity theory	Practice theory	Plug-and-play
Perspective	Context of purposefulness in which a practice is applied	Learning continuity across time and activities	An activity involves multiple practices (through the division of labour) and a practice is realised in multiple activities
What?	Object	Domain	Domain refers to areas of competence necessary for achieving the object of activities
Who?	Subject	Identity (participation)	Identity refers to the continuity of learning and becoming across contexts of subject–object relation
How?	Tool (mediation)	Artefact (reification)	A tool mediating an activity is usually an artefact that has meaning within one or more practices (beyond a single activity)
Why?	Good for locating contradictions that drive development	Good at focusing on learning opportunities in trajectories through the social landscape	Recognising the role of multiple drivers of learning, including contradictions, but also participation, boundary processes, inspiration, adoption, etc.

The compatibility of perspectives combined with the complementarity of purpose and technical terms make plug-and-play easily productive.

Bourdieu's habitus/field theory

Pierre Bourdieu's work is an attempt to create a sociocultural theory of stratification that uses a combination of economic and cultural factors to explain enduring dominance in social-class relationships (Bourdieu, 1984). Learning in a stratified society will confront stratification, whether to reproduce it or resist it. So a learning theory and a theory of stratification have usefully complementary purposes – they need each other. Because both theories are anchored in a practice-oriented perspective, they are a natural pair. However, there are some difficulties in the details of plug-and-play due to subtle differences in language generated by the two perspectives. What I call 'competence', for instance, Bourdieu would call 'cultural capital' because he is interested in the potential for stratification. As a learning theorist I am more interested in the content of learning as the ability to do something.

I believe that the notion of field could benefit from being seen as a landscape of different practices that constitute it. This would provide a more textured view of the geography of competence necessary to sustain a field. But Bourdieu (1992) and I make different uses of the term practice. I use it in the sense of a competence derived from a collective learning process that creates continuity across time and space, as in the expression 'medical practice'. Bourdieu uses it to refer to moments of engagement of the habitus in a field. So the use of the term practice requires great care if one run the theories through each other.

The closely related meanings of the terms habitus and identity also create some difficulties. It is not possible simply to equate them because habitus refers to embodied dispositions, largely beyond consciousness or volition. This is important for a theory that tries to account for the subconscious reproduction of stratification. Reflecting my focus on learning and becoming, my notion of identity is constituted by more active processes of identification, which are essential to my commitment to account for agency.[10] I sometimes think that habitus could be viewed as the subconscious aspect of identity, which would be useful because my theory misses this distinction, except perhaps implicitly in the participation/reification pair. In this sense, my use of the term participation may be closer to Bourdieu's habitus, but participation is a process while habitus is a state. In turn, learning as becoming through the construction of an identity would add an aspect of agency to habitus, something that Bourdieu's critics often claim is missing. These conceptual struggles reflect the conflict between my intuition that the two theories are made for each other and the practical subtleties of language involved in plug-and-play.

Organisational theory

Some people raise concerns that my theory does not include a theory of organisation, which they see as important since communities of practice often operate in organisational (or cross-organisational) contexts. 'Organisation' is not a technical term in social learning theory, but again there are many theories about organisations in economics and organisational studies. My theory's focus on learning and practice does offer a perspective on organisation. An organisation involves reification in the form of designed structures, policies and relationships. This design does not 'act' on its own. Organisational design, policies and hierarchies do not have agency. They need to be created, sustained and enforced through participation in specific practices (managerial, legal, accounting, plus all the practices that are necessary to do the work of the organisation). These practices reflect and involve localised social learning processes, both to be what they have become and for their continuation and adaptation. There are several theories of the firm to choose from, but I would insist that the one selected be compatible with this view, that is, that it be run through my theory, before I can take it on board. For instance, a knowledge-based theory of the firm would have to incorporate the view that knowledge resources are embodied in a complex landscape of practice, with different communities and boundaries between them.

Plug-and-play as a discipline of progress

If a theory has difficulty accounting for a phenomenon, the temptation is to create new technical terms. But one has to be parsimonious in creating technical terms because every new term makes the theory heavier and potentially unwieldy:

it would not be very useful to make the whole of English into technical terms. Social theories do not become useful by aspiring to universality or dominance, in the sense of explaining everything. Theories that try to explain everything tend to reduce the human experience to a simple principle: everything is social class, everything is sexual drive, everything is gender, everything is power. These theories deny that there are other stories to tell about the human world.

What this suggests is a notion of progress for social theory that does not aspire to simple accumulation, but does not entail mere fragmentation either. The nature of theorising in social theory makes it hard to build on each other's work cumulatively the way natural scientists aspire to. For them if a theory struggles with data or creates more problems than it solves, ideally it is replaced by another. Natural scientists can strive for one dominant theory at a time (even if the reality of practice is more complex) because they are telling a fairly well-defined story within the purview of their specific disciplines. The plug-and-play principle is an alternative to linear accumulation. It views social theorising as a puzzle, whose diversity reflects the complexity of human life.

From this perspective a good theory is not one that claims to cover everything, but on the contrary one that is well confined and with a well-defined place in the puzzle. It is one whose boundaries are easy to engage with from other theories. This requires specifying its location and shape in the theoretical puzzle:

- what it is good for, the kind of story it can help to tell, questions it forces one to ask and focus on; and where its limits are, what story it does not help to tell, questions it is not equipped to ask well, things it overemphasises;[11]
- what other theories will need to do (accept and provide) if they want to interface while doing justice to the fundamental tenets of its perspective;
- what terms are made technical and what restrictions this formalisation places on their use.

This goes beyond merely classifying theories into schools of thought. It entails searching for productive boundaries. In an academic world where accusations that one's theory does not do this or that can be so effective, the discipline of plug-and-play may be counter-cultural. This notion of plug-and-play progress entails a more humble definition of what makes a good theory. If you cannot stand on each other's shoulders, you do not have to walk on each other's toes. You can learn to dance.

Implications for research

If social theories are built for the purpose of enabling certain accounts about the human world, researchers need to choose a theoretical framework based on the account they want to give. But it is often the case that one theory is not sufficient: no single theory provides the conceptual tools to tell the full story researchers want to tell. It is necessary to adopt the plug-and-play principle to combine theories. Of course, the process is a bit more complex because both theory and data can suggest new stories worth telling. So it is not the case that you decide on the story and then decide on the theory. The browsing of theory gives you different ways of looking at your situation or data; so the process is iterative.

I am quite comfortable with the idea of people choosing some technical terms from one theory and some from another and concocting a mix that serves their account. The plug-and-play principle suggests that you can make your own assemblage, but you need to do justice to the DNA of each theory: its purpose, its stance, its language. When selecting terms, you need to consider the embeddedness of concepts in a broader theory: what else you need to take along to remain true to the concept as used in the theory.

Implications for practice

The view of theory as conceptual framework I have outlined here suggests a mutual relationship of theory and practice. The social sciences have the characteristic that our subjects can understand and use our theories.[12] I personally do not do much research in the traditional sense: a lot of my work consists in helping practitioners apply my theory.[13] However, I can offer this reflection as a challenge to the 'what works' agenda that has been addressed by other authors in this book: the mutual engagement of theory and practice works both ways.

I find my straddling of theory and practice quite productive for my own theorising. Working with practitioners is a good ground for exploring how theory changes the way people look at the world, and which theoretical language seems most productive for people who are trying to accomplish something concrete like supporting learning in or across organisations. I can test what reflective practitioners find useful in their attempts to make sense of what is happening and what they need to do. I often discover new technical terms in my attempts to make my work useful. I can then test the evocativeness of a concept by using it in various contexts. How useful is it in helping people think about a problem? Then I have to go back to the theoretical loom and see how the concept can be woven into the theoretical fabric in a coherent way. But the demands of practice provide a very fertile ground for theory generation and refinement.

If I gain theoretical insights from involvement in practice, practitioners gain new insights from theory. The notion of community of practice has changed the way many people look at learning and at organisations. Because practice is more complex than theory, using theory to guide practice often requires some plug-and-play. This also suggests that while theory can guide the perspective of the practitioner, it cannot replace it. Theory as I have presented it here is not a claim to truth that subsumes experience, but a claim to perspective that informs experience. In the realm of social theory, the role of theory can only be to propose conceptual perspectives that train the eye to see. Theory is not to be implemented; only adopted as a tool. The final say has to be left to practitioners in the field who can see the terrain. May theory give them good eyes to see; and may their seeing eyes rescue them from the tyranny of theory.

Notes

1 I will call the version of social learning theory I am working on 'my theory' for short, referring to my book on communities of practice (Wenger, 1998) as well as more recent work (e.g. Wenger-Trayner and Wenger-Trayner, in preparation). But of course it is rooted in my work with Jean Lave (Lave and Wenger, 1991), which was itself rooted in her earlier work (Lave, 1988); and many others have contributed to its evolution.

2 Progress in scientific knowledge is the subject of intense debates in the philosophy and sociology of science. Kuhn (1962) dismisses the notion of linear progress by noting dramatic shifts between incompatible paradigms. Larry Laudan (1977) argues that an ongoing problem-solving view explains the evolution of science better: scientific theories evolve by solving (and in doing so creating) not only external, empirical problems posed by data but also internal conceptual problems in the theory. Situating science in institutions, Latour and Woolgar (1979) look at the scientific and institutional practices that 'produce' facts in the laboratory. The controversies are too subtle to be discussed here, but my point does not depend on adopting a particular view of the evolution of the natural sciences.

3 The relationship is a bit more complicated. Knowledge that is unlikely to be derived from experience can also help explain experience and thus gain plausibility; for instance, when knowing that the earth is round helps explain why it appears that ships sink as they sail towards the horizon.

4 The natural sciences do this too, e.g. force or work in physics and function or axis in mathematics. Likewise, scientists can only use these terms in their vernacular sense when it is very clear that such is the case; for instance, if a physicist complains that writing a paper was a lot of work.

5 Wide recognisability in this sense is a form of generality. Here again, generality is defined in terms of being recognisable by many people by reference to their experience, as opposed to generality gained by accounting for a large dataset beyond experience.

6 By the way, this focus on technical terms that gain evocative power from the vernacular language makes translation very difficult. Fernand Gervais of Laval University, who translated one of my books into French, told me that it would have been easier to write a whole new book (personal communication).

7 The notion of 'plug-and-play' comes from a development in the design of peripherals that can easily add functionality to a computer system by interfacing with that system immediately upon connection.

8 I am avoiding talking about theoretical commitments in terms of schools of social thought because I am more interested in the craft of theorising than in classifying theories, even though I recognise that these classifications are useful as a way to understand what theories are trying to do and where they come from.

9 I have selected these particular theories because they have influenced me and I have struggled to figure out what the relationship was and, in many cases, whether there was any reason for my own theory at all.

10 Qasim and Williams (2012) argue that Bourdieu (1991) makes a distinction between habitus and identity and accepts that identity involves more negotiated processes of identification. I do not think, however, that Bourdieu would consider identity a technical term in his theory.

11 Theories always get into trouble; for instance, activity theory with its insistence on a single, well-defined object (Engeström, 2009), or my theory because it overemphasises issues of membership, as noted in Gee's critique (Gee, 2007).

12 As well as empirical findings, Giddens argues that the use of the social sciences for institutional design is a characteristic of modernity, which he calls *institutional reflexivity* (Giddens, 1991).
13 For a critique of the instrumental use of practice theory, see Vann and Bowker (2001).

Chapter 9

Using diverse system perspectives to develop policy and practice in an answerable way

The case of dyslexia support in higher education

Tim Deignan

In this chapter I describe a small-scale exploratory study (N=33) that investigated the views of dyslexic students and dyslexia support staff in relation to the learning support provided for students with dyslexia at a university in the north of England (see also Deignan, 2012a, 2012b). My study theorizes the interplay of activity and subjectivity at a range of levels, using a framework that gives multiple perspectives and diverse values a central role in the development of policy and practice. To model activity and subjectivity in relation to dyslexia support as seen by the participants, I used a blend of activity theory (Engeström, 1993) and Q methodology (Brown, 1980; Stephenson, 1953; Watts and Stenner, 2012), a technique for investigating viewpoints. I describe how policies and practices can have negative impacts and how top-down attempts to make systems work can be detrimental at many levels. I propose an approach to systems development that is multi-voiced and values-respecting. Drawing on the work of the Russian philosopher and literary theorist Mikhail Bakhtin (1895–1975), I argue that Bakhtinian concepts of dialogism and answerability, used in combination with activity theory and Q methodology, can support the development of more democratic and effective policy and practice in a range of contexts.

The motivation to conduct the study arose from my experience of working in post-compulsory education as a dyslexia support tutor. I was interested in the possibility of improving such support at a range of levels, from one-to-one tutorial support to national level policy design contexts. Within a university dyslexia support context, a wide diversity of dyslexic students with different personal profiles and needs follow a range of programmes with widely varying demands. In these circumstances, the desirability of a one-size-fits-all approach to learning support is questionable, as 'what works' may be contingent on individual and context-specific circumstances. Yet, at a national policy level, proposals have been made to standardize learning support for all dyslexic students (DSA-QAG, 2010). The study participants' views on this and other support issues are discussed later in the chapter.

My study took place against a changing national regulatory landscape in relation to dyslexia support. In England, specialist one-to-one tuition for students with dyslexia (until recently called 'study skills' tuition) is funded through the Disabled

Students' Allowance (DSA) (SFE, 2010). From their introduction in the early 1990s until the end of 2008, most DSA applications were processed by the individual student's Local Education Authority (LEA), since renamed as Local Authorities (LAs). A transfer of responsibility occurred with effect from the 2009–2010 funding cycle, when the Student Loans Company (SLC), also known as Student Finance England (SFE), took over the administration of the DSA application process for all Year 1 undergraduate students and postgraduate students (NADP, 2009, p. 3).

The study I describe here was conducted at the time of transition, shortly before responsibility for the administration of DSAs was passed formally from LAs to SFE. Following the transfer, disability organizations were critical of the SLC's DSA service provision, accusing it of failing to engage with key stakeholders (NADP, 2009; Skill, 2009). Similarly, The National Audit Office (2010, p. 10) reported an urgent need for 'mutual trust, open communication and shared understanding of how to deliver the service'. Following these criticisms, the Chief Executive and the Chairman of the SLC both resigned (BBC News, 2010). As a proposal to help avoid such problems, I outline a way in which diverse viewpoints may be better understood and, more importantly, used to inform policies and practices that work better because they are sensitive to context-specific issues and perspectives. I argue that policy and practice can be developed more successfully by incorporating systematically the multiple voices and perspectives that interact, and sometimes contradict each other, in a complex policy area. Engaging with multi-voicedness in an answerable way is, I argue, crucial for policies and practices to 'work'.

Conceptual framework

The conceptual framework for my study treated specialist one-to-one learning support for university students with dyslexia as activity that is socially situated (Engeström, 1999b). Understanding subjectivity is particularly significant in sociocultural research. For example, Lave and Wenger (1991, p. 113) describe multiple viewpoints as a characteristic feature of participation in a community of practice, where 'objective forms and systems of activity, on the one hand, and agents' subjective and intersubjective understandings of them, on the other, mutually constitute both the world and its experienced forms' (1991, p. 51). To model the university dyslexia support system, I used an activity theory framework (Engeström, 1993). Mediation plays a central role in activity theory, which is grounded in the notion that human beings use tools to work on an object, or problem space, in order to achieve a desired outcome. Engeström (2000, p. 964) describes how 'a collective activity system is driven by deeply communal motives. The motive is embedded in the object of the activity.' Accordingly, in Figure 9.1, the university is shown as a *subject* that uses dyslexia support as an educational *tool* (or mediating artefact) to work on an *object* (students with dyslexia) with the intended *outcome* being improved equality of opportunity, more independent learners and enhanced student achievement. This object-oriented activity involves a *community* with *rules* and a *division of labour* among the various participants.

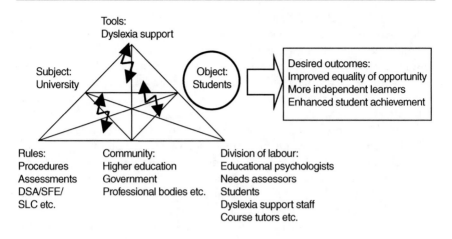

Figure 9.1 Object-oriented activity: dyslexia support in the university.

The lightning bolts in Figure 9.1, which are randomly placed, indicate potential 'contradictions' within and between the elements of the system. Contradictions, as described by Engeström (2001, p. 7), 'are not the same as problems or conflicts'; rather, they are 'historically accumulating structural tensions within and between activity systems'. Analysing the internal contradictions within an activity system is essential (Engeström, 1999b); they are described by Kangasoja (2002, p. 200) as:

> the driving force of development ... manifest in the daily practices as breakdowns, tensions, ruptures and innovations. They call for reworking, both conceptually and very concretely, the objects and motives that sustain the activity, and for re-mediating the activity system by way of improving and inventing new tools.

Engeström (2001, p. 138) also argues that 'in important transformations of our personal lives and organizational practices, we must learn new forms of activity which are not yet there. They are literally learned as they are being created'. This approach suggests to me a perspective on human development that acknowledges the specificity of individual contexts and viewpoints, and that resists simplistic reductionist prescriptions regarding 'what works'.

I will turn now to how Bakhtinian concepts relating to uniqueness, answerability and dialogue may be used to complement and strengthen the activity theoretical approach outlined thus far. Consistent with a respect for diversity in developmental contexts, Bakhtin (1993, p. 2) emphasized the 'never-repeatable uniqueness of actually lived and experienced life', in which the uniqueness of our being 'becomes a centre of answerability' (1993, p. 42). In emphasizing the moral imperative of acting in the world and the importance of dialogue within developmental contexts, Bakhtin's dialogism is described by Cheyne and Tarulli (1999, p. 11) as 'a way of thinking about ourselves and the world that always accepts non-coincidence of stance, understanding and consciousness'. Consistent with this, Bakhtin's concept of language is described by Holquist (1998, p. xviii) as involving a 'sense of opposition and struggle at the heart of existence, a ceaseless battle ... present in culture ... and in the specificity of individual consciousness'. These Bakhtinian tensions are very relevant to Vygotskyian perspectives on pedagogy and to activity theory. For example, Wegerif (2008, pp. 352–353) comments that 'a dialogic perspective argues that education more generally takes place within dialogic human relationships in which students learn to see things from at least two perspectives at once, their own point of view and that of their teacher'.

Such a view of education necessarily involves thinking about values, and indeed for Bakhtin, according to Emerson (1983, p. 248), 'every act of understanding involves an act of translation and a negotiation of values. It is essentially a phenomenon of interrelation and interaction.' This is clearly evident in Bakhtin's literary theory, in which novelistic discourse is theorized as a polyphony of contesting voices. Importantly, Bakhtin valued an interacting diversity of characters' voices over a monologic authorial voice and, as an exemplar of this, valorized Dostoevsky's polyphonic novel in which the author is on an equal footing with the characters. Morris (1997, p. 89) describes how Dostoevsky 'centres the whole novel upon the interactive consciousness of the characters'; this ceding of authorial power 'goes along with a shift of focus from seeing to hearing. Dostoevsky's new novelistic form is a design for discourse; a great dialogue of interacting voices, a polyphony'. This preference of Bakhtin's for heteroglossia over monoglossia has not only an aesthetic but also an ethical dimension, with wider implications beyond literature for our individual lives and public society.

In matters of policy and practice, the powerful do not always listen carefully or hear others clearly. Monologue, according to Bakhtin (cited in Todorov, 1998, p. 107) is 'deaf to the other's response; it does not await it and does not grant it any *decisive* force ... Monologue pretends to be the *last word*.' By contrast, Bakhtin emphasized the plural nature of subjectivity and the development of meaning and understanding through the interplay of multiple voices – a developmental process that requires respect for the voice and values of, and an answerable attitude toward, the other. I suggest that the Bakhtinian perspective on uniqueness, answerability and dialogue outlined above may be operationalized to challenge the validity, at a range of levels, of monologic 'one size fits all' approaches to policy and practice, while simultaneously pointing to solutions beyond their inherent limitations by emphasizing context-specific sensitivity. This respect and desire for multi-voicedness informed the choice of research methods for my study, as I describe in the next section.

Methodology

While Engeström (2000, 2010a, p. 18) emphasizes the importance of making manifest the multi-voicedness inherent in a collectively constructed activity system, he also acknowledges that a methodological approach for analysing the 'subjective problematic' has been lacking. Similarly, Roth *et al.* (2004) suggest that subjectivity is an important but overlooked feature of activity-theoretical studies, and emphasize the importance of a better understanding of subjective realities in activity systems. A multi-voiced theory of activity, in which the internal tensions and debates are an essential focus of analysis, requires 'tools that offer ways out of the internal contradictions' (Engeström, 1999b, p. 33). I suggest that Q methodology[1] is one such tool, and may be put to work successfully in activity theoretical studies (e.g. Deignan, 2009). As described by Barry and Proops (1999, p. 339), 'the basic distinctiveness of Q methodology is that, unlike standard survey analysis, it is interested in establishing patterns within and across individuals rather than patterns across individual traits, such as gender, age, class, etc.' Q methodology involves Q sorting, a data collection technique, followed by correlational and factor analysis of the Q sort data (Brown, 1980).

Q sorting

Procedurally, participants in a Q study represent their viewpoints on an issue by ranking, or 'sorting', a set of items along a dimension. In my study, the items were 48 statements on dyslexia support, ranked by the participants on a seven-point scale from 'disagree most' to 'agree most'. The set of statements used in the study was developed from an initial concourse of diverse views drawn from a wide range of sources including the academic literature, and communications with dyslexic students and other individuals from a range of backgrounds who had personal experience of dyslexia support in university settings. In selecting the final set of statements, care was taken to ensure that they provided thematic coverage of the different elements of the activity system as depicted in Figure 9.1. Accordingly, statements were selected that related to the *subject, tools, object, outcomes, rules, community* and *division of labour*. These relations were not exclusive, reflecting the dynamic and interconnected nature of the elements in the activity system. Below are some examples of the final set of statements sorted by the participants (see Table 9.1 for the full set).

- Students with dyslexia should be seen as having learning differences, not 'learning difficulties' (statement 1, relating to the *object*).
- Dyslexia support provision should be standardized to meet the needs of all dyslexic students (statement 10, relating to the *tools*).
- There is a danger of dyslexia support tutors doing their students' work for them (statement 36, relating to the *division of labour*).

The study participants (N=33) comprised 14 dyslexic students and 19 dyslexia support staff. Each participant was given the 48 statements printed on individual slips of paper. The sorting task required the participants to rank all the statements relative to each other along a scale from –3 to +3. The participants sorted the statements into three initial piles of 'disagree', 'agree' and 'neutral' before then assigning more finely graded degrees of feeling to the items. In a Q study, the response grid for recording a participant's ranking of the items usually employs a quasi-normal distribution,[2] with the statements in the grid columns being progressively fewer in number as they extend outwards from the middle point. A completed grid from the present study is shown in Figure 9.2. It can be seen, for instance, that statements 1, 10 and 36 (see above) were placed by this participant in columns –1, –2 and –3 respectively.

The participants' completed Q-sorts provided the raw data[3] for subsequent statistical analysis. Their views on dyslexia support as modelled in their individual Q-sorts can be considered in relation to Bakhtin's (1993, p. 45) comment on 'the emotional – volitional picture of the world' which 'presents itself to me in one way, whereas to someone else in another way'. Also resonating with the philosophy of Q methodology, Holquist (1990, p. 50) notes that Bakhtin's 'dialogism is very close to the thought of C.S. Peirce', and particularly in relation to 'what Bakhtin calls the science of ideologies, the study of differential relations between "I" and others'. William Stephenson, Q methodology's originator, drew on Peirce to emphasise the importance of subjective feeling in the formation of meaning and likewise in Q-sorting, where 'feeling is primordial' (1980, p. 9). The correlation of individual values and meanings, as modelled in participants' Q-sorts, is at the heart of Q methodology. This modelling of diverse value and belief systems in turn resonates strongly with Bakhtin's (1993, pp. 61–62) concept of novelistic discourse, which aims 'to provide … a representation, a description of the actual, concrete architectonic of value-governed experiencing of the world … the whole topos of values, the whole architectonic of seeing'.

Disagree most						Agree most
–3	–2	–1	0	+1	+2	+3
26	39	33	22	43	15	37
36	10	17	18	32	8	48
2	9	19	45	12	44	34
41	7	11	21	13	40	20
	4	6	47	14	3	
	42	38	28	16	25	
		1	35	46		
		24	5	23		
		31	29	27		
			30			

Figure 9.2 An example of the completed response grid, showing the rankings of the 48 statements as sorted by one participant in the study.

We can consider also Bakhtin's valorization of the polyphonic novel in relation to the potential of Q methodology to inform the development of a multi-voiced activity system. Bakhtin (1963, p. 102) describes how Dostoevsky 'thought not in thoughts but in points of view ... voices'. Dostoevsky's creation of a fundamentally new novelistic genre is described by Bakhtin (1963, p. 89) as one in which 'a character's word about himself and his world is just as fully weighted as the author's word'. Similarly with Q methodology, by completing and subjecting their respective Q-sorts to correlational and factor analysis, a university student's voice may be given the same weight in mathematical Q factor space as that of a support tutor or a government education minister. In this way, diverse stakeholders' views and the logic of their respective belief systems may be included, compared and contrasted, and weighed in the balance in relation to decision making on policy and practice issues.

Q factor analysis

Resonant with the Q-sorting process, Bakhtin (1993, p. 74) speaks of 'value-centers that are fundamentally and essentially different, yet are correlated with each other'. In Q methodology the shared subjectivity, i.e. viewpoints, of the participants is interpreted using Q factor analysis. Unlike conventional statistical procedures used in psychology, in Q methodology the participants are treated as variables and the items (i.e. here the set of 48 statements) are treated as cases (e.g. Stenner, Watts and Worrell, 2008). Using 'by-person' data, each person's entire Q sort is correlated with that of each other person. This intercorrelation of Q sorts shows how each Q sort's item rankings relate to that of each other Q sort. These data can then be subjected to a pattern analysis.[4] In essence, this is a data reduction process that identifies groups of Q sorts that are highly correlated. A cluster of such Q sorts points to persons sharing a similar viewpoint. These persons' Q-sorts, once identified, are merged to form a single synthetic or 'idealized' Q-sort, which represents a combined weighted average of their individual rankings of the statements (Brown, 1980). In this way, my study aimed to model shared *subjectivity* (i.e. viewpoints) among the participants and to relate this subjectivity to dyslexia support *activity* as modelled in Figure 9.1. The blend of activity theory and Q methodology is depicted in Figure 9.3. The triangle and oval shape, as in Figure 9.1, represent an activity system and its object, while the elliptical shapes represent the diversity of viewpoints within the activity system that may be modelled and interpreted using Q methodology.

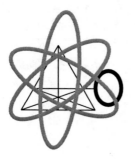

Figure 9.3 Activity/subjectivity.

I suggest that Q methodology, in combination with activity theory, offers a way for researchers to sample the diversity of interacting voices in a system and to render them mutually understandable in their polyphonic complexity. This in turn may enable the reinterpretation and overcoming of contradictions within and between activity systems. Using Q methodology with activity theory and drawing on the Bakhtinian concepts of dialogism and answerability may help us to better appreciate diverse values and perspectives and to build stakeholder consensus by, for example, co-producing a shared object for all partners to work on by using tools with shared values incorporated into their design.

Findings and discussion

Four distinct factors, representing four distinct viewpoints, were interpreted. The four columns, F1–F4 (shown in Table 9.1) represent the rankings of the statements in these four synthetic Q-sorts; each of the four is a product of the merging of strongly correlated Q-sorts. For example, the individual Q-sort shown in Figure 9.2 was one of a group that correlated strongly and contributed collectively to the creation of a single synthetic, or 'idealized' Q-sort for Factor 2 (shown in Figure 9.4). The values assigned to the 48 statements in the Factor 2 Q-sort are also displayed[5] in the F2 column in Table 9.1.

Q methodology is 'not concerned' with what proportions of a population might belong to any given factor (Brown, 1980, p. 192) and thus no claims are made here regarding generalizability.[6] As Robbins (2005, p. 215) notes, Q methodology is used to model 'characteristics of subjectivity rather than characteristics of populations'.

Disagree most						Agree most
−3	−2	−1	0	+1	+2	+3
2	1	5	6	11	20	3
26	4	17	7	12	32	8
36	10	24	9	14	37	16
41	19	28	13	23	43	25
	33	31	15	27	44	
	38	39	18	29	48	
		42	21	30		
		45	22	34		
		47	35	40		
			46			

Figure 9.4 The synthetic 'idealized' Q sort for Factor 2.

Table 9.1 Factor array showing the synthetic Q-sort values for factors 1–4

–3	–2	–1	0	+1	+2	+3
Disagree strongly	Disagree moderately	Disagree mildly	Neutral	Agree mildly	Agree moderately	Agree strongly

Note 1: *Italicized statements* indicate a consensus item (i.e. the rankings of that item by the four factors are all positive, or all negative, or all neutral).

Note 2: A **bold** ranking in the factor array indicates an item ranking difference of two or more points relative to the rankings of the same item by the other factors.

	Factor array			
	F1	F2	F3	F4
Students with dyslexia should be seen as having learning differences, not 'learning difficulties'. (1)	2	**–2**	**0**	3
Dyslexia support should concentrate on improving students' spelling. (2)	–1	–3	0	–2
Getting clear assignment feedback from course tutors is important to dyslexic students. (3)	3	3	**0**	2
Course tutors understand how to support students with dyslexia. (4)	–1	–2	–2	–2
With learning support provision, dyslexic students have a better chance of coping at university than non-dyslexic students. (5)	**–3**	–1	0	0
The main priority for dyslexic students is getting through their course. (6)	0	0	**3**	–1
Providing alternative forms of assessment for dyslexic students can undermine academic standards. (7)	0	0	–2	–3
Dyslexic students need help with developing their study skills. (8)	3	3	2	1
The university values the contribution that students with dyslexia can make. (9)	0	0	–1	0
Dyslexia support provision should be standardized to meet the needs of all dyslexic students. (10)	–2	–2	–1	–1
Dyslexia support should be mapped against critical moments in the student's learning programme. (11)	–1	1	1	0
Dyslexic students get the coursework grades that they deserve. (12)	–3	1	–2	0
Students with dyslexia can learn from hearing other students talk about their experiences of coping at university. (13)	1	0	0	1
The quality of dyslexia support provision in the university is satisfactory. (14)	0	1	1	0
Course tutors are explicit about what they expect from students. (15)	–1	0	–1	–2
Having effective learning support is important to dyslexic students. (16)	3	3	2	2

Continued

Table 9.1 Factor array showing the synthetic Q-sort values for factors 1–4, *continued*

Course tutors incorporate the needs of dyslexic students into the design and delivery of programmes. *(17)*	−1	−1	**−3**	−1
Dyslexia support should involve human contact, including counselling, so that the emotional effects on students' learning can be addressed. *(18)*	2	0	0	2
Course tutors have the training needed to support students with dyslexia. *(19)*	−2	−2	−2	−2
Students need specific help with understanding how dyslexia affects their learning. *(20)*	2	2	2	2
Dyslexia support provision should aim to reduce academic culture shock. *(21)*	0	0	0	0
The academic culture of the university makes it easy for dyslexic students to talk to other students and staff about their concerns. *(22)*	0	0	1	−1
The university's dyslexia support provision helps students to progress through their programme of learning. (23)	0	1	2	1
The importance of course tutors needing to take account of students' different learning styles is exaggerated. (24)	−1	−1	0	−2
Students with dyslexia waste time and energy because they do not know the best way to do things. *(25)*	2	3	2	1
Dyslexia support is really just about spoon-feeding weak students. *(26)*	−3	−3	−3	−3
Dyslexic students worry about not meeting their course tutors' expectations. (27)	2	1	2	0
The university meets all the needs of its dyslexic students. (28)	0	−1	−1	**−3**
Course tutors should help dyslexic students to improve their study skills. (29)	0	1	1	−1
Dyslexic students can be empowered by learning how to use appropriate information and communications technology. *(30)*	1	1	1	1
The informal peer support that dyslexic students get is more effective than the support provided by the university. (31)	0	−1	0	0
Dyslexia support should help students to cope holistically with the combinations of complex challenges that face them. (32)	**0**	2	2	3
Course tutors are aware of their dyslexic students' support needs. (33)	−2	−2	1	−1
On entry to a programme, a student's study skills should be good enough to cope with the academic demands of their course. (34)	−1	1	−1	−1
Students with dyslexia are sometimes unprepared for the academic demands of their university programme. (35)	1	0	3	1
There is a danger of dyslexia support tutors doing their students' work for them. (36)	−3	−3	−2	1
'Dyslexia' is a vague concept. (37)	−3	2	−3	2

The support that dyslexia tutors can provide over an academic year is not enough to substantially improve a student's academic performance. (38)	1	−2	−1	0
To combat the effects of dyslexia, non-standard or unorthodox methods of teaching are needed. (39)	1	−1	−1	−2
The transition from school or college to university is equally challenging for dyslexic and for non-dyslexic students. (40)	1	1	1	2
By being 'dyslexic-friendly', course tutors can actually discriminate against non-dyslexic students. (41)	−2	−3	−1	−1
The coordination between the dyslexic student's LEA and the university is satisfactory. (42)	−1	−1	−1	−1
The learning support offered to dyslexic students should help them to become independent learners. (43)	**−1**	2	1	3
Dyslexic students play a central role in determining the nature of the learning support they receive. (44)	1	2	0	0
When marking assignments, course tutors make sufficient allowance for the effects of dyslexia on their students' written work. (45)	1	−2	−3	0
University can be a frustrating and isolating experience for dyslexic students. (46)	**3**	0	1	1
Meeting the needs of dyslexic students requires huge amounts of additional work by course tutors. (47)	−2	−1	−2	−3
To be effective, university learning support needs a holistic and coherent approach to policy design which engages all those involved, including dyslexic students, non-dyslexic students, course tutors and support staff. (48)	1	2	2	3

Areas of consensus among the four interpreted viewpoints

The statements in italics in Table 9.1 show areas of consensus in terms of similar rankings of the statements by the four viewpoints represented by Factors 1–4. When considered in relation to the activity theory framework depicted in Figure 9.1, these consensus areas suggest the existence of several 'contradictions' or 'historically accumulating structural tensions' within the activity system (Engeström, 2001, p. 7). The consensus areas are depicted in Figure 9.5 and may be considered in relation to 'what works', or does not work, at a range of levels.

For example, among the consensus statements relating to system *tools*, the rankings of statement 10 challenge the wisdom of standardizing learning support for students with dyslexia. At a national level, SFE has proposed introducing a standardized support package for all dyslexic students in higher education. However, dyslexia support organizations have spoken out strongly against the SFE standardization proposal (DSA-QAG, 2010, p. 4). Similarly, the participants in the present study rejected the idea of a standardized support package (Table 9.2).

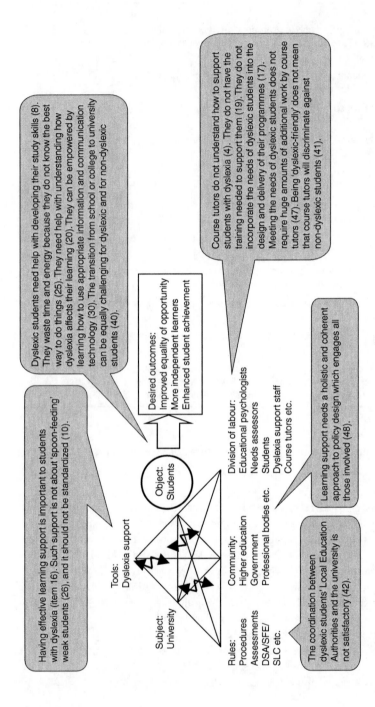

Figure 9.5 System voices: areas of consensus and near-consensus among the four interpreted viewpoints.[a]

[a] The statements in the voice bubbles point to relevant elements of the activity system.

Table 9.2 The rankings of statement 10 by the four viewpoints

Dyslexia support provision should be standardized to meet the needs of all dyslexic students. (statement 10)

Strongly disagree	Moderately disagree	Mildly disagree	Neutral	Mildly agree	Moderately agree	Strongly agree
	Factor 1	Factor 3				
	Factor 2	Factor 4				

A member of the dyslexia support staff commented as follows on statement 10:

> Well that's a load of rubbish because each dyslexic student is different and has different individual learning support needs. So if it's standardized it fails to meet their needs. What's really important in good dyslexia support provision is to identify what each individual student needs and organize the support to meet that.

A student in the study concurred that 'there's different types of dyslexia and certain people find different things difficult, basically, in a nutshell. Every single person is individual. You can't standardize something like that. You can't fit them all into the same box.' Another student commented, 'I don't think you can have one standardized approach for any student, with dyslexia or not.' Another felt that 'lots of holes could develop in it'. The risk of a standardized approach not working was explained by yet another student:

> If you just apply the standard issue kind of support it wouldn't work, because a lot of students would, you know, fall by the wayside. They wouldn't benefit from it ... dyslexia affects people in a lot of different ways ... it would be good if everyone could talk to each other basically ... to find out what the difficulties are ... sort of learning support strategies, sort of come up with individual learning support programmes.

This risk of students 'falling by the wayside' due to the imposition of monological assumptions about 'what works' is further exemplified in the case of policy on spelling at the university where the study took place. While dyslexia is commonly associated with spelling difficulties, none of the four interpreted viewpoints felt that improving students' spelling should be a priority (Table 9.3). A member of the support staff commented that 'it's not just about spelling ... It's a whole host of other things they might have problems with or, you know, do differently.'

Table 9.3 The rankings of statement 2 by the four viewpoints

Dyslexia support should be concentrate on improving students' spelling. (statement 2)

Strongly disagree	Moderately disagree	Mildly disagree	Neutral	Mildly agree	Moderately agree	Strongly agree
Factor 2	Factor 4	Factor 1	Factor 3			

A student who participated in the study explained how he very nearly did not access dyslexia support at all in his final year of university as he was concerned that the dyslexia support tutor would want to focus on improving his spelling:

> I can go into ways that dyslexia support has not helped me ... previous dyslexia tutors have worked on things like spelling and reading certain words. I don't really think that is what my problem is at all. You know, my problem is organizing stuff – organizing written work, structuring it – I think that's where my problems lie ... Certainly in the first year of uni it were just a bit of a waste looking at certain spellings of words and stuff. It's just not what I needed at all really ... I very nearly didn't come for any support this year based on all the things that have happened previous.

I think that this student's account is particularly significant given that, at the university where the study was conducted, and I believe in many other universities, the institutional guidelines for specialist dyslexia support tutors urged them to ensure that the support they offered was in line with the student's Educational Psychologist's report. This advice was exemplified with direct reference to students' spelling abilities. The guidelines noted that if a report identified spelling as an area of weakness then the support tutor should work with the student to find ways to help overcome their spelling difficulty in order to minimize the impact of their dyslexia. I see a real danger here in relation to this 'best practice' recommendation. Given that a difficulty with spelling might be expected to feature frequently on Educational Psychologists' reports relating to students with dyslexia, an institutional deficit model emphasis on remedial spelling, however well-meaning, may actually inadvertently discourage students from accessing learning support.

Finally, and again challenging monological assumptions about 'what works' in terms of official 'best practice', specialist support tutors at the university were expected to develop dyslexic students' study skills against the following specified 'learning outcomes': research, composition, proofreading, note-taking, time management and examinations. Accordingly, the university provided an 'Individual Development Plan' and 'Individual Development Review' for support tutors to identify and monitor the required 'learning outcomes' intended to result from the support.[7] However, from a sociocultural perspective, there is more to learning than skills and competence (e.g. Deignan, 2005), and again there is a danger that using a pre-specified and narrowly focused 'one size fits all' approach may actually constrain support by not being sufficiently sensitive to identify students' individual and context-specific needs.

Differences between the four interpreted viewpoints

Aside from consensus areas, the viewpoints as modelled in the factor arrays in Table 9.1 show some marked differences in the rankings of the statements. These differences again point tentatively to the location of internal contradictions within the activity system (Figure 9.6). For example, viewpoint 1 suggests that dyslexia support as *a tool* should involve unorthodox teaching methods.

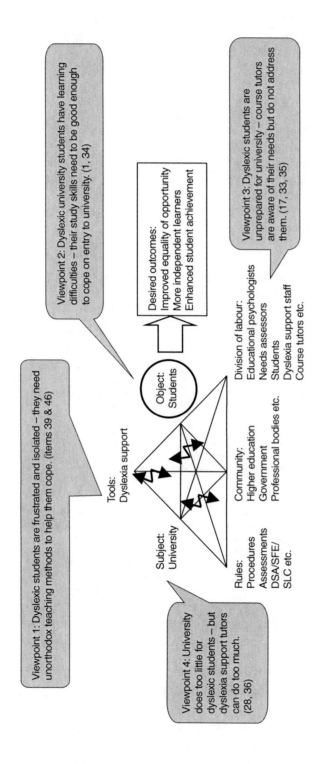

Figure 9.6 System voices: four viewpoints on dyslexia support.

Key: DSA Disabled Students Allowance; SFE Student Finance England; SLC Student Loans Company.

Note: The viewpoint voice bubbles point to elements of the system that appear particularly significant from their perspectives. For example, viewpoint 3 sees the role of course tutors as significant.

Other differences between the four viewpoints can be seen in the factor array (Table 9.1). For example, there were different views on the use of the terms 'learning differences' and 'learning difficulties' in relation to dyslexia (Table 9.4).

Similarly, there was near polarization in the ranking of statement 37, which suggested that 'dyslexia is a vague concept' (Table 9.5). One member of the support staff disagreed strongly with statement 37, and attributed such a view to 'people with their own internal political agendas'. He commented that dyslexia 'is not a middle-class construct' and added that statement 37 was 'one of the most insulting comments I've heard in a long time'. Other participants saw it differently. A student remarked that 'it just seems to be a label. It doesn't tell you specifically how everyone's affected. Everyone's affected differently and cope with that effect differently to varying degrees'.

Tensions such as those outlined above are a normal feature of activity, and their identification is a necessary step in enhancing system performance. Roth *et al.* (2004, pp. 50–51) describe contradictions as 'potential growth points that allow the system to improve'. However, developing a complex system in a way that ensures the trust and confidence of multiple stakeholders presents a challenge. The complexity of the issues involved and how they relate to stakeholder value systems need to be recognized.

Table 9.4 The rankings of statement 1 by the four viewpoints

Students with dyslexia should be seen as having 'learning differences', not 'learning difficulties'. (1)						
Strongly disagree	Moderately disagree	Mildly disagree	Neutral	Mildly agree	Moderately agree	Strongly agree
	Factor 2		Factor 3		Factor 1	Factor 4

Table 9.5 The rankings of statement 37 by the four viewpoints

'Dyslexia' is a vague concept. (37)						
Strongly disagree	Moderately disagree	Mildly disagree	Neutral	Mildly agree	Moderately agree	Strongly agree
Factor 1					Factor 2	
Factor 3					Factor 4	

Making a system work better

Values, according to Valsiner (2008, p. 73) are 'internal subjective meaning fields that totally capture and guide the person who has constructed them'. This is an important point as decisions at a range of levels, for example regarding dyslexia support interventions, will inevitably be influenced by how decision makers, including support tutors, HE institutions, national policy makers and others, define the problem space and how they perceive that which they seek to transform. Government and university policy perspectives, main course tutors' and specialist dyslexia support tutors' views on dyslexia all have implications. Interventions, however well-intentioned, may have potentially undesirable consequences. Therefore, by following a precautionary principle in understanding better how policies and practices 'work' or not, the modelling of diverse stakeholder viewpoints can offer developmental opportunities for all participants.

For example, as mentioned earlier in relation to difficulties in the provision of the DSA, the National Audit Office (2010) highlighted an urgent need at the national level for 'open communication and shared understanding' between the various stakeholders. Problems such as these may be avoided or minimized by giving multiple perspectives and diverse values a central role in the development of policy and practice. Accordingly, Figure 9.7 speaks to Bakhtin's (1981, p. 366) 'Galilean perception of language' which 'denies the absolutism of a single and unitary language' and 'refuses to acknowledge its own language as the sole verbal and semantic centre of the ideological world'. Using activity theoretical and Q methodological analyses of stakeholder activity and subjectivity, powerful voices such as the Department for Business, Innovation and Skills (BIS) and SFE/SLC may hear and understand more clearly less powerful but equally valid voices, and be influenced by them. In Bakhtinian terms, exposure to the other may have a moderating and democratizing effect, in which, as described by Crowley (2001, p. 180):

> [M]onoglossia is superseded by polyglossia when the self-sufficient language becomes conscious for the first time of otherness … once the perception of differences has entered then the self-enclosed Ptolemaic language becomes irreversibly transformed into the open Gallilean set of languages in a variety of relations with one another.

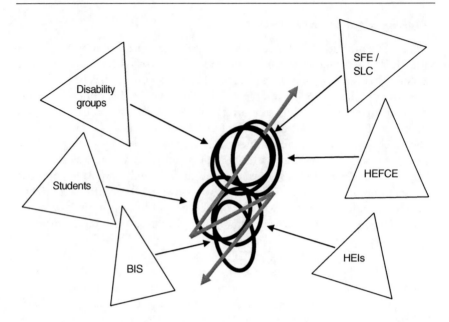

Figure 9.7 Interacting activity systems with object tensions: a zone of proximal development.

Key: SFE Student Finance England; SLC Student Loans Company; HEFCE Higher Education Funding Council for England; HEIs Higher Education Institutions; BIS Department for Business, Innovation and Skills.

In such a scenario, open communication and shared understanding may benefit all stakeholders, including the powerful, and avoid unintended consequences. As Bakhtin (1981, p. 368) notes, 'it is necessary that heteroglossia wash over a culture's awareness of itself and its language, penetrate to its core, relativize the primary language system underlying its ideology and literature and deprive it of its naive absence of conflict.' In this way, employing activity theoretical and Q methodological analyses, Figure 9.7 speaks to Bakhtin's (1981, pp. 414–415) description of 'languages of heteroglossia, like mirrors that face each other, each reflecting in its own way a piece, a tiny corner of the world' which 'force us to guess at and grasp for a world behind their mutually reflecting aspects that is broader, more multi-levelled, containing more and varied horizons than would be available to a single language or a single mirror'. 'Man's activity', according to Leont'ev (2009, p. 402), 'is regulated by mental images of reality.' In combining such images, Figure 9.7 hints at 'the reflection in the fairy-tale mirror' described by Leont'ev (2009, p. 40) 'in which is seen not only what is happening directly before it but also the whole real world, even that which has never directly thrown its rays on the mirror'.

Conclusion

There is a challenge for activity theory research, 'to develop conceptual tools to understand dialogue, multiple perspectives, and networks of interacting activity systems' (Engeström, 2001, p. 6). In this regard, I believe that Q methodology and activity theory, informed by Bakhtinian philosophy of language concepts, may be used to sensitize powerful stakeholders to the voices of others. The hearing and respecting of other voices is central not only to power relations in the polyphonic novel, but also to public sector policies and practices that are expected 'to work'. The approach is also consistent with Fischer's (2003, p. 173) comments on reframing public policy, where 'the analyst needs to identify the multitude of voices and hear their stories'. Similarly, it is consistent with Wenger's (1998, p. 218) views on harmonizing participation and reification, and the benefits of bringing 'various perspectives together in the process of creating some coordination between them'. It also resonates with Engeström's (1999b, p. 35) characterization of an activity system being 'by definition a multi-voiced formation', with development requiring 'a reorchestration of those voices, of the different viewpoints and approaches of the various participants'. The way in which we understand systems clearly influences our developmental possibilities for improving the shared worlds we inhabit. A cultural tool such as that described here, blending Q methodology with activity theory and informed by the Bakhtinian concepts of dialogism and answerability, may be used collectively to improve both our understanding and our ways of working in a wide range of policy and practice contexts.

Notes

1 The letter 'Q' is used to differentiate it from R methodology, named after Pearson's 'r' correlation. In Q, not traits but persons' individual rankings of items (i.e. their Q sorts) are correlated and factored. McKeown and Thomas (1988, p. 48) note that 'all observations in Q technique are premised on a common unit of measurement, namely, "self-significance"'.
2 For details of the minimal effects of using forced rather than free distributions on the resulting factors, see Brown (1971).
3 In addition to the statement rankings, qualitative data were also collected. Following the completion of their Q sorts, participants were asked to comment on their rankings of the statements. These qualitative data were included later in the interpretation of the shared viewpoints.
4 Principal Components Analysis followed by Varimax rotation was used for pattern analysis purposes. Only those factors with an eigenvalue greater than 1.0 and with a minimum of two Q-sorts loading on them were chosen for rotation (Donner, 2001). Four factors accounted for over half of the variance in the original 33 Q-sort data set. PQMethod (Schmolck, 2010), a statistical software package developed specifically for Q methodological research, was used for the analysis.

5 Statement 45 is ranked as –2 in the F2 column of Table 9.1. However, because of tied item z-scores it has been placed in the –1 column in the Figure 9.4 response grid as there were only six spaces available in the –2 column.
6 See Brown (2002) and Danielson (2009) for ways of investigating the prevalence of the viewpoints interpreted in a Q study in a wider population by using Q in combination with standard R survey analysis.
7 Similar approaches and documentation are used in many UK universities.

Chapter 10

Not just so stories

Practising discursive research for the benefit of educational practice

Anna Sfard

Few educational issues are as contentious these days as those that gave rise to the rhetoric of 'what works'. Imported into the discourse of educational research by politicians,[1] phrases such as 'scientific evidence', 'medical model' and 'randomized experiment' go against socioculturally minded scholars' basic understanding of what works in educational research. In the fervour for unifying, encompassing and objectifying, researchers who follow the medical model turn a blind eye to widely differing needs of individual students and classrooms. When numerous cases that have nothing in common with each other except a certain superficial feature coalesce under a single numerical label, our access to the diverse factors responsible for individual learners' success or failure is lost forever. To produce a picture that can count as truly helpful, an incomparably higher resolution is needed than can ever be attained in randomized experiments.

In this chapter, I present a vision of research that seems to have a better chance to work. For reasons that will be explained later in the chapter, I call this research discursive. My point of departure is that rather than counting superficial similarities in the quest after universals, the researcher must dig deep under the familiar and the obvious, looking for hitherto unsuspected, but in fact highly consequential differences; and rather than trying to tell teachers what is going to work in their classrooms, the researcher should help them craft tailor-made solutions for their specific problems. Within this context, the term 'scientific', if it is to be used at all, must be redefined as meaning simply that the researcher is accountable for what she says. Accountability, in turn, rather than implying adherence to a strict protocol, signals that the researcher has provided her audiences with what they need in order to see what she is seeing.

Discursive research, one that celebrates variation and change, is presented in the rest of this chapter as an avenue to take in the pursuit of the thus understood utility, scientificity and accountability of research. The adjective *discursive* signals that, whatever questions are asked in this research, the focus is on communication. The attention to discourses originates in the assumption that understanding human communication, its inner working and its relation to other things people do, is crucial for our grasp of all things human. In this chapter, after outlining the origins of discursive research and specifying its distinctive features, I will zoom in on its most consistent, 'radical' version, the approach that explicitly rejects the problematic thinking/communicating dichotomy, pervasive both in our everyday talk (we speak, for example, about 'expressing our thoughts in words' or about 'putting the same thought in a different way') and in the traditional discourses of educational research. The focus will be on ways in which discursive investigators avoid objectifying, and thus perpetuating, what is in fact transient and subject to intentional change. I would not finish without pointing to some of the challenges facing the researcher who pursues this type of endeavour. My illustrative examples come from research dealing with teaching and learning in mathematics.

Discursive research: its origins, features and forms

Even before defining radical discursivism, it is useful to take a look at how this relatively new line of research emerged from the contemporary theory of knowledge and, in particular, from the sociocultural tradition in human studies. For the sake of this brief summary, two interrelated developments have to be considered, with one of them responsible for revolutionizing our view of research as a human endeavour, and the other to be credited with reshaping our ideas about what it is that constitutes the object of human studies.

Let me begin with the first of the two developments, the epistemological. The postmodern rejection of the notion of 'absolute truth', the promise of which fuelled positivist science, is probably the first historical occurrence we need to consider when trying to answer the question of what put human sciences on a path towards the discursive turn. Rather than seeing the products of scientists' work as originating in nature itself and arising from a direct encounter between the researcher and reality, postmodern thinkers began picturing these products as human constructs, originating in interpersonal exchanges. Nowhere is this latter vision of knowledge more explicit than in the postmodern philosophers' declarations that knowledge is 'a kind of discourse' (Lyotard, 1979, p. 3), a 'conversation of mankind' (Rorty, 1979, p. 389) or 'those familiar yet enigmatic groups of statements that are known as medicine, political economy, and biology' (Foucault, 1972, back cover).

Replete with communication-related terms such as *conversation*, *sentences* and *discourse*, these different proposals can be summarized as saying that *research is the activity of collective storytelling*. In the postmodern world, we are fully sovereign in choosing our narratives, and this is true even with regard to those stories that we call 'scientific'. This does not mean that there are no restrictions on what can be told by researchers. To be endorsed as 'scientific' and trustworthy, the narrative must count as at least potentially useful. In addition, there are constraints related to the researchers' wish to achieve consensus within their community. While doing research, one participates in a special *discourse* – in a well-defined type of communication, recognizable by four characteristics, the first three of which are its specialized vocabulary, visual mediators and routines. All these, if applied properly, result in narratives that the research community endorses and regards as 'facts'. These narratives are the fourth special characteristic by which we recognize discourses. Also noteworthy is the fact that the researcher's constant effort to enrich and improve her stories is accompanied by an ongoing meta-level attempt to perfect the tools of the storytelling trade. As a result, there is continuous change not only in the stories told, but also in the discourses that make them possible. Every so often, the communicational meta-rules that regulate research practices change so drastically as to end up producing a new discourse incommensurable with the one that has been practised so far. In the newly created discourse, old words will be put to novel uses and many of the hitherto endorsed narratives will have to be rejected.

Postmodernism, therefore, portrayed research as the double activity of telling specialized stories and refining the ways in which these stories are told. The revolutionized epistemology required a matching change in the vision of the object of research, that is, of what human studies are all about. Slowly but surely, researchers interested in uniquely human forms of life began considering all those things that people say to each other as worth attention in their own right. This was quite a change, considering the fact that ever since the Cartesian decree about the separateness of the bodily and the mental, people's talk was seen as a mere 'window' to something else – to the 'contents' of the human mind, composed of entities qualitatively different from all that is directly accessible to an observer. It is this new type of research, one that takes discourses as 'the things' to explore, that will be labelled here with the adjective 'discursive'.

In the last few decades, the interest in discourses began crossing disciplinary boundaries and established itself gradually as a motif unifying all human sciences, psychology, sociology and anthropology. Whatever the questions asked in research, different aspects of human communication invariably come to the fore as an object of study. It is probably not surprising that of all human activities, communication is the one to get the lion's share of researchers' attention. Much of what people do is either purely discursive or imbued with discourse. Indeed, since discourse is the main arena of all those occurrences that count as 'social', one can say that discursivity is the hallmark of humanity. But the acknowledgement of this fact is only a part of what the discursive turn is all about. For many discursively minded researchers, even if not for all, the shift to discourse means seeing old phenomena in a dramatically new way. As instantiated with the story of changes in our thinking about science and knowledge at large (which, let's not forget, can serve as a good example of a uniquely human undertaking!), many of those activities that, so far, were considered to be merely 'mediated' or 'helped' by concomitant discursive actions may now be rethought as being communicational in nature. In other words, discourse became a principal medium in which all things human originate and remain embedded, in one way or another. In particular, as an immediate entailment of viewing research as a communicational practice, one can now say that the research disciplines known as mathematics and history are discourses, and thus learning of mathematics or history is a discursive activity as well. Indeed, research and learning are quite alike. Both consist of telling and endorsing stories and changing discourses, except that in research this change happens at the level of community and is mainly productive (creative), whereas in the case of learning it is predominantly reproductive and occurs in discourses of individuals or of small communities.

This non-dualist stance on the issue of ontogeny has its independent roots in the work of Lev Vygotsky, who claimed the developmental primacy of speech over thought and illustrated their subsequent inseparability by comparing an attempt to study thought (or meaning) and words as autonomous entities to trying to understand properties of water by investigating those of hydrogen and of oxygen. The demise of the sharp thought–communication dichotomy can also be linked to Wittgenstein's rejection of the idea of 'pure thought', this amorphous entity that is supposed to preserve its identity through a variety of verbal and non-verbal expressions. Indeed, the untenability of the thought/speech divide is clearly what Wittgenstein had in mind while stating that 'Thought is not an incorporeal process which lends life and sense to speaking, and which it would be possible to detach from speaking' (Wittgenstein, 1953, p. 109). All this comes to say that the translation of the 'cognitive' into 'discursive' does not mean any omission – it does not entail, for example, that there is no such thing as processes that happen inside human heads. It only means that discourse became the superordinate category and mental phenomena have lost their separate – and special – ontological status.

In spite of the fact that the rejection of the thinking–communicating dichotomy has been heralded by some writers as the beginning of the 'second cognitive revolution' (Harré and Gillett, 1995; see also Edwards and Potter, 1992; Edwards, 1997), non-dualism cannot be seen as a general feature of discursive research. I will now propose a subdivision by distinguishing between *moderate* and *radical* discursive positions, with the latter being characterized by an explicit commitment to the non-dualist stance. By equating thinking with communicating, adherents of radical discursivism become, by default, members of the sociocultural camp: they recognize the fact that even the most private of human activities, such as thinking or feeling, can be understood only if conceived as a part of wider collective activities. Thus, learning mathematics or physics is seen as a process of becoming a participant of the historically developed forms of discourse known as mathematics or physics. As is made clear by the word *participation*, and as famously stated by Vygotsky (1978), whatever is uniquely human originates on the 'social plane' rather than directly in the world. The diversity of the foundational positions notwithstanding, this latter point seems to constitute this one basic assumption with which no discursively minded researcher, whether moderate or radical, would be likely to argue. Radical discursive research, its basic tenets and these tenets' implications for how research should be carried out, is the theme of the next part of this chapter.

Radical discursive research: its features, advantages and challenges

Being radical means following the entailments of non-dualism all the way through. The task may sometimes be dauntingly difficult. Converting oneself into a participant of a new discourse, incommensurable with one's everyday ways of talking, requires utmost discursive discipline and a constant conscious effort to avoid slipping into old habits. Only those who firmly believe that the new discourse holds the promise of better, more helpful stories are likely to persist. Personally, I am sufficiently convinced of these future rewards to fully commit to the demanding principles of radical discursivity. In what follows, before offering a substantiation of my conviction, I briefly describe some of these principles.

Let me reiterate: doing research means participating in a well-defined discourse. Consequently, one way to delineate a certain kind of research is to specify its main discursive characteristics: its vocabulary and syntax, its mediators, routines and endorsed narratives. In what follows, I describe radical discursive research in these terms. My claims are illustrated with examples from a recent study by Einat Heyd-Metzuyanim (Heyd-Metzuyanim, 2012; Heyd-Metzuyanim and Sfard, 2012). In that investigation, the researcher, who acted also as a teacher, followed a group of four middle-school students as they were learning a number of mathematical topics. The principal aim of the study was to pinpoint those aspects of learning–teaching interactions that could be held responsible for the occasional ineffectiveness of the process. The data included in Heyd-Metzuyanim and Sfard (2012) come from a lesson during which the students were trying to solve a word problem expected to usher them into discourse on fractions.

The use of words (conceptual framework)

The discursive researcher wants to tell helpful stories about what people do. Her first principle is to construct her accounts so as to make it clear that these are, indeed, narratives about doing, about people in action. If this requirement, which may, at first, sound self-evident, needs to be explicitly stated, it is because we all have a strong propensity for *objectification*, for turning stories about properties of human actions into stories about properties of the actors. Thus, we speak about students as being mathematically *gifted* or *learning disabled* whenever we observe them participating in mathematical discourse in ways that deviate from what we consider as a 'norm'. Similarly, we present learners as having a 'well-developed *conception* of fractions' whenever we see them dealing successfully with the majority of fraction-related problems. Moreover, all those nouns that transform stories about doing into stories about being or having – *gift, learning disability, conception, mental schema*, etc. – are often used as if they signified self-sustained entities, the existence of which is a matter of independent facts rather than of a researcher's decision to speak about people's actions in a certain way.

The discursivist can see at least two reasons for attempting *disobjectification* of her talk – for avoiding verbs-turned-into-nouns, supposedly signifying object-like entities. First, talk on mental objects, such as conceptions, is at odds with her non-dualist stance. Second, objectified stories about people, as opposed to those about the inanimate world around us, are often unhelpful, and sometimes downright harmful (Sfard, 2009). Unfortunately, to see the risks one needs to look very closely, and this is something we rarely do in a spontaneous manner. The difference between a story about actions and a supposedly 'equivalent' story about the actor is subtle but important. Whereas what people do is transient, personal properties are usually conceived as rather permanent. Whereas the responsibility for individual actions can rarely be treated as the actor's own – think, for example, about the collective effort that goes into shaping a student's participation in mathematical discourse – objectified statements about how a person *is* imply that the responsibility for the given state of affairs rests either on this person's shoulders or in her genes. It is thus clear that stories about actions and those about actors inform our deeds in different ways: whereas the former invite intervention and change and leave all the options open, the latter doom individuals to special life trajectories. Indeed, the label of being affected with a 'learning disability' redirects the student to a path quite different from that of her 'normal' peers. And if all this is not enough to convince about the need for disobjectification, let me mention the risk of logical fallacies that come with contrived process–object dichotomies and lead to phony explanations and illusory dilemmas. These aftermaths of objectification may well be what Wittgenstein had in mind while warning against misuses of language disguised as deep philosophical quandaries (see also Sfard, 2008, 2009).

The work of disobjectifying is never easy, but it is not altogether impossible. One can try either to omit some nouns or redefine them in such a way as to make clear that they refer to forms of participation rather than to participants. In this latter case, it is also important to be explicit about the fact that these nouns signify discursive constructs rather than entities that pre-exist discourse, and that they have been created solely for the sake of communicational effectiveness (objectification squeezes lengthy descriptions of processes into concise statements on objects). Thus, descriptions of students' learning in Heyd-Metzuyanim's study are free from objectifying terms such as *able* or *learning disabled*; instead, the author speaks about histories of successful or unsuccessful participation in mathematical discourse. She also avoids words such as *conception* or *meaning*. This abstention does not preclude the talk about students' participation in mathematical discourse as more or less *meaningful*, with this latter adjective referring either to the participants' own evaluation of the experience or to its interpretation by an observer. To say that much, however, one does not need such undefined entities as conception or meaning and can, instead, speak directly about forms of participation (the adjectives *ritualized* vs. *explorative* are used by Heyd-Metzuyanim for making the relevant distinctions in forms of participation). Similarly, to deal with the emotional side of students' participation, the researcher speaks about property of discourses that she calls *emotional hue*. Finally, the currently popular term *identity* is defined explicitly as a discursive construct – as a collection of objectifying, emotionally hued stories one tells on different occasions about oneself (first person identity) or about other people (second or third person identities).

For the sake of those who, at this point, may mistakenly conclude that radical discursivism is a form of behaviourism, let me immediately add a disclaimer: due to the foundational assumption that equates thinking with a form of communication, looking exclusively at discourse does not mean ignoring what is going on inside one's head. On the contrary, the discursivist is trying to reconstruct the 'missing parts' of a conversation – those segments of communication that happen between a person and herself as a part of any exchange with others. She does this just as an archaeologist reconstructs an old bowl: by adding small pieces that are of the same kind exactly as the remnants she has found and that, together with the available parts, combine into a cogent whole. The only feature of radical discursivism that distinguishes it from traditional cognitivism is its stress on the fact that the 'inside' and 'outside' pieces are ontologically indistinguishable. As said before, for the radical discursivist, discourse is a superordinate category.

The requirement of disobjectification is complemented by another one, that of *operationality*: whatever terms are used, they must come with definitions that determine in a clear, unambiguous way situations in which these terms may be used as descriptors of participants' actions.[2] One of the principal challenges of Heyd-Metzuyanim's research was to disobjectify and operationalize the notions of *emotion* (this is where the term emotional hue came from) and *identity*. She did this by specifying those properties of participants' discourse that must be present if any of these terms is to be used. To understand the nature of this kind of criteria, one needs a better grasp of the medium, known as *data*, with which the researcher is working.

Perceptual mediators (data)

We can think about mediators as 'perceptual proxies' of things we are talking about. Thus, in Heyd-Metzuyanim's study, the researcher wanted to get a good grasp of students' problem-solving processes, but while conducting her analyses she was actually looking at segments of video and transcriptions, neither of which was the event itself, and each of which brought her back to that event in a different way, with different types of omissions. Video recordings that were taken simultaneously with three differently situated cameras preserved much of what happened, but still provided only a selective view of events. Even more, of course, was lost in transcriptions.

In discursive research, videos and transcriptions rather than events as such are considered as data, and the researchers, therefore, are the constructors of the materials they are supposed to investigate. Two principles are worth mentioning with regard to the work of transcribing. First, there is the requirement of *verbal fidelity*: the researcher does not re-voice the participants of her study or at least tries not to. She documents what was said verbatim, as accurately as she can. This stress on accuracy stems from the recognition of the fact that words do not have to be used in the same way by different people, and two utterances that count as 'saying the same thing' in somebody's eyes may lead somebody else to claim the opposite. Catching this kind of difference is one of the main goals of the discursivist, who knows only too well that people live by the words they use.[3] The second requirement with regard to transcriptions can be called *the principle of multimodality*: for obvious reasons, discursive researchers have to document selected aspects of participants' non-verbal actions as richly and completely as possible. The adjective 'selective' has been added to stress that one cannot possibly document everything, and the choice depends on the questions asked. Heyd-Metzuyanim had to devise a method for documenting the emotional hue of utterances. Needless to say, whatever technique she eventually came up with allowed for only limited richness of description and went only so far in ensuring commonality of interpretation.

Routines (data collecting and analysing)

Probably the most important principle worth mentioning when it comes to discursivist routines of data collecting and analysing is that of *discourse completeness*. This rule breaks with the tradition of studying 'concept formation' and requires that when one wishes to explore learning of a given topic, say, fractions, one has to investigate the development of the entire discourse related to this topic. Thus, the discourse within which the concept emerges, rather than the concept as such, is the unit of analysis. This is in tune with the holistic vision of communicational activity, one that precludes the possibility of a change that affects the use of a single word and leaves the use of related words intact. This also removes the sharp distinction between 'the individual' and 'the collective' that, as long as mental and public phenomena were accorded differing ontological statuses, separated research on learning from historical study of 'concept formation'.[4]

There is also the *principle of interdiscursivity*, which acknowledges the fact that instances of 'pure' discourses are rare, that real-life conversations make use of multiple discourses, and that our participation in one discourse is affected, sometimes only from afar, by a plethora of other discourses. Data collected in Heyd-Metzuyanim's study have shown that only too often, learners' mathematical discourse – their talk about mathematical objects – is inextricably intertwined with discourses of identity – talk about people and, in particular, about the participants themselves. In her study, Heyd-Metzuyanim listed all identifying utterances made by the participants spontaneously in the midst of painstaking mathematizing. Considering the intensity of identifying, the researcher decided that her interest in factors encouraging or inhibiting students' participation in mathematical discourse obliged her to gear her analyses towards the question of how each of the two discourses, that of mathematizing and that of identifying, influenced students' participation in the other.

Finally, the radical discursivist activity of analysing data is guided by the principle of alternating perspectives. The analyst, always mindful of the possibility of incommensurability between her mathematical discourse and the discourse of those who participate in her study, constantly zigzags between being an insider and an outsider to her own ways of using words. To help herself to bracket her immediate understandings and notice particularities of study participants' word use, the researcher, usually committed to considering every utterance in its discursive context, may now do the exact opposite: she may collect all the appearances of the given word 'thorn' from the transcript together with some surrounding verbal 'tissue'; or she may construct an inventory of all utterances of a certain kind. This is what Heyd-Metzuyanim did when she collected in one place the participants' identifying statements about one of them, Ziv (and this included Ziv's claims about himself). In real-life exchanges, and also in traditional research on classroom discourse, the repetitiveness – or perhaps the very presence – of such brief personal exclamations tends to be ignored; if identifying utterances are noticed at all, they are dismissed as momentary digressions, unlikely to have a noticeable impact on the ongoing conversation. Presenting these utterances one next to another and away from the 'diluting' context brings their potential significance to the fore.

Endorsed narratives (conclusions from research)

The final set of meta-rules for radical discursive research regards the form, construction and endorsement of its narratives. The first distinctive feature of these stories is the careful way in which they portray the ontological nature of the entities they deal with, as well as their own epistemological status. According to the principle of ontological fidelity, the discursivist makes it clear that her narratives are stories about the participants' stories, not about the world as such. In colloquial discourses and in many traditional studies, we regularly fall victim to ontological collapse – we confuse a story about a story with the story as such. This fallacy can be compared to mistaking a person's portrait for the person herself. We commit ontological collapse when we re-voice somebody's statement about something – say a student's declaration 'I understood fractions' – as a direct, authorless statement about this something, in this case, as the assertion: 'The student understood fractions.'[5]

The radical discursivist tries to do everything in her power to prevent ontological collapse. How can she do this? An answer is simple to formulate, but it is difficult to implement: she should never let the authors of the stories that constitute her data disappear. Thus, in the example above, rather than saying 'The student understood fractions', the discursivist should be careful to say 'The student said he understood fractions' (in some situations, it would be still better to say 'The student said "I understood fractions"'; indeed, reported speech is an act of interpretation, and for some purposes we should keep our interpretive actions to a bare minimum). By presenting her own stories in the first person, the researcher also remains true to the principle of epistemological fidelity: she presents herself as a creative storyteller rather than the world's ventriloquist (Bakhtin, 1986). An additional disobjectifying technique is to be explicit about the nature of the object of one's research. Thus, Heyd-Metzuyanim did not attempt her own assessments of the participants' understanding, neither was she trying to construct her own identifying stories about the participants. By indexing practically every narrative in her article with its author and addressee, she created a clear-cut distinction between stories she was telling as a researcher and those told by the participants of her study. She also explicitly declared that the former narratives were about the latter – that as a researcher, she was informing the readers about participants' own evaluations of their understanding and about identifying stories they built for themselves and for others.

Another question regards the worthiness of the considerable effort one needs to invest in keeping ontological collapse at bay and preventing statements that present what people say about themselves and their world as if it was a result of the researcher's own observations or as if it was the Truth. Against what may be expected, my justification is not concerned with the possibly questionable reliability of study participants' own accounts. The stories people tell are, themselves, a part of their lives, and a very important part, at that. One can say, in fact, that we live in and by the stories we tell. Being knowledgeable about these stories, about their mutual relations and about ways in which our narratives and our actions co-constitute each other is a key to many of the dilemmas that have always been bewildering the best of thinkers. This key is what Heyd-Metzuyanim was looking for in her study, when she focused her gaze, squarely and explicitly, on the reflexive relationship between participants' mathematizing and their identifying storytelling activity. While doing so, she was trying to fathom hidden mechanisms of success and failure in school mathematics.

The last batch of rules I wish to mention comes to ensure the optimal usefulness of discursivist stories. The principle of generalizability requires that these narratives provide insights going beyond the specific cases at hand. Let me immediately remark that there is no contradiction between this principle and my former claim about discursivists' refusal to foreground commonalities at the expense of differences. As any researcher, the discursivist looks for patterns, that is, for occurrences that repeat themselves; unlike many others, though, she splits her attention equitably between the common and the distinctive. If the patterns that she detects in her data have never been noticed before, her study can count as an existence proof of a new phenomenon. To claim the existence of a pattern, the analyst must honour the principle of evidential accountability: she must be able to point – quite literally, with her finger – to those places in the transcriptions where specific, unambiguous instances of the phenomenon are visible (this explains, once again, the need for the operationality of the researcher's vocabulary). This is what Heyd-Metzuyanim has done to support her conclusion that 'The activity of identifying can prevent the student from taking advantage of what appears as a particularly promising opportunity for learning' (Heyd-Metzuyanim and Sfard, 2012, p. 128; note the existential character of this proposition).

Another need, that of *theoretical accountability*, arises when one tries to justify her generalizing stories. To claim a degree of generality, one may do either of the following: seek analytic explanation or support her local story with similar stories from additional sources (this, if you wish, is the quantitative component of discursive research). A combination of these two techniques was applied by Heyd-Metzuyanim when she generalized her stories of 'local' patterns, clearly visible in her data, into a general claim about the collective production of the individual student's success or failure. In the fine-grained analysis of her classroom data, she was able to identify a number of 'vicious circles' propelled by emotions on the one hand, and by gradually solidifying patterns of doing mathematics on the other. Here, the term *vicious circle* refers to the discursive mechanism through which failure perpetuated failure and success begot success. The researcher grounded the claim about the generalizability of her findings; first, by showing a high occurrence of the self-aggravating circularities all along her data and, second, by proposing a theoretical model that explained how a student's failure (or success) to mathematize and the stories of her 'learning disability' (or 'giftedness') told by teachers, parents and the learners themselves dialectically co-constituted each other.

Concluding remark

In this chapter, I formulated a list of principles that we need to observe if we want to make sure that our research-inspired stories are useful. True, living up to these principles is hard work, and this may be why not every discourse-minded researcher is prepared to comply. But only by investing the necessary effort do we remain true to ourselves. No less important, many rewards seem to be waiting at the end of the discursive researcher's uneasy journey. Let me count but a few of them.

First, discursive research brings together within one conceptual and methodological framework what, so far, belonged to separate – and often unbridgeable – domains of study. As put by Heyd-Metzuyanim, in this research 'cognitive and affective, as well as intra-personal and inter-personal (or individual and social) aspects of learning processes [become] members of the same ontological category, to be studied with an integrated system of tools, grounded in a single set of foundational assumptions' (2012, pp. 128–129). This, when combined with the requirement for operationality, greatly increases communicational cohesiveness of the research community, reduces fragmentation of research and facilitates collaborations. In the final account, it increases the coherence of the stories we tell as researchers. The sustained effort to use verbs instead of nouns is an effective defence against the numerous traps of objectification and, above all, against narratives that perpetuate what the researcher might rather wish to change. The resulting high-definition picture shows as different what so far appeared as the same, and reveals rationality in what until now appeared as senseless. The combined effect of all those advantages is the unprecedented potency of the researcher's narratives. Indeed, if well done, discursivist stories are stories that work.

By way of summarizing, let me conclude with the personal credo: for me, the utmost attention to our own discourses as researchers is the obligation that comes with nobility. If our basic tenet is that discourses are what makes humans human and what plays a major role in their well-being, then we are obliged to mind our own discourse as much as we mind those of the participants of our studies.

Notes

1 The 2001 No Child Left Behind (NCLB) Act, the US Act of Congress proposed by President George W. Bush and signed into law in 2002, 'calls for education policy to rely on a foundation of scientifically based research', with the latter type of research understood as adhering to experimental or quasi-experimental design (see http://en.wikipedia.org/wiki/No_Child_Left_Behind_Act and http://www.nber.org/reporter/summer03/angrist.html, both retrieved on 12 August 2012).

2 The principle of operationality may sound self-evident and not at all specific to a radical discursive approach. And yet, operationality is a rare virtue in educational research. In private conversations, I have heard colleagues trying to rationalize their unwillingness to deal with questions about what is meant by the words they use. But if you are a researcher, and if your job it is to tell stories that are supposed to shape practice in useful ways, such unwillingness can hardly be justified – just imagine an engineer whose story about ways of building bridges is so ambiguous as to be interpretable according to one's whim.

3 At this point, it is worth mentioning that the study of people's differing interpretations of seemingly equivalent utterances (as opposed to studying differing 'conceptions') is a rather recent addition to the repertoire of central questions asked by educational researchers. In fact, the very realization of how common it is that the same words are used in different ways by different people was made possible by the advent of audio- and video-recordings. One can hardly become aware of such differences as long as one has to rely on memory or on notes prepared during or after events. Thus, one can say that radical discursive research owes its existence, to a great extent, to recent technological developments.

4 This is not to say that these two types of developments, the ontogenetic and the historical, can be considered as identical. It only means that they affect the same kind of entity, the discourse. This latter claim goes against the traditional view according to which learning concerns the growth of a child, whereas historical concept formation concerns the evolution of an ill-defined entity known as 'human knowledge'.

5 Nowhere is such collapse more commonplace than in attitude surveys that regularly transform their respondents' statements into impersonal claims implying a certain 'objective' state of affairs. Consider, for example, the assertion 'Women, by and large, are slightly happier than men', which the author of an article published on 16 December 2011 in *The Economist* (www.economist.com/node/17722567, retrieved on 10 July 2012) made while summarizing a number of surveys on the issue of well-being. This formulation obliterates the fact that the survey participants were offering their personal vision, grounded in their personal interpretations of the question, and especially of terms such as happiness and well-being.

Chapter 11

Research cannot define 'best practice' but it can offer tools for considering 'which practice'

Working through theories of identity and curriculum

Valerie Farnsworth

In this chapter, I work through theories of identity to consider issues in curriculum design. The contexts for these theoretical and practical considerations are two rather different case studies of learning in which I explore the relationship between the learner and the curriculum as it is reflected in discourse. I reference the concept of identity in three ways using three different terms. First, I will use 'identity' to refer to the various social constructs that characterise different kinds of people in relation to their affiliation with particular social groups or institutions (for example, those who teach in schools are identified as 'teachers'). This use of 'identity' is similar to Gee's notion of Discourse with a big 'D', such as an urban teenager Discourse or a university professor Discourse (Gee, 1999).[1] However, my use of 'identity' differs from Gee's use of Discourse because I focus only on the shared or socially distributed meaning of particular Discourses, as ways of thinking, valuing, feeling and believing, but am not necessarily considering how they act and interact or use tools and objects 'to enact and recognise different identities' (Gee, 1999, p. 13) in the context of particular practices (i.e. personal financial management in the first case, and teaching in the second case). Instead of focusing my lens on social interactions, I draw attention to the negotiation of meaning and beliefs in the context of identification which I infer from interview data. This notion of 'identification' is the second way I reference identity, and is similar to Wenger's use of the term (1998) when talking about the role of identification in learning which involves becoming a member of a 'community of practice'. I situate 'identification' in relation to learning and want to suggest that this is one way to approximate learning outcomes. Thus, I assess the extent to which the curriculum in each of my two case studies supported the intended learning outcomes by considering learners' identifications with the practices and meanings represented by the curriculum. My third use of the concept of identity is implied in my appropriation of Bakhtin's focus on 'ideological becoming'. Specifically, Bakhtin's (1986) notion of addressivity highlights the way in which identity 'performances' are for others, even if an imagined other. The 'other' is also present in our voice and the language we use as we negotiate our identification with (or appropriation of) available identities. As Bakhtin argues (1981, pp. 293–294):

> The word in language is half someone else's. It becomes 'one's own' only when the speaker populates it with his [sic] own intention, his own accent, when he appropriates the word, adapting it to his own semantic and expressive intention.

The process of 'ideological becoming' occurs when a person borrows or ventriloquates multiple, pre-existing voices (*heteroglossia*) and externalises this achievement in discourse.

   In summary, I use 'ideological becoming' to characterise the process of 'identification' which is an indicator of learning. I am particularly interested in the 'identities' the learners appropriated in their 'ideological becoming'. In the first case, which examines learning in the context of a financial capability education course for 16–18 year olds,[2] I found that the identity of someone financially capable was constructed in particular ways in the curriculum materials and that the learners adapted but also rejected aspects of this identity construct. In the second case, which focuses on one aspect of a teacher education course designed to support future teachers to become culturally responsive, I found that the learners appropriated specific identities that were rooted in their experiences prior to, and often separate from, their engagement in the course. By comparing these two cases, I highlight the ways 'ideological becoming' is related to curriculum design. In particular, I point to qualities of a curriculum that can be seen as more or less dialogic. Following is a brief presentation of my analysis of learning which focused on the language used by the learners in the context of research interviews, as well as language evoked in related curricular materials, such as teacher guides and handouts distributed to students.[3] I draw on this analysis to conceptualise a potentially useful descriptor for characterising curricula. The distinction is rooted in the dialogic aspects of the curriculum which builds on and applies concepts from Bakhtin (1981). I conclude by considering the trade-offs prompted by different types of curricula and their implications for learning.

Methodological considerations regarding language, identity and learning

Methodologically, I focus on identity as the performative act of self-presentation in interviews. This particular theoretical and methodological standpoint challenges a common critique of discourse approaches, whereby the validity of the analyst's interpretation is assumed to be found in the researcher making claims about the 'true' feelings or 'self' of the researched. My response to this critique is integral to the methodology, which does not attempt to capture a 'true' self but, rather, aims to unpack the social reality reflected in discourse, to produce a conceptual understanding of the social world as it relates to, and thus affects, learning. The process of identification as it is expressed in discourse is a pivotal concept for this kind of analysis.

My analysis explores the cultural storylines or cultural models of the social world that the research participants inevitably draw upon when they express their 'disposition, social identification, and even personification' (Holland *et al.*, 1998, p. 271) within this social world. By looking across the interview data of each individual participant, I then analyse the cultural models in relation to each other, and in relation to other 'voices' that similarly reflect cultural models and identities. The ways learners appropriated these other 'voices' – directly or by adapting them to their own 'voice' – was indicative of the 'authoritative' or 'internally persuasive' qualities of these 'voices' (Bakhtin, 1981). More specifically, authoritative voices are not as amenable to reflexive appropriation and adaptation as 'internally persuasive' voices. Thus, I interpreted those instances in which the participant re-voiced the cultural models of the curriculum (or of a particular community of practice), without obvious adaptation, as indexing an 'authoritative' voice. Methodologically, this means also collecting personal narratives from research participants as these signal personal adaptations. Based on the idea that learning can be interpreted from 'ideological becoming', authoritative discourse potentially limits learning in the sense that its meanings are fixed and the opportunity for adaptation and 'merging' among discourses, which is the basis for 'ideological becoming', is curtailed. On the other hand, an 'internally persuasive discourse' is dialogic because it is characterised by words that are 'half-ours and half-someone else's' (Bakhtin, 1981, p. 345), and allows for a creative and productive process of appropriation in order to construct a new discourse or voice.

The learner and the curriculum: a look at financial capability identities

My first example is an analysis of the relationship between the learner and the field of financial capability as it was constructed in a qualification certified by the *ifs* School of Finance. The *ifs* School of Finance is a not-for-profit organisation that provides professional financial education in the UK. One of the qualifications they offer has been designed as a provision for young people, typically aged between 16 and 18. This particular qualification, which was available as a certificate and, as a more advanced option, a diploma,[4] aimed to introduce students to the financial services industry and to develop their financial literacy and personal financial management practices. Such courses have been considered important as individual debt increases and financial systems become more complex (Miller, Godfrey, Levesque and Stark, 2009).

The primary data used for this analysis draws on the longitudinal interviews our team conducted with a sample of students who took this course in 2005–2006. Thirty students from 11 different institutions across the UK participated in a series of interviews, conducted during their course participation and then ten and 22 months after the first-year course completion. We asked students to tell us why they chose the course and how they were finding the course as well as how they reflected back on it after completion. We analysed the interview data for cultural models which we identified using Gee's approach to discourse analysis (Gee, 1999); that is, in telling us about their experience with the course, many students presented themselves or performed their identities as financially capable or as becoming financially capable (Farnsworth *et al.*, 2011). Here, I briefly recount my analysis of the relationship between these identity enactments (and related cultural models) and the cultural models of personal finance evoked in the course materials, specifically the teacher guides which, along with a complementary set of online materials for students (for example, worksheets), provided the framework for the course curriculum. This analysis involved looking for expressions of the course narratives and cultural models (explicitly or implicitly in the materials) as they matched with student discourse in interviews.

The first-year course (Certificate level) consists of three Units. From each Unit, excerpts describing the aims of the Unit were analysed. As these materials were kept on a password protected website available only to institutions that offered this provision, I have paraphrased the text rather than providing direct quotes. Unit 1 aimed to orient the young person to their long-term goals and to relate those to a financial plan for their future. A key part of having money to meet those aspirations across their life cycle was being able to recognise the difference between their individual needs and their wants. A recurring theme was to establish the importance of money and the role of the financial services industry in managing personal finances. The storyline of personal finance that is being constructed in this Unit, or the cultural model expressed in the materials, implies that a person should take personal responsibility for their finances and consider personal circumstances when making financial decisions. By referencing the life cycle, the curriculum guidance indicates that the student is expected to consider themselves in terms of their growing responsibilities and increasing social expectations as they are transitioning to adulthood where they need to make money (and responsibly manage their money). The underlying normative directive of what a young person 'should' do exemplifies an authoritative voice that is not open to dispute. However, the reference to *highlighting* 'the importance of money' and *introducing* students 'to the financial services industry' is less directive in terms of the storyline that the teacher is intended to follow. As I will argue later, this way of framing 'money' and the 'financial services industry' with minimal direction leaves more room for students to make the 'voice' of this course their own by appropriating it in negotiation with their existing, internally persuasive cultural models. However, some aspects of the curriculum, I will show, are more 'authoritative' and hence offer less opportunity for dialogue.

The primary directives and knowledge boundaries marking out the field of financial capability are framed in terms of decision making. That is, students are directed to make 'informed' financial decisions. Being informed seems to involve being aware of larger economic trends, as expressed in the aims of Unit 1, and understanding their finances in terms of their personal life cycle. There is also an emphasis on how students should make decisions about what to do with their money based on their knowledge of the financial products available to them. For example, Chapter 4 established the specific aim of enhancing students' ability to distinguish needs from wants and to know about various financial products and practices, such as savings accounts, investments, overdraft protection and borrowing. The course focus on personal financial management (PFM) in terms of individual responsibility and consumer choice is summed up in one of the Key Topics outlined in the final chapter for Unit 1 of the teacher's guide. In this chapter, teachers were advised to explain that protection does not mean they are absolved from personal responsibility. The emphasis was on making informed choices and understanding the options available to them.

The storyline presented in the materials establishes a link between personal choice and knowledge of the financial services industry (e.g. options to invest, save or borrow money). The implied storyline is that, if a student is informed, they will be able to (and are expected to) make the right decisions that are appropriate for their own personal circumstances and goals. Once they make those decisions they also enter into an agreement with the financial provider and it is the responsibility of the customer to know the terms of that agreement. The emphasis on personal choice is juxtaposed with normative or moralistic aspects of decisions, outlining the 'right' or 'responsible' way to be financially capable and literate. However, by presenting students with multiple financial decision options and product choices, the curricular voice leaves open the opportunity for dialogue as students appropriate the identity of being someone who is seen as financially capable.

The discourse of students, and the cultural models evoked, supports this conjecture that the curriculum supported a process of 'ideological becoming'. I found that the cultural models expressed by students reflected many of the storylines carried through the course materials. A particularly common identity was one used to express themselves as consumer aware. For example, Mahmood told us he would now look for

> who offers the best deal and the different points, like I wouldn't consider [that] before because, if I wasn't doing financial studies I wouldn't really know that, which points I want to consider, what to look at when I'm comparing, so it helps.

The cultural models that presented PFM as knowing about products and making informed choices among products were appropriated in Mahmood's discourse. The self-admissions and uses of 'I' are indicators of his own accent applied to his re-voicing of these cultural models.

There was also a distinct emphasis by students on the personal and individual aspects of finance which reflected the course storyline. If there was a reference to society it was with regard to debt as a social problem and something to avoid.

The dominance of an individualistic approach to personal finance suggests that this aspect of the shared cultural models was non-negotiable and hence authoritative. However, within this framework of PFM as personal, there were nevertheless opportunities for the students to appropriate the voice of the curriculum and weave it into their other cultural models and values.

For example, Salima told us how she 'learned not to borrow' and 'take[s] care of money now'; she also noted that she does not save money in a bank but with her mother. Thus she does not fully take up the cultural model of PFM as a question of making use of available financial products:

> Yes I actually save a lot of money now, I do a lot of saving. I don't have an account I have actually saved money with my mother. I give it to her and she saves it for me now. I think it's a bit safer than an account because then I could go and take the money out, but with my mum she just won't give it back.

Ultimately, we find that students evoke the cultural models that are found within the course materials, but we also note personal variations that are attributable to the weaving of course and personal narratives. The consumer-aware cultural model was perhaps 'internally persuasive' to the young people, given its affinity to dominant consumerist discourses of modern capitalist societies. Thus, students engaged with broader social identity constructions and storylines. To represent this process of weaving, and to account for the variations in cultural models expressed by students, I look to Bakhtin's notions of dialogism and heteroglossia. I will suggest that learning is a dialogic process, and that the implication of this is that if learners are engaged in a curriculum, there will be evidence that they weave narratives of the curriculum together with their own experiences and accent.

This argument rests on the notion that cultural models afford individuals' ways of identifying within the 'figured worlds' they construct (Holland et al., 1998). Thus, a curriculum can support students in thinking in particular ways about a subject, such as personal finance, but the learners' self-positioning (or self-authoring) with regard to the subject may also be influenced by their personal experiences, lives and cultures.

Ayesha, for example, wove the course narrative with a personal narrative about her relatives' experience with financial investments:

> My aunty bought stocks and shares because someone told her they'd double within a year but they actually went down. What she invested went down nearly a half and she thought, 'when I get back my capital I'll withdraw out of it' ... I would just [use] savings accounts or bonds or something but it depends on what kind of bonds they are.

In this brief narrative, Ayesha shows her knowledge of financial products when she comments 'it depends on what kind of bonds they are', evoking the cultural model expressed in the course materials which indicates that PFM is about being an informed consumer of financial products, such as bonds. At the same moment, she references her aunt's experience with stocks and shares, implying that for her this is the most convincing argument for using savings accounts instead of bonds. Although she appropriates the course cultural model of personal finance as a matter of making appropriate and informed choices, she rejects the cultural model about how stocks can be a good way to make money grow. She is able to adapt the discourse of the knowledgeable consumer by integrating it with her knowledge of her aunt's experience. These multiple storylines, not all of which are authoritative, enable this dialogue and her learning as 'ideological becoming'.

The student-teacher and ideological influences on 'ideological becoming'

My second illustrative study enables further exploration of the relationship between learning as ideological becoming and structured learning experiences provided by the curriculum. The study was conducted in the US and examined trainee teachers' narratives about their learning experiences during the final year of their primary teacher education course. I was interested in how the community-based learning (CBL) component of the course contributed to their identities as teachers and, more specifically, as social justice-oriented teachers. The CBL experience was integral to their programme, which followed the Professional Development School (PDS) model[5] and required trainee teachers to participate in community events or identify other ways to engage with local families.

The programme's narrative,[6] which elaborated this requirement and the expectations of students, is represented by the following excerpt from a handout distributed to students that described 'CBL' as

> for student teachers to learn more about the communities in which their students live (e.g., funds of knowledge, social networks, ways of interacting and of seeing the world). We want our students to learn how to learn about the communities where their students come from and how to translate this knowledge back into their classrooms as culturally relevant/responsive teaching practices.

The students were left to their own devices to identify and engage in appropriate 'community experiences' which they would reflect on in a 'log book' periodically submitted to their tutor. They were placed in groups of approximately 12 trainee teachers and met weekly at the primary school where they had their placement. These meetings were a chance to discuss the placement as well as various topics related to teaching in ethnically and linguistically diverse communities. The CBL component was the focus topic for three of the sessions in the academic year that I conducted the study. The tutor invited guest speakers, including professionals who had hosted trainee teachers previously in their organisations (e.g. a group of volunteers providing weekend sessions for children to learn about African American culture and history).

In general, the CBL requirement was loosely structured in order to allow the trainee teachers to make the experience their own. However, the regular group meetings also helped to construct a common repertoire and identification with common goals of teaching with a social justice orientation. In other words, the group formed a community of practice whose shared goal was to support each other in becoming 'good', social-justice oriented primary school teachers.

The curriculum was diverse. The students took part in a suite of course modules and activities over three years,[7] and not all students took the same modules other than the placement seminars already described above. By contrast to the financial capability curriculum, the CBL element, which was my main research interest, focused less on knowledge in books or course materials and more on practice or knowledge obtained through engagement with local community members. I suggest that this less structured and more diverse curriculum meant that the tutor was not authoritatively voicing particular cultural models such as cultural models of social justice. As such, these cultural models were more multi-voiced than were the cultural models of PFM from the previous example. Given the US context and historical racism, I intentionally followed up on or interrogated data reflecting racial ideologies. In fact, my interest in the CBL approach was because of its aim of challenging racial stereotypes and enabling 'culturally relevant pedagogy' (Ladson-Billings, 1994).

As with the financial capability study, my focus was on the cultural models represented and reconfigured by the research participants, who in this case were the trainee teachers. Given a key theme in research literature on teacher education that highlights the importance of teacher biography and identity (Alsup, 2006; Goodson, 2008), a narrative approach to interview data collection was taken. The student teachers were asked to tell stories about their prior educational experiences as well as their experiences of CBL in the context of becoming a qualified teacher.

The research story I was then able to tell was about the ways the trainee teachers made meaning of their CBL experiences. In particular, I found that their discourse and reflections on their experiences often referred to their prior school experiences. Their approaches to the CBL assignments differed in ways that signalled diverse appropriations of the programme and tutors' storylines. These individual appropriations signalled different perspectives on social justice (Farnsworth, 2010) and pointed to the process that Bakhtin refers to as 'ideological becoming'.

My research suggests that the loose framework approach provided the trainee teachers with an opportunity to play with ideas and try on identities as teachers who learned from the community and parents (Farnsworth, 2010). However, the internal negotiations that took place (evident in the narrative interview data) also revealed a tendency to privilege (Wertsch, 1991) particular constructions of a teacher identity or social justice activist that they had learned prior to the teacher training course (e.g. in their own schooling) or through other activities. Their identification as members of their community of practice also came across in their discourse, suggesting that the storyline of their programme, PDS, was 'internally persuasive', at least among the four student-teachers I interviewed. A key storyline was the 'community' perspective and intention to teach in disadvantaged schools.

In my analysis, I explored how learners appropriated the 'voice' of the programme as part of their identity negotiations in becoming teachers (Farnsworth, 2006). I focused on a range of stories told by the four trainee teachers, interviewing them over the course of the year on multiple occasions, so allowing for variation and trust building between myself and the research participants. I focus here on two of the trainee teachers – Sam and Patrick, with a brief mention of a third – Aerykah. To exemplify this approach to analysis, I have selected two stories about their prior experiences of growing up that also resonated with the ways they enacted their identities as social justice teachers in other moments of the interviews.

Sam's story of her youth

Yeah [my school] was very high academic like very well-achieving kids, they pushed us a lot I think but um I mean athletics was very, everything there, the clubs, athletics, theatre, like we were pretty lucky, like we had pretty much everything [Val: resources, yeah] you can ask for, yeah, we really did. So it was good, we had, I liked my teachers, I felt they were well-educated um, I was a cheerleader so I was really involved in like that and um National Honors Society and like that kind of stuff. So I was pretty involved, and and yeah I mean, I feel lucky, I think I grew up in a really good high school, had a really good experience as far as – it's funny though looking back on it now because it wasn't very diverse and seeing as how now I want to teach in a diverse setting, [Val: uh hm] like I do see a lot of the stuff that I might have missed out on. [Val: uh hm] Like I had really good academics, because we had really good funding and all of that, but like I didn't, never had that experience about learning about other cultures maybe as much as other people would have, and so I kind of look down on that aspect of it now, but, I mean it got me into a good college, where I'm learning about that now.

Patrick's story of his youth

I guess once either my sister or I asked just because all of our friends would go to the other [shopping] mall, I mean they're only like five miles apart from each other, but it's a 45-minute drive to either one for us and why are we going to this one when everyone else always goes to that one? And this, the mall that we went to they had different empty stores and just 'cause people avoided it. So well back to where I was, either my sister or I, one of us at one point asked, you know why do we go to this one when all our friends go to that one? It was like, 'because there's only White people there and you need to see that sometimes people look different than you'.

I noticed that most of the stories Sam told, either in relation to general reflections on her prior school experiences or her current teacher training experiences,
focused on what I termed 'academic' topics. She tended to construct her identity
as a teacher in relation to cultural models of teaching and learning ratified by
formal educational institutions and emphasising academic learning. By contrast,
Patrick's stories typically covered what I called 'community' topics. Thus, even
if I asked Patrick specifically about school experiences he would inevitably reference the wider community, beyond the school itself. Patrick's identity as a
teacher typically emphasised his relationships with people in the school and the
local community. Both trainee teachers, however, expressed a commitment to
an 'ethic of service' (Boyle-Baise and McIntyre, 2008) to the communities they
taught, which reflected the institutional discourse of their university programme.
The difference was in the identity construction they privileged when expressing
this 'ethic of service'.

A key question for me in this research was how they adapted, accented and
appropriated the notion of 'social justice' as they engaged in CBL. I found that
Sam's academic privileging betrayed an affiliation with a group of people who
value academic learning, while Patrick revealed his identification with a group
that might be called community activists. These identities can be said to include
ideological accents in the sense that ideologies are sets of factual and evaluative
beliefs that help to define social groups and group identities (van Dijk, 1998).
This meant that, as they negotiated their identities as teachers through their participation in PDS and CBL, they ventriloquated 'voices' and beliefs associated
with the group voice they privileged.

Another pair of narratives further illustrates the ideological aspects of their
discourse and their identity negotiations – this time giving us insight into the
identity constructions of a social, justice-oriented teacher. In separate interviews,
Sam and Patrick, recounted the same event – a conversation Sam had with a
'Republican' in a bar in their university town. In telling these stories they again
incorporated their respective cultural models of what it means to be social,
justice-oriented teachers and also made clear their identification with their
teacher education programme and, in particular, PDS and the PDS emphasis
on teaching in disadvantaged schools. The Republican encounter narrative was
particularly revealing of their cultural models of social justice to the extent that
they both dis-identified and disagreed with the Republican's support of school
voucher policies. Both Sam and Patrick took issue with his positioning of certain
students who 'wouldn't have a chance to learn anyways' (Sam quoting the
Republican) and the Republican's reference to certain kids who 'are never going
to be successful anyway' (quote from Patrick). For Sam, this was an attack on her
sense of social justice and, in telling this story, she re-established her affinity with
a cultural model of social justice education as providing 'good' teaching to non-
dominant or non-privileged students (e.g. in 'urban' schools). In her narrative,
Sam takes up the Republican's reference to 'failing schools' and does not redefine
this concept or characterise them in more positive ways, other than to say they are

the schools where she wants to teach so she can 'give 'em a chance'. The danger in this cultural model is that it does not necessarily challenge deficit models (King, 1991) of non-dominant children and families. Both of Patrick's narratives re-present another cultural model of social justice education in which the aim is to resist and redefine dominant views of students and dominating policies and practices. That is, Patrick's story about the Republican focused on the need to 'go in and just at least stop people from pitying them or thinking that people are not worthy'. This cultural model more directly addresses and challenges the notion of a deficit model.

Their different cultural models of social justice are formed from different cultural life experiences and 'figured worlds'. They drew on these cultural models in presenting themselves as certain kinds of social justice teachers, where social justice may be enacted through 'good' teaching on the one hand, or through political and economic participation on the other hand.

The conclusion I make is that learners come to any learning experience already having appropriated cultural models and ideologies that will be drawn upon in the process of making the cultural models, identity constructions or 'voices' of a course 'internally persuasive'. The learning process is a complex intersection of identities and cultural models that the learner appropriates and accents in various ways. While educational institutions may provide structure to learning and 'ideological becoming', these are only one part of the dialogue that constructs a teacher's identity. The outcome is that educational institutions, such as universities and their teacher education departments, do not have a monopoly on the learning of learners. In other words, input does not lead to output as in a factory production line.

An important implication of this analysis of learning as a process of ideological becoming is that there may be a tendency for learning to be limited to recycling or reconfiguring old knowledge and ways of doing things (aka practices). The challenge of creating learning experiences that expand the learner's repertoire and engage them in new practices remains. Based on the more extensive analysis, which I do not have space to recount here (see Farnsworth, 2010), I propose that ideologically informed identifications can be a barrier to this more expansive learning. That is, identification with a group such as PDS or certain kinds of 'social justice' teachers seemed to be privileged by Sam and Patrick in their sense-making of CBL and their engagement with the activities they chose as their CBL experiences. From a perspective of 'ideological becoming', this privileging of a particular voice can be seen as problematic for learning. My proposal is that we consider these privileged voices to be authoritative in the context of CBL, where the expectation is that the student-teacher dialogically constructs localised interpretations and meanings of cultural practices of their students, their families and their communities in order to counter stereotypes and to inform culturally relevant pedagogy.

However, these authoritative voices are not internal to the curriculum or course or CBL, but represent wider professional or social group identities; these are voices the student-teachers bring with them from their past. The absence of similar ideological discourse (in terms of identification with PDS or other groups) within transcripts of interviews with another student-teacher, Aerykah, suggests that participation in CBL can be negotiated in other, more dialogic ways. That is, Aerykah chose to approach CBL as a chance to learn new things about herself, rather than as a way to enhance her developing identity as a social justice teacher. So, Aerykah, when she described her community experiences, tended to position herself in relation to others as a discursive participant. For example, she told me:

> I learned places where I feel really uncomfortable like I learned um that it's really hard for me to just to cold go up to a parent and say I know your kid, great to meet you. And beyond that it's really hard for me ... I just don't know how to be appropriate all the time and I want to be appropriate and then I recognise too that my appropriate is not going to be everybody's appropriate. So I've learned how to make mistakes. And how to be as neutral as possible and how to be as sensitive as possible so I could try and fit in but also understand that I'm not going to fit in everywhere.

I conclude that ideologies can become authoritative voices that can limit the potential for dialogic learning in the context of CBL. From my analysis I have come to understand the ideal CBL to be one that engages with localised identities grounded in their CBL experiences, rather than ideological group identities (Farnsworth, 2010). A dialogue with the learner's prior experiences and their identification with PDS or appropriation of socially shared cultural models of social justice can support learning, but will not necessarily take the learner as far into the learning spaces that were intended by the CBL requirement.[8] The implication is that, when the learning goal involves challenging dominant ideologies (e.g. racist stereotypes and deficit models), the curriculum may need to be designed in such a way that ideological identities can be put aside so that new identities can be explored.

Concluding reflections on learning, useful research and methodology

The Bakhtinian perspective can help us to understand learning as a process in which the learner works to weave together the various cultural artefacts, such as cultural models, available to them along with ideological commitments, all of which are also learned and developed through experiences over time. (This is what I consider identity 'work'.) In the first example, the relationship between the learner and the curriculum was more tightly structured, with more authoritative voices, than the loosely coupled relationship between the trainee teacher and their curricular requirements of the second example. However, in both examples, the learner identifies with particular cultural models that contribute to their 'figured world' (Holland *et al.*, 1998, p. 271) and ultimately their identity performances (Gee, 1999).

Bakhtin's concept of 'ideological becoming' helps to overcome the deterministic aspects of a structuralist perspective, whereby identification is seen as determined by 'structuring structures' (Bourdieu, 1977, p. 72). A social theory of learning (Lave and Wenger, 1991; Wenger, 1998) helps us to see how this may have implications for learning because identification is considered to contribute to the learning process through participation in situated practices. This learning theory, combined with Bakhtin's dialogic perspective, provides an antidote for determinism by orientating us towards what might be called a *dialogic curriculum* (Higham and Farnsworth, 2012) which is a curriculum defined and structured in ways that support individual negotiations of identity or ideological becoming, and hence promote learning. The analysis here suggests that the goal of education and teaching should be to provide a curriculum that supports dialogic learning and ideological becoming. Further consideration may also need to be given to the use of monologic or authoritative voices that may limit the learning potential by restricting the voices and opportunities for learners to appropriate voices of the curriculum with their own accents in the process of identifying with a learning activity or curriculum. However, monologues may be appropriate in some instances. For example, the rules and regulations set by financial institutions cannot be rewritten by consumers; hence, some voices have more authority than others and are best recognised as such (which is not to say they are not also open to challenge and critique). Thus, the conclusion is not that one approach to curriculum design is better than another (e.g. promotes learning better) but that there are trade-offs to all approaches, and theory can help to identify those trade-offs.

The implication is that research cannot simply provide the answers to educational concerns, such as curriculum design, and hence cannot tell us 'what works'. It does perhaps allow us to give grace and understanding to those responsible for change when they are not successful or when policies and interventions do not 'work' as expected. Research thus can help to illustrate the ways that education operates as a complex system of ideas, practices, identities and goals. This brief review of two projects shows how theory and method[9] can work together to develop further conceptual tools that can be added to the tool box used to address educational concerns.

A key challenge for curriculum designers and teachers is to determine the voices that should be available for learners to appropriate in ways that support their learning of new knowledge and practices. For the financial capability curriculum, it was important to include the voices of the financial industry as a way to give students access to, and opportunity to reflect upon, a discourse that is a powerful and inescapable voice in our societies. A multiplicity of voices and cultural models in that curriculum supported dialogic engagement with the dominant voices of the financial services industry and capitalism (albeit not quite critical engagement, see Farnsworth *et al.*, 2011). For the CBL curriculum, an effort was made to limit the structure of the requirement in order to allow for more emergent voices of the learners to develop. However, authoritative voices that referenced teacher and social justice identities and ideologies were also implied in the ways the trainee teachers talked about CBL. The privileging of these voices may have restricted the opportunity to learn new ways of thinking about social justice.

The analysis is not presented to provide a blanket rule that can be applied to all curriculum design. The role of theory in this instance is to draw our attention to particular features of learning and relationships that produce learning and learners in these contexts. Theory also helps us to make distinctions that may be useful in curriculum design. We have examples of researchers, for example, using Bernstein's distinctions between 'vertical' and 'horizontal' knowledge to explore the 'strong' and 'weak' grammars of curricula (Luckett, 2012). In a similar vein, I am proposing that Bakhtin's distinction between 'authoritative' discourse and 'internally persuasive' discourse can provide useful ways of also thinking about curricula.

In summary, this research can point us towards areas to consider when making curriculum decisions. For example, a less structured curriculum may leave more room for 'ideological becoming' but it may also mean greater variability in terms of learning experience and outcomes. If the curriculum is based on the premise that an established knowledge base should be learned by all, this variability may present problems in terms of equity. On the other hand, if the expectation is that knowledge is individually constructed through practice, activity or social interaction, then variability is not as problematic. In the latter case, the challenge may be in attempting to orchestrate a balance of 'voices' so that authoritative voices are not privileged. Similarly, the challenge with the former case may be to provide a set of materials and activities that alternate or vary the authoritative voice to enable a dialogue with more marginal voices, such as those voicing critical, social and political implications of financial decisions. The key question for a curriculum designer is then: what kind of dialogue do I want to promote among the learners?

Notes

1 I have chosen to refer to 'identity constructions' throughout this chapter rather than Discourses in order to focus on just two conceptual tools – identity and dialogue. However, this concept of Discourse is underpinning the methodological approach I have taken.
2 Financial capability, sometimes referred to as financial literacy, is about knowing the practices and expectations of the world of finance. It includes things such as knowing how to open a bank account and which type of account to purchase etc. The research presented here was funded by the *ifs* School of Finance and led by Pauline Davis and Sue Ralph.
3 All names used are pseudonyms.
4 National Certificates/Diplomas are Level 3 qualifications that prepare students for a career in a specific occupational area. They were also designed to have equivalencies to A Levels which are the qualifications that enable access to higher education.
5 A key aim of the PDS initiative was to strengthen the relationship between public schools and universities (Holmes Group, 1990). This PDS worked collaboratively with the local schools to train teachers, situating the pre-service teachers' field seminars in the school, rather than the university, and appointing a tutor who was employed by the school and the university to lead the seminar.

6 The students were part of the PDS programme which was a sub-programme of the teacher education course at their university. The programme limited entry through an application procedure and sought to enrol students with explicit interests in social justice. The students followed the same modules as other students except for their placement tutorial meetings, which were uniquely held on the school campus with a tutor who was employed by both the school and the university.

7 The first year comprised studies in 'general education' completed prior to a 'major' specialism that they complete in the final three years of undergraduate study, as is common in many US universities.

8 The handout quoted earlier notes: 'we want our students to learn to learn about communities'. This learning to learn quality is what I consider to be emergent. This focus on the importance of ongoing learning entails a more dynamic view of culture than one entailed by learning about cultural norms which are assumed to be established norms rather than practices lived out daily by people in their communities.

9 Methodologies that combine discourse analysis with more ethnographic research can expand this complex system visualisation to include practices not captured by discourse analysis alone (e.g. by accounting for the mediation of other cultural tools or artefacts).

Chapter 12

Research knowledge production and educational activity

A 'research path' approach

Seth Chaiklin

What is the relation between educational research and educational practice? It may be tempting to seek, once and for all, a comprehensive image, model or vision of how they should be related to each other, but this temptation is stimulated by or predicated on highly abstract views about educational practice and educational research that do not recognise or address adequately the complicated societal arrangements and diverse activities covered by these two general expressions.

This relation is viewed as a permanent problem for individual educational researchers precisely because of this diversity. All educational research is conducted under specific relations between researcher, organisation, academic discipline, state and civil society. Researchers are caught in a web of demands, interests and expectations that arise from these sources including patronage relations (e.g. their employer, public and private funding), different disciplinary interests and traditions, and public opinion.

The demands and interests that arise from these relations (e.g. relevance, cost-effectiveness, choice of particular topics, theoretical position) influence the form or content of one's research, even if they do not impinge on its day-to-day conduct. These demands are particularly consequential when individual researchers must account for or justify their research choices, especially in relation to educational practice. These moments of accountability challenge individual researchers to find justifiable strategies or conceptions for responding to these often conflicting demands and interests. The diversity of these structural tensions speaks against the likelihood of finding a singular general model for conceptualising the relation between educational research and educational practice. The kind of answer sought or accepted when addressing this question about their relation often depends on who is asking the question and for what purpose (e.g. a politician trying to justify expenditure or a researcher seeking to justify a line of investigation will often emphasise different criteria).

In this chapter, the analytic focus is on educational research that aims explicitly to improve or develop educational practice. The idea of *research path* is proposed as a general strategy that can address this focus, while responding to the general tensions raised here. This idea is grounded in a general theoretical perspective that draws on the concepts of *practice* and *activity* as developed in cultural–historical science (Chaiklin, 2011). The presentation first introduces this perspective for characterising general properties of educational research and educational practice more concretely. Then the general idea of research path is explained, and illustrated with a specific path for subject-matter teaching research. The brief concluding section outlines some implications and consequences of the research path idea.

Analysing the relation between educational research and educational practice

Box 12.1 presents a series of historical and ontological assumptions involved in conceptualising educational research and educational practice as *practices* (i.e. a historically developed tradition of action). The first two points describe some basic relations between educational research and educational practice. Specific practices are defined by their products, where these products are oriented to and legitimated by societal need (point 3). This conception of practice helps to differentiate the abstract phrase *educational practice* into many different practices, which might include primary, secondary, tertiary or vocational practice, where each practice is oriented to different needs.

Box 12.1 Some assumptions about educational research and educational practice, with implications for understanding their relation

1   Educational practice is autonomous. It does not depend upon or require educational research. Historically, educational practice has preceded educational research.

2   Educational research depends on educational practice, in the sense that educational practice (or activities within the practice) are an object of investigation.

3   All practices are organised around production, where the production responds to a societal need.

4   All practices are manifest in activity.

5   All activity depends on knowledge.

6   Knowledge production is the key feature of educational research practice.

7   Knowledge (produced from educational research) can be relevant to both educational practice and/or activities within that practice.

8   *Basic problem:* How is knowledge produced in one practice (educational research) going to be used in another practice (or activity)?

Individuals (educators and researchers) are engaged in activity in relation to these practices (point 4). *Activity* refers to a meaningful whole of actions organised in relation to a practice. Within each practice, there are likely to be many different activities organised in relation to these practices. For example, primary education is a practice, where school as an institutional form of this practice appears with variations in content and funding, usually with some form of accreditation and/or state regulation. Many activities are involved in primary school practice (e.g. classroom teaching, school leadership and administration, addressing behavioural and academic problems, political policy making), where general activities (e.g. classroom teaching) have specific forms (e.g. mathematics teaching, history teaching). An individual teacher may be engaged in several activities (e.g. subject-matter teaching, socialisation) that have definite goals and procedures, where these activities are necessary for realising the need(s) that underpin the practice (e.g. educated, well-behaved children). Similarly, the many activities of academic researchers (e.g. classroom teaching, attending conferences, peer review, collecting data) are related to disciplinary and university practices.

As far as theoretical distinctions go, *practice* and *activity* – as explained so far – may appear trivially obvious, just another pair of theoretical concepts to express the idea that educational researchers and educational practitioners have different professional objectives. This distinction (for many kinds of professional research and practice) – well-known from everyday experience – is often framed analytically with spatial metaphors, perhaps inspired by or grounded in a 'two-worlds' model (Boggs, 1992; Caplan, 1979; Wingens, 1990), which implies mutually exclusive or parallel practices. Researchers have characterised these differences with such expressions as two groups (Levin, 2004), two communities (Caplan, 1979), different social systems (e.g. Kieser and Leiner, 2009; Simon, 1967), different modes of professional practice (Labaree, 2008), a group of knowers and a group of actors (Rein and White, 1981, pp. 1–2), and so forth.

The purpose and value of these concepts appears when they are used systematically to conceptualise (rather than merely describe) educational research and educational practice as examples of practices that are manifest in persons' activity in relation to these practices (point 4). Educational activity is dependent in part on knowledge, whether or not this knowledge was produced in or supported by research (point 5). The main objective of social science research (as a practice) is production of new knowledge (point 6). Note that the last two points provide a more precise characterisation of the potential relationship between these two worlds.

Since at least the beginning of the twentieth century, educational researchers could engage meaningfully in research practice, without having the intention to produce something that could be used directly in another practice. At the same time, given that educational research is focused on educational practice (point 2), then some of the knowledge production from educational research is likely to be relevant to educational practice and activity (point 7). The basic question or problem (point 8) to pose is how this happens: 'How does knowledge move from one practice to another?' Or in relation to individual researchers: 'How does knowledge produced in research activity become part of educational activity?' This question provides a critical reformulation and sharpening of the initial question about the relation between educational research and educational practice, highlighting a pragmatic point that 'knowledge' is the medium through which research practice and educational practice are related. The main argument (and key idea) for addressing the specific focus in this chapter is that individual researchers must be able to give an account for how specific, research-produced knowledge is going to be materialised in a specific educational practice or activity.

This focus on knowledge use is consistent with the extensive research literature – in both the social and natural sciences – that discusses the general question about the relation between research and practice. Many of the existing analytic approaches to this relation tend to treat knowledge as an 'undifferentiated substance' to be transferred, with little or no attention to the content or characteristics of research results (i.e. knowledge); the main problem is simply to get any research results into practice (e.g. Broekkamp and van Hout-Wolters, 2007; Hutchinson and Huberman, 1994). As a rough generalisation, this orientation reflects an underlying idea of translation, in which research-generated knowledge is supposed to be 'moved' into practice. This conception may be encouraged by a two-world metaphor, with its implied division of labour, which inclines one to note 'gaps' between the two worlds, and seek ways for knowledge produced in one world to 'bridge the gap' to another. Many strategies focus on the transfer of knowledge to practitioners, in the belief that the primary problem is to inform practitioners about research results. This bridging idea reflects a long-standing linear model of innovation (Godin, 2006), which seems to persist both in popular and researcher understanding, despite occasional critiques of this metaphor (e.g. Davies, Nutley and Walter, 2008).

When the meaning of *knowledge* is not specified (e.g. such as in point 5, Box 12.1), then it is unproblematic to hold a linear model or to assert that knowledge is a necessary part of activity. To address the key idea (i.e. to give an account for how specific research-produced knowledge is going to be materialised in a specific educational practice or activity), a more differentiated concept of knowledge is needed – including the function that research-based knowledge plays in educational practice, the forms of knowledge produced from research, and ways or processes by which particular kinds of knowledge become part of activity. The following discussion highlights some of these issues.

Functions of knowledge in educational practice

Research knowledge is used in practice in different ways. In one analysis, Pelz (1978) notes instrumental, conceptual and symbolic uses. Instrumental uses reflect the popular understanding of research use (i.e. where a specific result is used immediately and directly in practice). Conceptual uses often involve the use of conceptual frameworks to interpret practical situations, where the value of research is justified in terms of general ideas or concepts adopted from a research field, rather than a specific study (e.g. Astley and Zammuto, 1992; Suppes, 1978). For example, teachers who use an idea such as zone of proximal development or communities of practice to think about their classroom teaching reflect a conceptual rather than instrumental use, because their actions are coming indirectly from these conceptions rather than from specific results. Symbolic uses involve using research to support ideas that one already believes (e.g. early adopters of 'multiple intelligences' ideas viewed these ideas as confirming what they already believed – see Kornhaber and Gardner, 2006).

These simple differentiations provide ways to elaborate many choices that an individual researcher must face in choosing a research strategy that aims to improve practice. Which uses of knowledge is one seeking? Are political demands only focusing on or accepting instrumental uses? Are seemingly instrumental uses actually symbolic? And so forth.

Forms of research-produced knowledge

The abstract term *knowledge* covers many different forms (e.g. empirical facts, theoretical concepts, narrative accounts). These forms are used for many different purposes (e.g. description, analysis, hypothesis formation, evaluation). Within research activity, one might produce written reports, which is described as knowledge (e.g. because it produces particular empirical facts, gives new interpretations of existing observations, introduces or elaborates theoretical concepts). Often these knowledge products do not exemplify any of the just-named instrumental, conceptual and symbolic uses. This implies that many results from educational research may be considered knowledge (in relation to research activity) but not in relation to educational activity. These situations provide one way to interpret or understand the so-called 'gap' between practices.

Consequences of the differentiated view of knowledge

These differentiations about functions and forms of knowledge highlight the inadequacy of interpreting the basic problem as a simple matter of knowledge transmission. The idea of knowledge transmission is grounded in an empirically inadequate assumption that research-based ideas can be realised appropriately in practice provided that researchers make this knowledge available (to practitioners). Verbal explanation (e.g. that the practitioner should read research results, or attend lectures or training sessions where they are explained) followed by action that reflects appropriately the intention of the verbal description is rarely effective for supporting change in action (see Putnam and Boys, 2006).

A second inadequacy to the knowledge transmission idea is that most research does not have the quality of being a 'nugget' (Weiss and Bucuvalas, 1980, p. 10), where a good idea (i.e. nugget) goes directly from its discovery or formulation by an individual researcher to its realisation in policy or practice (i.e. the instrumental use). A common response to the non-nugget-like status of most educational research is to argue for the value of educational research in general (e.g. that it contributes to sustaining a large, robust community of well-functioning, productive educational researchers who will ultimately provide results that will make a difference for some educational practice) (i.e. the conceptual use).

This kind of generic argument may produce warm and noble feelings among many educational researchers, but it is not particularly persuasive (to non-researchers), because it does not engage sufficiently with a general expectation that research can be relevant to practice (e.g. it only promises vaguely to contribute, without explaining specific ways). This leaves individual educational researchers with a problem of justifying research that does not (appear) to have immediate application.

Arguments for the value of educational research that does not have immediate application must be elaborated in relation to different kinds and purposes of research, and include an explanation of how some (though not necessarily all) of its knowledge production can come into educational activity. This approach to analysing the relation between educational research and educational practice reflects a conclusion, developed from analyses of the historical development of theories of knowledge use, that context-sensitive models (Gibbons, 2000) or adaptive models (Jacobson, 2007) are more promising. In other words, it is necessary to develop analyses about how to bring research-based knowledge into specific educational activity, rather than seek a universal model of this relation. To exemplify, the remainder of the chapter focuses on pedagogical innovation and diffusion of ideas into educational practice, where the idea is to improve or develop practice.

Improving or developing educational practice

The underlying question that motivates the analysis is: If we, as individual researchers, want to use educational research to improve or develop educational practice – and have free hands to do what we want (within typically existing resources and conditions), regardless of current political or organisational demands, or interest in or support for such efforts – then is there a general strategy we would use?

Production of knowledge is the primary activity for educational researchers aiming to improve or develop educational practice. If educational researchers can only produce knowledge, then how can this improve or develop an educational practice? The strategy question raises two challenges. First, it requires an explanation or account of the significance of each investigation. It is not sufficient to produce a 'piece of the puzzle' (i.e. instrumental use) or a useful idea that might give some inspiration (i.e. conceptual or symbolic use). Second, it seeks conceptual principles appropriate to all cases, rather than seeking a unique solution for each investigation.

If a practice is embodied in and realised through activity, then improving or developing an educational practice depends critically on changes in the activity of educational practitioners (see Dewey, 1929, p. 47 for a similar argument,[1] from a different theoretical perspective). Change in activity comes about through changes in specific actions, so it is not necessarily a matter of a complete redesign of activity. Change in action is the way through which new knowledge is introduced into activity. This key idea, grounded in the activity perspective, gives a slight, but important, shift in emphasis from transmitting information to focusing on the action of practitioners (who may or may not be conscious of the research-based arguments for these actions). Researchers must be able to give an account for how knowledge produced in research will yield changes in action in educational activity, or as I sometimes prefer to say, how an activity must change to allow (research-based) theoretical knowledge to be there.

Simply asserting an envisioned better way for activity leaves the ideas hanging in the air, in the hope that others will solve the problem of how to realise that vision in activity. An expression such as 'putting theory into practice' must be recognised as a research problem about how knowledge can be embedded in activity (i.e. through changed action). Changes in individual activity often depend critically on changes in working conditions (e.g. access to resources, support, time), where enabling these conditions may be as important as the knowledge for action for improving or developing activity. Researchers do not usually have direct control over working conditions, but research knowledge may help to clarify aspects of an organisational form that can support or hinder the use of knowledge (i.e. changed action). Once again this is not likely to be achieved by simple verbal transmission, where one can explain to administrators why there is a need to change working conditions. That simply shifts the original mistake from front-line practitioners to another part of the working organisation.

Research path as a general strategy

The proposal is that individual researchers should work with an integrated, self-conscious general perspective (i.e. a comprehensive critical imagination) that conceptualises the entire 'path' by which research-produced knowledge is going to be used to improve or develop educational practice, where this conception must have a plausible (i.e. empirically grounded) analysis of the process by which a specific practice is going to change.

A general path for improving or developing practice involves an account of (a) the function or use of specific kinds of knowledge in relation to the practice or activity, (b) what knowledge is likely to improve or develop the practice or activity, and (c) the process by which this knowledge might actually become part of that practice or activity. These three parts are found already in existing research activity, but not usually in an integrated way. That is, the first part is often included in concluding discussions of 'implications for practice', where the second part is often left implicit; the third part is often treated as a separate (research) problem of 'utilisation', 'transfer' or 'translation' of knowledge. But these three parts are not viewed as necessary aspects for a researcher to consider in conceptualising a single research work.

Experience shows that it is likely to be important for the single researcher to consider all these aspects, because demands from each one will have important consequences or challenges for how other aspects are developed (see Hackman, 2003 for a related argument). The basic challenge is to give an integrated account of the specific process by which research-produced knowledge is going to be used to develop an educational practice. For convenience, the expression *research path* is used to refer to this collection of accounts, where a more precise expression might be *research path to practice development.*

The 'path' imagery is chosen to highlight that research is oriented to a destination (i.e. improvement or development of practice), where a specific activity within that practice is in focus, and where the path is concerned with knowledge movement from one practice (embodied in research activity) to another (embodied in educational activity).

I have not seen a comparable integrated proposal in my wide-ranging search of research literature on knowledge utilisation. Some have noted the importance of the different aspects in their models about research in relation to innovation (e.g. Gideonse, 1968 in education; Thomas and Rothman, 1994 in social work), but without the strong demand that the individual researcher conceptualise all aspects. This demand involves a change in the underlying conception about the relation between educational research and educational practice, which may explain why no previous proposals were found. The path conception dissolves or avoids the 'two worlds' problem, giving the researcher full responsibility to consider the entire activity being addressed, and the full movement of ideas into that activity. This idea also provides a way for individual researchers to address the political tensions raised in the opening discussion.

Shove and Rip (2000), experts in research use and science policy, advocate giving up the fairy tale of the research user, and call for creativity in finding other strategies to encourage 'a variety of academic and non-academic interaction' (p. 182), but they do not provide a specific alternative. The 'research path' is one candidate, where the responsibility turns back on the researcher, to articulate and justify the assumptions in a comprehensive theoretical model for how research-based ideas will be realised in improving practice.

A variety of general strategies are used in the social sciences to bring knowledge into practice. These include specific 'engineering' efforts to design and implement innovations (e.g. Burkhardt and Schoenfeld, 2003), indirect strategies aimed at changing policy in a variety of organisations and general popular diffusion strategies (e.g. producing materials, books, film). The remaining discussion in this section elaborates the general idea of path in relation to an engineering strategy (i.e. how research-based knowledge can be used to improve or develop a practice). Other general path characteristics are likely to be needed for other objectives (e.g. policy change) and diffusion strategies (e.g. publishing relevant materials).

General construction of a research path for improving or developing practice

In forming a research path, individual researchers do not need to organise their investigations in a way that presupposes or reproduces the current division of labour between educational researchers and educational practitioners. A *division of labour* arises as a consequence of specialisation of work roles, often reflecting a historically conditioned, rather than a necessary or natural, organisation (Llorente, 2006).

The idea of division of labour is introduced here to highlight both the historical origins of the present division of activities embedded in research and educational practices, and the possibility for different kinds of divisions. At present, there is a 'social division of labour', reflected in the idea that researchers and educators are engaged in different practices, with the activity of researchers directed to one practice and the activity of educators directed to another.

One can envision a technical rather than a social division of labour (i.e. where persons are engaged in the same practice, with each contributing their part to the whole production process (Llorente, 2006). That is, research can be viewed as an activity within the practice of education, rather than a separate practice in its own right.

A technical division of labour contrasts with dominant images that put practitioners in one world and researchers in another. The current social division of labour makes this organisation harder to imagine, but it does not preclude conceptualising research from this point of view. That is, we already operate with a convenient fiction that researchers are supposed to produce knowledge while practitioners are supposed to use it (despite many analyses showing the inadequacy of this conception, both theoretically and empirically). So it should not be difficult to adopt another convenient fiction (or background assumption) that educational activity is the common object of investigation for both researchers and practitioners, but with different responsibilities in relation to that object. (Bulterman-Bos, 2008 makes a similar argument for treating educational activity as the object of investigation, but her proposal places all responsibility on clinical researchers, which eliminates the division.)

By viewing research as part of educational practice, the role of research and the role of knowledge in relation to that practice change from more typical linear models (e.g. knowledge translation) to one in which a researcher aims to understand how to make changes in action (which reflects knowledge). As noted before, an educational practice involves many activities. A research path should engage with a meaningful whole within a practice (i.e. an activity), with a bias to considering the essential aspects of the activity, and an aim to identify what knowledge needs to be introduced into activity (to support its improvement or development) and how to achieve that introduction.

I expect at least one 'research path' for each activity within a practice, where a specific path does not have to be limited by currently existing activities or goals within an actual practice, or restricted to being instrumental in relation to existing conditions and goals of the activity. The 'research path' provides, in effect, a guide for action for the individual researcher, describing what knowledge is needed both to act in and to develop educational activity.

In working with a research path, many actions (i.e. research projects and interpretation of results) may be taken along the way, involving many different kinds of knowledge, both knowledge for actions in the educational activity, as well as knowledge about how to create conditions to support this knowledge in the activity. Usually each project by itself will be insufficient to improve or develop practice. The meaning or significance of each research product or project is understood in relation to the path. For example, if a science education researcher studies children's expressed conceptions about the free fall of objects, then it would be necessary to explain the role of this research knowledge in a path that aims at (for example) development of children's theoretical understanding of physics concepts, where this aim is a meaningful whole in the practitioner's activity.

An important implication of this conception is that much knowledge produced through research may be used, in the first instance, by researchers to mediate their own actions in relation to educational practitioners' activity (e.g. to identify what changes in action one should strive for and how these changes might be realised). In other words, not all knowledge produced from research practice should necessarily become part of educational activity. This conception provides a way to explain or justify why some kinds of research are needed, even if not producing the 'nugget' of action that can be transmitted directly to practitioners.

A 'research path' for subject-matter teaching

This final part discusses a research path for the activity of subject-matter teaching, concentrating on illuminating the idea of 'research path' and how it is constructed and used. The discussion presupposes the focus on the individual researcher, but it is both possible and meaningful for other persons to be involved in working with a specific research path, which is consistent with conceiving research as a part of the educational practice.

A research path for an activity is always described with two layers. A *general layer* describes general features of the path necessary to develop the particular activity in focus (where the aim is a description likely to be accepted by all practitioners, including researchers and teachers). The *specific layer* involves specific theoretical assumptions and principles that operationalise and concretise the demands in the general layer. The imagery of layers is used to convey the idea that increasing specification and adaptation is needed for concrete research projects, while keeping clear about the role or significance of the particular details of a specific investigation in relation to the entire path.

General layer of a specific path for subject-matter teaching

Subject-matter teaching is an activity within an educational practice, hence a meaningful focus for a research path. Research about subject-matter teaching is another activity, usually organised in relation to a different (research) practice, where both are examples of societal practice. The activity of subject-matter teaching is carried out under specific conditions (e.g. in school classrooms, 45 minutes per day, with about 25 children and one teacher). The research path seeks to outline the kinds of knowledge needed for a comprehensive approach to developing subject-matter teaching in actual conditions, and that reflects the whole of subject-matter teaching activity.

The general layer is always the starting point for any research path. The general layer for the research path for subject-matter teaching outlines the general knowledge requirements for developing this particular activity. Box 12.2 presents an initial proposal. Note that the general layer can be used across different subject matters, age groups and educational levels.

Ideally this path would be accepted by most educational researchers and teachers working with developing subject-matter teaching as reflecting the basic knowledge needs for developing this activity, even if individual researchers or teachers may personally prefer only some parts of the path (or may want to add interpersonal or social–relational aspects). The acceptability is an important strength because it provides a common ground for communication among persons oriented to subject-matter teaching activity, whether as researchers or as practitioners, which makes a technical division of labour meaningful. This commonality provides a way to formulate, interpret and evaluate specific research projects, because they must be meaningful in relation to this general path.

The acceptability of the general layer may derive in part because it is formulated in abstract (or general) terms. But this abstraction is also a weakness because it does not provide specific guidance for how to realise the general ideas. The specific layer addresses this weakness.

Box 12.2 A general path for subject-matter teaching

1   Toward what goals (in terms of pupil capability) are we working?
2   What principles do we have to create instructional interventions that realise those goals?
3   What conditions are needed for teachers to make instructional interventions that realise the goals?
4   How can those conditions be realised within existing organisational conditions?

Specific layer for specific research path for subject-matter teaching

The specific layer concretises the general layer, reflecting specific theoretical ideas about how to address the points in the general layer. The specific layer is likely to be more contentious, as it becomes grounded in specific theoretical commitments and implications, but this gives the possibility for individual researchers to pursue their conceptual ideas about the practice under analysis.

The following discussion outlines the specific path I use for my research on subject-matter teaching. The four points in the general path are taken as the organising frame, while the specific path outlines a concrete way to address the demands of the general path. For present purposes, the presentation is intentionally abbreviated (i.e. meant to communicate the spirit of making a specific layer in relation to the general layer, without going into all the practical details and problems found in the fuller version).

Goals

Activity is always in a specific historical condition. In a specific research path, researchers and practitioners are working in relation to the same societal totality, where subject-matter teaching goals are political, embedded with demands from local or national authorities, and more indirectly from civil society. In making a specific path, one needs to argue for the validity of particular goals, beyond the desires or opinions of individual researchers or teachers. Personally I would prefer a political process for establishing goals, with all relevant stakeholders involved in a substantial way. Others have also argued for the need for such an approach, and the difficulty in realising it (e.g. Bruner, 1999, pp. 405–408; Martin, 1996, pp. 9–10).

In the absence of that ideal, it is often necessary (as a researcher) to formulate and justify choices about goals (e.g. drawing on documents from national curriculum, professional associations) as though these goals were going to be accepted and then concretise the specific path in relation to those goals. It is possible, even likely, that these goals reflect intentions that are not widespread in current teaching activity – which is consistent with a focus on improving or developing practice.

These goals may include requirements to work with general aspects of subject matter beyond factual content, and aspects that arise as a consequence of subject-matter teaching such as the personal development of pupils or critical thinking. For example, in my specific path for primary and secondary school teaching after about the age of nine, and drawing on the cultural–historical tradition, I would include a requirement to always work towards developing theoretical thinking in relation to theoretical concepts, giving access to historically developed traditions of knowledge (e.g. Chaiklin, Hedegaard, Davydov) and relating everyday experience with theoretical content (Hedegaard and Chaiklin, 2005). At the same time,

I would think about how to use the specific subject-matter teaching for personality development or development of whole person (Hedegaard, 1988; Chaiklin, 2001) or human flourishing (Chaiklin, 2012).

Principles for instructional interventions

Davydov (1986/2008) developed principles about developmental teaching, where a key aspect is developing theoretical thinking in relation to subject-matter content. Hedegaard (2002) developed these ideas further. And I have joined in that tradition, where we have developed the radical-local principle (Hedegaard and Chaiklin, 2005), with a focus on relating theoretical thinking to content from children's life worlds.

Conditions needed for realising activity

To realise the goals in a specific subject-matter teaching, a teacher must be able to:

* understand theoretical thinking (at least in a particular subject-matter area);
* create tasks for pupils that are designed to develop theoretical thinking in relation to the specific subject-matter;
* interpret children's responses and proposals in relation to conceptual ideas, and create new tasks that draw on those responses.

Support for teachers

The just-described conditions reflect some of the craft knowledge needed to realise the activity of effective subject-matter teaching (according to this specific path). Principles are needed for how to support teachers to develop those capabilities, and how to realise that support within their existing working conditions.

Training methods that remain rational or verbal are usually weak. Even if a person understands intellectually what is required, one often falls short when it comes to acting in accord with those understandings, or is not able to start at all. The key idea is to organise tasks that aim to change a teacher's activity (which implies appropriate action) so that it reflects the theoretical conception.

In relation to working within existing conditions, there is a better chance to engage teachers if one is working with topics that matter to them (see Lingwood, 1979 for an example). Research on school improvement has focused on the need for change at the level of the whole school, rather than the single classroom (e.g. Fullan, 2007; Hopkins, 2001). This point might be taken into account in the specific research path.

A specific proposal, showing how a specific research path is used

Consider a specific project where one wants to develop primary school mathematics teaching in Ghana.[2] The general and specific layers of the subject-matter teaching research path provide an orientation. In this particular case, goals are chosen relatively quickly – to accept the goals formulated in the national syllabus (because this should make it easier to engage with the third and fourth points in the general layer), while including the idea of radical-local teaching and learning (which is seen as developing the practice). The specific research focus is how to teach measurement concepts so that schoolchildren acquire a theoretical understanding of measurement in relation to their life practice. Many teachers in Ghana find measurement difficult to teach, so the research is engaging a topic that they want or need to solve (i.e. the researcher's intervention is not imposing or introducing a new task into their activity, just a new way of addressing it). In this project, the second point in the general path about instructional principles becomes critical: Do I have good ideas for being able to realise those goals?

In this case, I believe we have good theoretical ideas about instructional principles, but now the problem is how to concretise them in this specific situation. Specific research tasks are still needed, even though the general ideas are relatively well understood. For example, I need an analysis of measurement as a theoretical concept. This analysis may appear as a journal article. By itself, such an article is likely to be criticised as irrelevant or unusable in practice. I agree; the analysis by itself is not usable. Its relevance comes from its role in the path, providing a necessary requirement in relation to developing instructional activities that develop theoretical understanding of the concept. This analysis may not be used directly (e.g. as content for an in-service training session); rather its 'visible' use (in the senses of *use* found in school or political vernacular) will depend on many other parts of the path being developed, where the ideas may be embedded in other concrete tasks for teachers.

I expect that it will be possible to develop an effective way of teaching measurement (which could be demonstrated in a teaching experiment in a Ghanaian primary school classroom, working under the typical conditions that teachers would face there). The problem is how to address the third and fourth points in the path – to make those ideas accessible to other teachers. In working with school teachers in Ghana, I would draw on research that indicates that many teachers are now oriented to constructivist approaches – even if they do not know how to work this way (Akyeampong, Pryor and Ampiah, 2006). I would ask them to produce some tasks for their pupils, where these tasks must fulfil certain requirements (motivated by the belief that teachers will be oriented to an intervention that allows them to act in relation to their professional motives).

In creating such tasks, the teachers would get fairly immediate feedback on their own (supported) creations – which is expected to develop their motivation, and to initiate questions for clarification. The intervention would be coordinated with the school authorities, and introduced to the teachers so that they could see genuine support from their leadership (cf. just-mentioned research about change for a whole school, rather than an individual classroom). This example illustrates one way to approach a specific research path for subject-matter teaching, providing a way to understand the complex relation between educational research and development of educational practice.

Concluding remarks

This chapter has focused on the issue of educational research where there is an interest in improving or developing practice, but many of the arguments could also be applied where the interest is only to be relevant to practice. One of the motivating themes is a hypothesis that models of research use have tended to be too abstract, with implicit assumptions that are often overextended and empirically unsound, which has created confusions and unrealistic expectations for individual researchers. The idea of 'research path' was introduced as one way to make more explicit models that would be viable for the individual researcher.

Special characteristics of the 'research path'

1   It outlines principles, rather than universal solutions. The path encompasses an analysis of what knowledge is needed to support activity in a practice, and an analysis of how that knowledge can come to be present in a particular activity.
2   The path provides a conceptual strategy for planning research and interventions.
3   Both the general and specific layers are viewed as a research object, where the focus is on elaborating a viable model, which can be examined, challenged and developed further through its use in research.
4   Research developments include establishing a need to expand or elaborate the specification of the general layer. In some cases this may involve adopting assumptions from the specific layer as requirements in the general layer.[3]

Implications and consequences of the 'research path' idea

1   It presupposes that a research orientation is always needed in educational activity because of the need to adapt general principles in specific situations.
2   It gives a way to explicate the general significance of particular research projects, and provides a way to justify specific research projects that are not immediately usable in practice (e.g. focuses on one aspect of a meaningful practice), because its relation to the path can be explained.

3 It encourages (or challenges) researchers to be able to explain the significance of their individual work in relation to 'research paths' by which this knowledge would be used (even if they are not going to attempt to complete the path).
4 Those who ask for direct solutions to improving practice from research (e.g. 'what works') must also justify the 'path' they are envisioning.

Notes

1 'For these teachers are the ones in direct contact with pupils and hence the ones through whom the results of scientific findings finally reach students. They are the channels through which the consequences of educational theory come into the lives of those at school' (Dewey, 1929, p. 47).
2 This project is a collaboration with Dr Ernest Davis at the University of Cape Coast.
3 For example, aspects in the specific path for subject-matter teaching presented here (e.g. theoretical thinking for all subject-matter teaching, or full-school development) may be accepted as an explicit requirement of the general layer, where implications of that change would ripple through to other aspects in the general path.

Dialogue IV

Cautionary tales on research use, theory and practice

Thus far in the book, several proposals for the role of research in informing practice have been put forward: examination of how things work as a way of uncovering unintended consequences of policies and practices; explanation of why implementing a new programme or changing a practice is not straight-forward; and the development of new ways to organise teaching and learning or to coordinate multi-agency and multi-institutional work practices. Theory, method and the voices and experiences of those engaged in educational practices and decisions have been foregrounded as key ingredients for a new research agenda.

As a final rejoinder to the book, the authors in this section revisit the theme that sociocultural theoretical perspectives can provide an alternative to 'what works' by explicitly using theory to reflect on ways research, policy and practice can work together to improve education. However, the authors of this Dialogue raise critical issues for theory, method and research practice as they are situated in, and responsive to, complex political, social and cultural contexts.

In his chapter, James Avis focuses on the possibilities and limitations of Cultural Historical Activity Theory (CHAT) in terms of enabling change that is radical. He warns that even in the context of radical activity, there is a danger that the CHAT approach simultaneously downplays wider structural relations of capitalist production and alienation. His cautionary tale, grounded in an example of Further Education in England, is potentially relevant to any attempt to integrate theory, research, policy and practice where the goal is change or reform in education. That is, the limitations he identifies for CHAT could be viewed as unintended consequences of taking a pragmatic approach to research use. His argument suggests that as theories become appropriated in the use of practical and pragmatic projects, they may be reorganised in ways that limit the more radical possibilities initially imagined.

Julian Williams and Julie Ryan conclude the book by both looking back over the issues raised by the authors and by offering a potential way forward that could, at least temporarily, overcome the alienation of teaching–learning from research. Drawing on an activity theoretical perspective to engage with the issues, they argue that the alienation between these activities is rooted in their division of labour. They propose overcoming these divisions through the design of joint activity in third spaces in which practices can hybridise and multiple voices can inter-animate. Using the example of a mathematics 'lesson study' they describe what might be viewed as a third space in which practices are brokered across boundaries and where a new hybrid relationship between theory, research, policy and practice is developed.

We conclude the dialogue there with the hope that others will continue.

Chapter 13

Policy, mediation and practice in Further Education

The contribution of CHAT[1]

James Avis

> If activity theory is stripped of its historical analysis of contradictions of capitalism, the theory becomes either another management toolkit or another psychological approach without potential for radical transformations.
> (Engeström, 2008, p. 258; and see Miettenen, 2009, p. 160)

> Education plays a key role in the perpetuation of the capital relation; this is the skeleton in capitalist education's dank basement. It is just one of the many reasons why, in contemporary capitalist society, education assumes a grotesque and perverted form. It links the chains that bind our souls to capital.
> (Allman, McLaren and Rikowski, 2003, pp. 149–150)

This chapter engages critically with Engeström's version of activity theory that is centrally concerned with expansive learning in the workplace. It sets itself two key and interrelated tasks: to develop a theoretically informed critique of this version while simultaneously considering the way it can be used to make sense of English Further Education (FE). English FE has some similarities to Community Colleges in the US and Canada, Technical and Further Education Colleges (TAFE) in Australia and similar provision in New Zealand. English FE nestles between the end of compulsory schooling and degree level study, and has been orientated towards the provision of non-advanced vocational/technical and general education as well as adult and community education. However, it has never been an easily definable sector, characterised by diversity, shifting boundaries and delivered not only in FE colleges but by a variety of providers. Provision can range from basic skills to degree level work, with providers being marked by their particular histories as well as their local and regional contexts.

The chapter examines policy, mediation and practice in FE. Policy, as well as conceptualisations of 'best practice' are mediated and reconstituted by teachers through practice, in ways that accommodate, resist or ignore these demands. For some years English FE has been set within a turbulent environment marked by policy hysteria (Avis, 2009a). Policy changes have come thick and fast, being set within an overly complex and somewhat inchoate system of governance that draws on a range of constituencies and stakeholders. Figure 13.1 derives from a

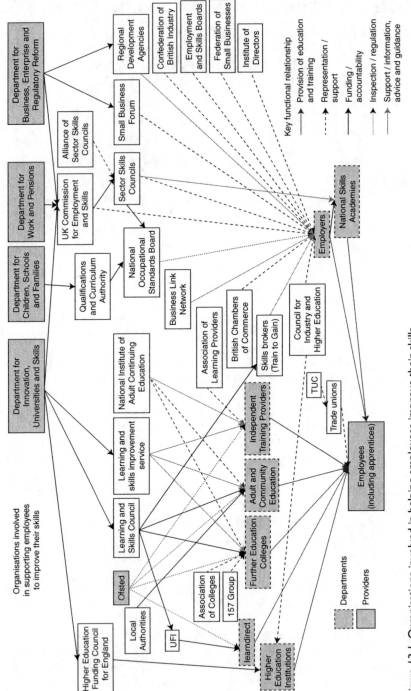

Organisations involved in supporting employees to improve their skills

Key functional relationship
→ Provision of education and training
⇢ Representation / support
→ Funding / accountability
⋯> Inspection / regulation
→ Support / information, advice and guidance

Departments
Providers

Figure 13.1 Organisations involved in helping employees improve their skills
Source: House of Commons Innovation, Universities, Science and Skills Committee, 2009: 97.

report prepared in 2009 and will no doubt be out of date at the time of publication but its purpose is to illustrate the complexity of the FE system. The UK Coalition government[2] is currently in the process of restructuring English FE.

There are, however, thematic continuities with the previous Labour government. A familiar concern addressing education in general and FE in particular is competitiveness and the need to continually up-skill the labour force. Education is deemed to have a pivotal role in the development of human capital which aligns with its concern with social inclusion and cohesion, both subject to the hegemony of the economic. The interest in social cohesion and inclusion has become more prominent following the urban riots of August 2011[3] but has nevertheless been a ubiquitous feature of Labour's (1997–2010) education and social policy landscape. The consequence for FE practitioners is that their roles are continually being expanded, often in the direction of inter-professionality, for example, social work and counselling. In addition there is, at least rhetorically, a common interest in localism that seeks to devolve decision making to as near to practice as is practicable. This current aligns with a desire to empower users of social and education services. For Labour the interest in user empowerment and provider accountability touches upon the role of local authorities and local democracy, whereas for the Coalition this is rather more centred on market forces. However, for both parties too much power still resides with central government at the apparent cost of the efficient delivery of services. This sits alongside a critique of the use of centrally driven targets and performance indicators that are construed as leading providers to become overly concerned with meeting targets at the expense of the effective delivery of services. While the Coalition may extol the benefits of the market, previous Labour governments similarly valued various forms of private educational provision (see Blair, 1998, p. 4 cited in Newman, 2001, p. 145). FE teachers confront a range of inconsistent policy demands ranging from competitiveness through to social inclusion.

Undoubtedly, and as illustrated by many studies of workplace learning, Engeström's activity theory provides a powerful analytic and heuristic device. In the following I briefly illustrate its potential when allied to 'development work research' and 'change laboratories', which place in a pivotal position dialogic engagement between researchers and practitioners. Fundamental to this particular version of activity theory is a reading of Marx that prioritises the commodity form and the contradiction between use and exchange value. These are expressed by disturbances or tensions that arise in any aspect of the activity system (AS) but can be traced back to the commodity and the contradiction between use and exchange value. The resolution of such contradictions leads to expansive learning and offers the potential to transform practice. The resolution of these tensions, disturbances or contradictions promises transformation and the development of new forms of practice. However, before considering FE it is necessary to comment upon activity theory.

Activity systems

In *Learning by Expanding* Engeström (1987) explores the development of activity theory which is now in its third and fourth generation (Engeström, 2010c; and see Avis 2007, 2009b). To describe the AS he draws on the familiar triangular representation. Figure 13.2 not only illustrates Engeström's minimal model for the third generation of activity theory but also incorporates its first and second generation.

The upper part of the triangle represents individual and group actions embedded in an AS, with the lower part referring to the division of labour between members of the community, the community who share the general object of activity and finally the rules that regulate action. The oval representations are used to indicate that object-orientated actions are 'characterised by ambiguity, surprise, interpretation, sense making, and potential for change' (Engeström, 2001, p. 134).

For Engeström, five principles underpin activity theory. In their description we can discern their Marxist and Vygotskyian origins.

> *The first principle* is that a collective, artifact-mediated and object orientated activity system, seen in its network relations to other activity systems, is taken as the prime unit of analysis.
>
> (Engeström, 2001, p. 136)

The focus is upon the AS as a whole and the manner in which the object is collectively formulated through the mediation of cultural tools and artefacts.

> *The second principle* is the multi-voicedness of activity systems ... The division of labor in an activity creates different positions for participants, the participants carry their own diverse histories, and the activity system itself carries multiple layers and strands of history engraven in its artifacts, rules and conventions.
>
> (Engeström, 2001, p. 136)

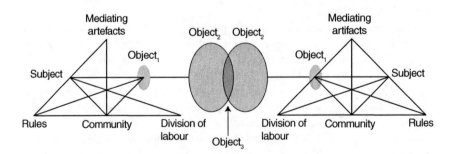

Figure 13.2 Two interacting activity systems as minimal model for the third generation of activity theory.
Source: Engeström, 2001, Figure 3, p. 136.

The division of labour within an AS creates different positions and therefore may give rise to various tensions, contradictions and conflicts. However, the way in which the division of labour is mobilised plays down managerial relations of power and it is for this reason contradictions and tensions can be resolved consensually. Although the importance of history is stressed, it is that of the AS and its participants. The concern with 'historicity' is set at this localised level, being reflected in the third principal.

> *The third principle* is historicity. Activity systems take shape and get transformed over lengthy periods of time … History itself needs to be studied as local history of the activity and its objects, and as history of the theoretical ideas and tools that have shaped the activity.
>
> (Engeström, 2001, pp. 136–137)

For Engeström such historical analysis needs 'to be focused on units of manageable size'. He suggests that 'if a collective activity system is taken as the unit, history becomes manageable' while at the same time moving 'beyond the confines of individual biography' (Engeström, 1999a, p. 36).

> *The fourth principle* is the central role of contradiction as sources of change and development. Contradictions are not the same as problems or conflicts. Contradictions are historically accumulating structural tensions within and between activity systems. The primary contradiction of activities in capitalism is that between the use value and exchange value of commodities … Activities are open systems. When an activity system adopts a new element from the outside … it often leads to an aggravated secondary contradiction where some old element … collides with the new one. Such contradictions generate disturbances and conflicts, but also innovative attempts to change the activity.
>
> (Engeström, 2001, p. 137)

The fifth principle of activity theory anticipates expansive learning and the dialectical resolution of contradictions. It hints at the modernist underpinnings of activity theory as well as an orientation that relates the transformative resolution of contradiction to the progressive development of the AS in an almost Hegelian fashion (see Langemeyer and Roth, 2006).

> *The fifth principle* proclaims the possibility of expansive transformation in activity systems. Activity systems move through relatively long cycles of qualitative transformations. As the contradictions of an activity system are aggravated, some individual participants begin to question and deviate from its established norms. In some cases this escalates into collaborative envisioning and as deliberate collective change effort. A full cycle of expansive transformation … is the distance between the present day everyday actions of the individuals and the historically new form of the societal activity that can

be collectively generated as a solution to the double bind potential [i.e. the contradictions, tensions or dilemmas] embedded in the everyday actions.

(Engeström, 1987, p. 174; cited in Engeström, 2001, p. 137)

Engeström's fourth and fifth principles point to the mechanisms through which ASs are transformed. This is closely aligned with his concept of expansive learning which arises through the resolution of contradictions. It emerges from processes of questioning where participants in an AS or cluster of systems question current practices, ultimately moving beyond these to generate new conceptualisations and forms of practice. 'A crucial triggering action in the expansive learning process … [is] the conflictual *questioning* of the existing standard practice' (Engeström, 2001, p. 151). The cycle of expansive learning is illustrated in Figure 13.3 and it can rest alongside developmental work research as well as change laboratories whereby practitioners connected to an AS or cluster of systems explore tensions with a view to their resolution.

The outcome of such collective and dialogic processes could be the development of not only more effective work-based or indeed pedagogic practices in FE, but also as a result of their transformation, more benign ones. However, despite the radical rhetoric, such possibilities are nevertheless set within an acceptance, or at least tolerance, of capitalist relations.

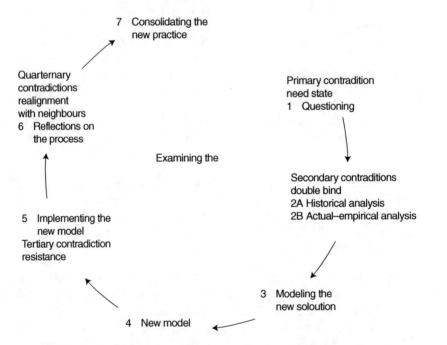

Figure 13.3 Strategic learning actions and corresponding contradictions in the cycle of expansive learning.
Source: Engeström, 2001, Figure 11, p. 152.

Further education, activity theory and transformation

Activity theory can be readily applied to FE, which provides a valuable test bed for the theory and its potential contribution to practice. Managerialism and performativity have been rife in the sector, leading to a series of disturbances or tensions within the system. These have been expressed at various levels from course teams in colleges through to national issues. They have also been met with conflictual responses that map onto the contradiction between use and exchange value. Gleeson and Shain (1999; Shain and Gleeson, 1999) explored the responses of those working in a college of FE to managerialism. They drew attention to the forms of compliance developed by staff ranging from unwilling to willing compliance that reflected either the wholesale rejection or acceptance of the new managerialism through to what they describe as strategic compliance. Importantly managerialism was multifaceted, arising in part as a response to changes in the type of students entering FE as a result of the growth of youth unemployment and a contraction in the labour market for un- and semi-skilled labour. These students encountered complacent institutions that served in many ways to reproduce classed, gendered and raced inequalities (see Avis, 2009, pp. 145–156). Disturbances and tension arose because of discrepancies between various ASs such as the youth labour market and college system. These discrepancies provided the terrain upon which managerialism developed. At an institutional level, managerialism was accompanied by regimes of performativity and the pursuit of targets that became ends in themselves.

Much has been written about the way in which lecturers in FE experienced these changes. Randle and Brady (1997) discuss proletarianisation and deskilling, with Gleeson, Davies and Wheeler (2005) adopting a more nuanced account that touches not only upon deskilling but also re-professionalisation (see Gleeson and James, 2007; Page, 2011a, 2011b). Managerialism was experienced by those working in FE in very particular ways. It is here that Gleeson and Shain's discussion of strategic compliance is important. At college level, contradictions were experienced between the aspiration to provide a valid educational experience for students and the distortions that arose out of the performative context in which institutions were placed. Strategic compliance was one of the ways in which progressive possibilities were sought. Notably, and as with other forms of compliance, these can straddle institutional positions and be found among principals, middle managers, and rank and file lecturers. Strategic compliers work with the progressive possibilities that change opens up and are characterised by a form of pragmatism that accepts some aspects of the new conditions as non-negotiable while others can be worked on progressively. Strategic compliers have, for example, developed collaborative relations with teachers, developing common materials, thereby overcoming some of the excesses of managerialism and performativity. Inter- and intra-college collaboration is a means by which lecturers attempt to regain some control over their labour process and mitigate the intensification of work through sharing course materials and so on. In a not dissimilar manner collaborative relationships have been developed across institutions. Such practices challenge the dominance of neoliberalism and managerialism with their emphasis upon competitive markets.

An exploration of such processes is well within the scope of Engeström's theory, which can readily understand and engage with such processes, pointing towards expansive learning. Disturbances and tensions and their resolution result in new and transformative practices. In a similar vein, policy makers have become alerted to the contradictions surrounding the use of targets and the micro management of educational institutions from the centre. This current is reflected in the emphasis accorded to the locality in education policy (see Avis, 2011). Importantly, these interventions in part illustrate expansive learning and the potentiality surrounding the use of developmental work research as well as change laboratories in the pursuit of 'best practice'. Within activity theory, what constitutes 'best practice' is a potentiality that develops out of the contradictions surrounding ASs and their resolution, which cannot be known in advance. In some respects there is an affinity between this understanding of practice and that of 'next practice' developed by the UK government's Cabinet Office Innovation Unit. As represented in Box 13.1, the Unit contrasts the improvement and innovation paradigms with *Next Practice*, aligning with the latter.

Reflecting the Innovation Unit's model of *Next Practice*, O'Leary and Craig write:

> Supposed empirical solutions to problems have their limits in any case because participants in systems see issues through *frames*. Where an individual is in a system will have an important influence on which problems they identify and how they frame solutions.
>
> (O'Leary and Craig, 2007, p. 8, emphasis in original)

Box 13.1 The improvement and innovation paradigms

Best Practice	Next Practice
Current Focus	Future Focus
Academic/policy generated	Practitioner/user generated
Adoptive	Adaptive
Fidelity emphasised	Context sensitive
R&D	D&R
Pilots	Trials

Source: Innovation Unit (undated).

Hence, 'Central to overcoming problems within a system is the process of disrupting these frames ... and supporting *learning* over time to build the *capacity* of the system to achieve a goal or set of goals' (Ibid.). Such processes can be easily translated into the language of activity theory and align with the ongoing changes that are impacting upon education in general and FE in particular. Change laboratories could be seen as disrupting frames by drawing together practitioners working within a particular AS thereby exposing contradictions. Turbulent environments characterised by open, if not chaotic, systems become the norm. Uncertainty and fluidity as well as the presence of poorly understood 'runaway objects' (such as climate change) that are not under the control of anybody become a feature of the environment (see Engeström, 2010b, p. 227). Such a contextualisation is echoed by the 2020 Public Service Hub's (2011) discussion of social productivity:

> The idea of social productivity represents a long-term culture change in public services – shifting from a culture of top-down, silo-based delivery of services, to a culture that recognises that social value is co-created between the service and user. It is an approach that puts engagement, co-production and civic responsibility at the heart of public services – creating sustainable systems that build social capacity, foster community resilience, and work with the grain of people's lives ... At root, it is the idea that 'public services should explicitly be judged by the extent to which they help citizens, families and communities to achieve the social outcomes they desire' [citing Commission on 2020 Public Services, 2010] ... This means focusing less on the particular services that are being – or have always been – delivered, and more on how the confluence of citizen agency, civil society and the state can collaboratively create the right conditions to improve social and economic outcomes.
>
> (2020 Public Service Hub, 2011, pp. 7, 8)

Unsurprisingly, these notions echo the interest in co-configuration and what Engeström describes as social production. For Engeström social production goes beyond the limits of bounded, firm-based models of production, extending co-configuration to include such practices as the development of open source software (2010b, p. 209). Activity theory has much to contribute towards the analysis of educational processes, workplace learning and, more specifically, expansive learning. These possibilities can be gleaned when examining analyses of the workplace that draw on activity theory. Engeström's extensive body of work comes to mind as does Lambert's (2003) on the educators of vocational trainers and the work of Daniels and others (2010) on inter-professionality. While this particular version of activity theory holds radical possibilities it is nevertheless marred by a form of comfort radicalism (Hayes, 2003), whereby its progressivism can also serve capitalist interest. It is marked by the same contradictions as those located within ASs, that is to say between use and exchange value.

Limitations

A number of issues arise from the manner in which activity theory and systems are conceptualised in the preceding discussion. For Gleeson and others who discuss strategic compliance there is a move towards a consensual model. This is echoed in some of Engeström's work focused on workplace learning and the resolution of problems in the workplace. While there is some recognition of conflicting interests at the site of waged labour, this tends to be domesticated and resolved through the ongoing development of the AS. The transformation of workplace relations seems to be set within a progressive direction and more often than not is presented as serving the interests of all. This is reflected in the cycle of expansive learning (see Figure 13.3) as well as in the use of change laboratories. It is as if the development of the forces of production move inexorably towards more progressive relations, that is to say those marked by more collaborative and democratic practices. While conflictual interests are embodied in the division of labour these are domesticated and not viewed as fundamental, in the sense that it is the forces of production that are being developed. The work of Adler (2006) is helpful here, suggesting that the progressive transformation of ASs can be construed as reflecting the development and socialisation of the forces of production allied to the ongoing development of the collective worker. Such a stance serves to play down the salience of conflict in the development of ASs and the resolution of contradictions.

For Adler, labour process theorists, through their emphasis on social antagonism at the site of waged labour, have ignored or failed to acknowledge the development of the collective worker and anticipatory socialisation of the means of production (and see Livingstone, 2006). Such a stance can be used to explain the underlying consensual nature of Engeström's theory and its tendency to treat conflict as resolvable through rational dialogue, as found, for example, in the use of change laboratories

Adler's position offers a particular take on transformative processes. On one level it reflects the constant 'revolutionising [of] the instruments of production, and thereby the relations of production, and with them the whole relations of society' (Marx and Engels, 1973, p. 38). Social antagonism is not present in the development of the forces of production or that of the collective worker. If these ideas were applied to the FE AS together with developmental work research, we could envisage a range of participants uncovering contradictions and working on their resolution, thus contributing to the development of the forces of production. For Adler this process stands apart from the antagonisms present in capitalism. However, if we understand the worker as 'the human made capital' (Rikowski, 1999) or that the labour process faces in more than one direction, mirroring the dual nature of the commodity, we can then begin to grasp the social antagonisms that surround the collective worker. Such a stance would recognise not only social antagonism but also raise questions of power. This would serve to problematise the manner in which Engeström understands ASs and their division of labour, revealing the ideological dimension of his argument.

Contradiction and questioning

For Engeström, contradiction is crucial to the development of ASs, providing the mechanism through which they are transformed over time. This process is linked to the questioning of current arrangements and can result in expansive learning. Such learning carries with it the development of new forms of knowledge and identity as well as changes in the division of labour. However, while emphasis is placed on the contradiction between use and exchange value, the political implications of this are rarely addressed. In the FE context this could be between the use value that derives from the forms of knowledge and experience students encounter and their exchange value in terms of the fee income they generate for the college. In studies on the delivery of health care, Engeström is at pains to point out the contradiction between the use value of medication as agents of healing and its exchange value. While this contradiction is seen as primary, much of the resulting analysis is focused on peripheral contradictions. This results in a failure to consider the political and radical implications of an analysis of the commodity form. Livingstone reminds us, 'without sustained attention to the central contradictory relationships serving to reproduce capitalist societies and generating the potential for their transformation, the basic objectives of Marxist inquiry are missed' (Livingstone, 2006, p. 147). This tension in Engeström's work is present in the following passage where there is a move away from a focus on primary contradiction to what could be construed as disturbances within an AS that are amenable to localised resolution:

> In activity theory, developmental transformations are seen as attempts to reorganize, or re-mediate, the activity system in order to resolve its pressing inner contradictions. While the primary contradiction between the use value and exchange value of the object does not go away, it evolves and takes the form of specific secondary contradictions. The emergence, aggravation of these secondary contradictions may be regarded as a developmental cycle in the life of the activity system (Engeström, 1987) ... If actors are able to identify and analyze the secondary contradictions of their activity system, they may focus their energy onto the crucial task of resolving those contradictions ... The contradictions do not manifest themselves directly. They manifest themselves through disturbances, ruptures and small innovations in practitioners' everyday work actions.
>
> (Engeström, 2005, pp. 180, 181)

Expansive learning is tied to the resolution of contradiction at the site of a specific and localised AS or cluster. If primary contradictions are central to the analysis this serves both to point towards the attempted resolution of these within the specific cluster of ASs as well as those present in the wider system. If these primary contradictions are to be addressed, this would necessitate forms of political mobilisation that extend beyond a particular cluster to wider society. Engeström's theory, as a consequence of its failure to push its analysis far enough, becomes domesticated and tied to 'transformist' practices, failing to transform itself into what Sawchuk (2006) describes as 'revolutionary activity':

> [I]f we accept, as I do, that ultimately expansive learning is defined by the progressive resolution of systemic contradictions, then paradoxically one can engage in processes of expansive learning by resolving a range of more peripheral contradictions only to the point of the most primary contradiction; that of use/exchange value. To move beyond this point is the dividing line between epochal and truly historical activity – that is revolutionary activity.
>
> (Sawchuk, 2006, p. 251)

As a consequence, Engeström's theory veers towards a form of comfort radicalism, its transformative rhetoric has a progressive appeal but ultimately readily lends itself to becoming no more than a management technique (Hayes, 2003, p. 38). Through the use of developmental work research and change laboratories, worker knowledge can be appropriated and used to transform the labour process in the interest of capital. It is important to recognise that such a consequence is not predetermined but is the outcome of struggle. Engeström's theory, despite its use of Marxist conceptualisations, has difficulty in accommodating class struggle as this requires recognition of social antagonism at the site of waged labour and undercuts the consensual dialogic processes embodied in this particular understanding. For some writers the manner in which ASs are described rests with a generalised model of up-skilling and the development of the collective worker (Adler, 2006). But, this collective worker is 'capital made human' and embodies the contradictions of capitalism. While new knowledge may arise, ASs are as much about the formation of the required dispositions of labour in contemporary capitalism as about the development of highly skilled workers (Daniels and Warmington, 2007; Warmington, 2005). It is also important to recognise that, while analytically it is possible to distinguish skill from social relations, the two are in practice intertwined (see Avis, 1981). Such tensions can readily be mapped onto FE in relation to the contradiction between use and exchange value, the marginalisation of social antagonism, as well as to 'the human made capital', whereby teachers become complicit in their own exploitation.

Miettinen's discussion of Engeström's use of contradiction illustrates the importance of locating these within the development of capitalism, as well as within a particular AS. This is important for two reasons:

> If empirical studies of local activity systems focus on secondary contradictions distinct or abstracted from the primary contradictions, the approach is subject to criticism, in that it tends to degenerate into a version of adaptive systems theory ... secondly analysis of the contradictions of capitalism is also important to avoid linear visions of the development of the organization of work, exemplified by the 'right path' suggested by Victor and Boynton (1998).
>
> (Miettinen, 2009, pp. 167–168)

There is much discussion of the relationship between primary and secondary contradictions, the tension between use and exchange value, as well as the salience of struggle, particularly when set against determinist accounts. Paradoxically, such tensions are present in Engeström's work and derive from its central interest in workplace learning and the transformation of practice. In order to accomplish this, some sort of 'accommodation' has to be made with capital. This is reflected in arguments that suggest the transformation of work anticipates progressive developments, the socialisation of the means of production and the development of the collective worker, that is to say the skills, knowledge and identities of those involved in the AS. In other words, there is an incipient logic surrounding the development of ASs, whereby their ongoing improvement moves towards the development of more collaborative and democratic practices as illustrated by co-configuration and social production. This position implies there is a community of interest between capital and labour and that, when contested, this would be by atavistic forms out of step with capitalist development. In addition, there is a tendency to emphasise the logic surrounding the development of capitalism as illustrated in Figure 13.4, in which social production is construed as a higher level of development that, at least for some writers, anticipates the socialisation of the means of production and the transformation of social relations.

This is linked to arguments that address the development of the knowledge/ information society and the increased salience of science in the production of use and exchange value. These arguments suggest that the knowledge society anticipates, in Engeström's (2010b; 2011, Chapter 9) terms, social production and a fundamental change in the way in which surplus value is created, this being generated externally to the firm through the appropriation of science, as well as the knowledge and skills of those engaged in social production. A raft of writers have addressed these concerns, many of whom draw upon Marx's (1973) discussion in *Grundrisse* on the development of the collective worker and the application of science to the forces of production (Adler and Heckscher, 2006; Gorz, 2010; Hardt and Negri, 2009; Miettinen, 2009; Virkkunen, 2009). There are at least two points to be made. First, older sedimented forms of production will exist alongside emerging social production. Second, and as these authors will partly acknowledge, these developments are a site of struggle and will not necessarily follow an inexorable logic. This is in part because of the tensions deriving from the commodity, those between use and exchange value. Yet, these analyses can easily fold over into a form of capitalist modernisation. This is because the interest in overcoming contradiction at the site of the local AS, cluster of systems or indeed swarm of systems, addresses disturbances or tensions manifested in that particular context. The use of developmental work research or change laboratories compounds this tendency. Such an analysis could readily be applied to FE exploring the tensions that exist within it and its related ASs leading to change. However, as a result of the focus upon the development of the AS and the resolution of contradictions therein, implicit in these practices is an assumption that it is possible to resolve tensions and to move the AS towards more effective practices. While there is recognition of primary contradictions, these are in effect bracketed and it is this that lends itself to the transformist thrust of such arguments and their domestication (Gramsci, 1971, pp. 58, 106).

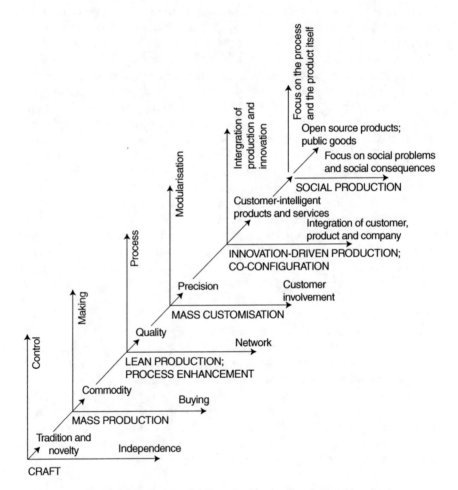

Figure 13.4 Historical types of production completed: towards social production.
Source: Engeström, 2010b, Figure 9.2, p. 232.

Conclusion

This chapter has examined policy, mediation and practice in FE. Policy as well as conceptualisations of 'best practice' are mediated and reconstituted by teachers through practice, in ways that accommodate, resist or ignore such demands. An exploration of these processes is well within the scope of Engeström's activity theory and there is much to commend in this. The use of change laboratories allows practitioners to explore the contradictions and tensions in the AS and through dialogue enables a reconceptualisation of workplace practices. The theory can address local specificity, but as a result of its tendency to downplay or domesticate questions of power and social antagonism, the resulting analyses can readily fold over into a transformist and overly conservative practice. This tension is expressed well in the quotation that opened the chapter: 'If activity theory is stripped of its historical analysis of contradictions of capitalism, the theory becomes either another management toolkit or another psychological approach without potential for radical transformations' (Engeström, 2008, p. 258). If this version of activity theory is to fulfil its potential it needs to be set within a broader politics that adopts a relational understanding of educational processes that challenge the structures of power in which FE is set.

Notes

1 Parts of this chapter draw upon Avis (2007, 2009b).
2 In May 2010 following the British general election and a hung result, a Coalition government was formed between the Conservatives and Liberal Democrats. David Cameron (Conservative) became the prime minister with Nick Clegg (Liberal Democrat) becoming his deputy.
3 Riots took place in a number of English cities including London, Manchester and Wolverhampton in August 2011, resulting in looting, destruction of property and in some cases death (BBC, 2011a). On 15 August David Cameron announced a review of government policy to ensure that they address and remedy what he describes as the 'broken society' (BBC, 2011b; Cameron, 2011; and see Avis, 2011).

Chapter 14

Research, policy and professional development

Designing hybrid activities in third spaces

Julian Williams and Julie Ryan

The literature (e.g. Hammersley, 1997; Hargreaves, 1997, 1996; and papers in this volume) and much previous professional experience suggest deep conflicts between researchers, professional practitioners and policy makers in education. Many educational researchers (e.g. Burkhardt and Schoenfeld, 2003; Pollard, 2006) are on record as arguing that research needs to be better designed, executed and communicated if it is to inform or influence practice and policy: most recently the English research council, ESRC,[1] and their Teaching and Learning Research Programme in particular scripted aims and criteria to intentionally inform policy and practice. They say research should find out 'what works' and so impact society and the economy in order to justify the government's expenditure. Thus, 'impact' is on all our research agendas now.

However, the impact agenda in education is predominantly discoursed in terms of measurable effectiveness: there is a presumption that research should identify the effect of definable practices, which can then be described as 'good', and which policy can then impose across the profession by means of various incentives and surveillance technologies. Unfortunately, it is too often assumed that good practice can be made to work across contexts. But whole swathes of research have shown how badly coordinated policy and practice can be. Indeed, some educational research views its main mission to reveal how the educational policy leads to negative, presumably unintended consequences for learning, just as it has for outcomes across the public sector (in health, in policing, in banking, tax, etc.). Such research typically employs case studies of how things *really* work, when practice often turns out to be not so good. Often such research shows how the richness of local context needs to be understood, and how professionals need to be able to make judgements in learners' best interests, some cases of which are shown in this volume.

In this chapter we will analyse the relationships between policy, professional practice and research. We will try to reveal the source of the alienation between these three, and show how activity might overcome such alienation, even if only temporarily. We look for solutions in third spaces between these activities, where new hybridised practices and discourses can be developed. (For more on 'third spaces' and 'hybridised practices' see Gutierrez, Baquedano-Lopez and Tejeda, 1999; and Williams *et al.*, under review.)

Activity theory, contradictions between research, policy and professional practice

An activity theory perspective suggests that we should seek the source of conflicts between these practices in their contradictory 'activity systems' (see Avis and Daniels, this volume). Let us consider 'learning research' and 'classroom teaching practice' activities, for instance (cf. Chaiklin, this volume). A simple analysis of the object and intended outcomes of these two activities suggests that they have different and contradictory 'objects', including their motives, goals and intended outcomes. Research on learning aims to produce new insights and understandings about learners and learning processes with knowledge outcomes to be published addressing a variety of communities, including teachers who might benefit (but then sometimes one can just say the immediate goal is to produce some academic papers for the next review without which the researcher's contract and research time may be curtailed). Classroom teaching, though, aims to produce new understandings of benefit to learners in classrooms (but then similarly one could say the goal is to produce test scores purporting to reflect such knowledge and understanding, without which the school will be in trouble, and the teachers responsible 'brought to account').

One does not need to go much further to see how different and contradictory these activities can be, and, as we indicated, each activity is itself contested and perhaps self-contradictory (does teaching/research aim to improve understanding or produce better immediate performance on assessments and reviews?). Furthermore, following Engeström (1987; 1991) let us consider some of the *mediations* of the two activity systems: academic research activity is mediated by data recording/producing tools, academic analyses, and personnel and institutional structures involving a hierarchy of various professionals and assistants and students, over timescales sometimes of years. In contrast, classroom teaching is mediated by a quite different set of relational structures, communities, norms, rules and timescales in schools. It is easy to see how separated research and teaching can become, with practical boundaries growing between them over time, including growing division of labour and increasingly specialist and alienated discourse genres.

However, in *joint* work involving researchers and teachers, we argue that the division of labour between teachers and researchers can facilitate reflection in ways separate work often cannot, for example, by providing analyses of videos and video-stimulated interview reflections for the joint group to discuss; but we are never naive enough to think that teachers and researchers are normally engaged in 'the same' activity.

Then there is also policy. In policy-making activity, politicians or policy makers (subjects) act to make or remake policy (objects), where motives regarding education are distinct from those of teaching-and-learning or research. At the 'top' of the policy hierarchy, this is not least due to the fact that policy information is largely mediated by statistics: the 'results' of policy are measured in exam results, league tables, in party conferences, and opinion and electoral polls. They have their own mediations and timescales: activity is often said to be shaped – we say mediated – by 'the media', and by the announcement for the next news conference, and above all the next election.

In the 'middle', we have layers of management caught in vertical chains of accountability (Wenger, 2009). The government adviser, regional analyst, head teacher, principal, head of department or subject coordinator, and, yes, often the classroom teacher too, are often all policy makers (see Williams, Corbin and McNamara, 2007). Each is responsible for the monitoring and supervision of results that account for their work, and provide evidence for a claim for a continuing flow of resources (which we here loosely call the exchange value). But, all the same, the impact of the whole professional system on the learning outcomes of learners can also be held to account: even the Minister of State is embarrassed if the unintended consequences of 'his/her' policy are shown not to be working in some functional, 'use' value sense. Thus performance and accountability works to some degree in both directions (see Williams, 2011b).

We intend here then to explore the conflict between the agendas and discourses such as 'what works' and 'how do things work' in relation to these conflicting policy and professional practices and activity systems. We argue that the alienation between research, teaching–learning and policy results from separation between and lack of freedom within these systems. We will then look at our own research in a third space 'between teaching and research' systems. Finally, we offer some 'ways forward' in terms of constructing new hybrid activity in third spaces, ways that at least temporarily alleviate alienation between activities, and at best might offer a microcosm of a new, reformed, less alienated education profession.

Subjectivity, dialogue and multi-voicedness within and between activities

The three main activities, or perhaps sets of activities, we need in focus are: (i) educational policy formation and implementation activity by politicians and their advisors, including curricula, assessment and accreditation structures, policies on funding, schools, teaching, professional structures of management, and so on; (ii) teaching and learning activities – or perhaps teaching–learning joint activity, and their assistance and support in classrooms, schools and colleges; and (iii) research activity of professional educational researchers, of their students and assistants and so on. Of course, in reality these overlap – teachers also 'research', and researchers also sometimes teach; as commented above, managers in school also make policy, and this can extend to the grass roots, even to teachers and children/learners. These three activities, 'policy', 'research' and 'teaching-and-learning' for short, each have broadly their own logic, community, motive and, in fact, 'ensembles of social relations' that Leont'ev (1978, 1981) called an 'activity system'. Yet, they are complex and multi-voiced, with actors bringing their experiences and discourses into the community from other activities.

Close analysis will show that in each main activity there may even be several interrelated activities: even the singular joint name for 'teaching–learning' gives this away. Sometimes teaching and learning appear as a joint activity of dialogue where teacher and learner are meaningfully engaged together, perhaps in an effort to achieve some joint understanding. But at other times it breaks down, teacher and learner become decoupled and perhaps alienated from each other: the teacher simply transmits, say, and the learner may just listen or copy. Further the activity of learning itself (or teaching) can have multiple motives and meanings, at one moment directed to 'grade getting' and at another to 'problem solving', for instance (Williams, 2011a refers to 'exchange value' and 'use value' in this regard).

In addition to these we might learn a lot through considering those who cross the boundaries of these communities/activities, especially when they bring practices and discourses from elsewhere. We argue that truly joint activity of teaching-and-learning involves learners in teaching (at least explaining, but even really teaching) and teachers in learning (at least listening and trying to understand the learner, but even really researching the learner). This joint activity becomes truly dialogic in a Bakhtinian sense when the joint object of activity becomes mutual understanding of the subject (Bakhtin, 1981, 1986; and see Ryan and Williams, 2007, 2012).

By extension of this argument, following Williams *et al.* (under review) and Williams *et al.* (2011b), we suggest learning from those who broker or work across the three categories, or who engage in and broker multiple activities, or who form hybrid activities in third spaces. In the context of the two activities of teaching-and-learning and research, think of inquiry groups including teachers who are researching their practice of teaching, for instance, or researchers who teach about researching teaching. An analysis of such activities and how the various subjects of these activities are positioned may explain their interests in the different formulation of agendas such as 'what works', versus 'how things work'. The point here is that a 'policy maker' is an acting subject engaged in policy making (with its own distinct subjectivity), whether they be a teacher/head teacher or researcher by profession: naturally their discourse on policy is ventriloquated by their teacherly or researcher professional voice!

As has been argued by others in this volume, a 'what works' educational agenda usually assumes an essentially policy perspective: it assumes that there is some policy or practice to be identified, described or constructed, formulated, disseminated or implemented that will deliver common outcomes, assumed implicitly to be, to some degree, invariant across context, across social geography, across institutions, teachers and learners. This is what policy desires. Policy has an interest in showing that it has made a difference by supporting (e.g. funding) or enforcing 'what works' across the wider system it governs, but also over which it can be held accountable (to their party or government, to their media, to their electorate, etc.).

The emphasis here that is interesting is the 'invariance across context' requirement of policy. In such a world it has to be assumed from the perspective of politicians funding policy-orientated research that policy is the tool, government is the acting subject with agency, and the education system (and its institutions, teachers and learners) are the object of activity. As the object of policy activity the teachers and learners may be deprived of agency. In this discourse the curriculum is non-negotiable to the learner, the pedagogy is non-negotiable to the teacher, the English 'three-part lesson' may be a non-negotiable law for the inspectorate, and performance management may be non-negotiable for the head teacher, governor or middle manager.

This lack of freedom in the process and product of one's activity is precisely how Marx defines 'alienation' (see Marx, 1844; Meszaros, 2005; see also Williams, 2012). Thus, the invariance and inflexibility of a policy on, say, the practice of teaching across contexts implies that 'what works' must be made to work across this variation of context, with 'good' and 'bad' schools and teachers, for instance. But the paradox is that – by alienating the teachers and learners in the process – 'what works' may come to not work after all! This raises the question: can policy be developed that allows for the free and unalienated engagement of the professional?

The medical analogue is clear in Pearson *et al.* (Chapter 4 in this volume): there are certain practices that are established as effective across patients and contexts (e.g. prescribe drug X for patients showing symptoms s1, s2, s3 ... and never prescribe the two drugs X1 and X2 together as this will likely cause harmful side effects, Y1 and Y2, or they may even cancel out). The purpose of policy and management is to establish such rules and enforce them rigorously across practice. The purpose of research is to enquire systematically, for example through experimentation and survey, to establish the 'good practices' that policy subsequently enforces: very NICE[2] (Hammersley, 1997; Hargreaves, 1996, 1997).

But what if following such standard, recommended practices do not work in practice? Even in medical systems it is well known that such practices break down when humans are involved. The criticism of this approach is that it reduces the agency of the professional (and patient) to act in their own context in ways that take account of that particular context and how it is progressing in a non-deterministic, and non-linear, dynamic system. Thus, as immunity rates rise in the population, individuals judge it not worth the risk to immunise their own children: the population as policy 'object' becomes a collection of active 'subjects' with their own agency, and pushes back, nullifying policy.

On the other hand, in contrast, the idea behind the 'how things work' agenda suggests that practice is complex and its effects are intersectionally contingent on many contextual factors, because all humans involved in a social system have agency and subjectivity. Rich description of and analyses of cases are required to capture how things *can* be made to work out in practice. This requires professionals with the agency to mediate policy and if necessary modify it or invent new solutions. Experimental conditions that simplify and rigidly control such behaviour are then anathema because they oversimplify. 'Life isn't like that', or only unfree, controlled and conditioned, alienating, life is like that.

But, for others, and typically for policy, this professional agency can be regarded as dangerous: can 'we' trust the professional to invent and reinvent their practice in local conditions, day by day? It is argued that professionalism requires the development of a bedrock of accepted standard, prescribed 'good' practice to 'apply' in normal circumstances – even if it is accepted the professional needs to think creatively when unusual or new cases/problems arise. Thus, a good doctor might need to think creatively about why a patient is not responding to treatment (perhaps they forget to take their anti-dementia tablets?) but they still need to know the right, normal dose to prescribe, or where to look it up. Even the creative artist works with standard, practised, basic skills honed through their ten thousand hours of practice of life drawing, or musical scales, they say.

Therefore, prescription of policy in professional standards is contradictory and problematic, but it is not going to go away: the genie is out of the bottle! We suggest that, in the context of such contradictions, we must look to generate new activities as a source of creative solutions, in third space social systems of activity that can motivate and create the kind of dialogues that might imagine solutions. Thus, the arguments for BOTH a 'what works' and a 'how do things work' agenda seem to have some merit in fuelling a dialogue about practice. But how can we make a new activity that expands or supersedes each of these one-sided discourses? This would require a new joint agenda that acknowledges the need for agency or freedom for all sides, but that requires a resolution of the underlying contradictions between these separate activity systems.

Activity theory: development of new subjectivity, consciousness and agency

The account given of activity theory so far is a little simplistic: we spoke of subject, object, and mediating tools, norms and division of labour (again: see Avis for details). In order to tackle our problem we need to understand how activity theory accounts for change and development, that is, its dynamic and social–psychological side. For Leont'ev, an activity system has a three-level structure that may be pertinent to understanding our problem: an operational level (below conscious level: behaviour), an action level (conscious level: goal) and a societal activity level (social level: motive). As activity unfolds, the consciousness of the subject may evolve and change due to contradictions within the activity, or between activities. On the one hand, the subject may suddenly attend and become conscious of operational 'moments' of the whole activity (the software suddenly does not work and the navigator's attention is drawn to programming problems and how to get round the crisis, e.g. Hutchins, 1995). On the other hand, one's attention is drawn from the immediate goal of action to the wider societal motive of the activity (e.g. the astronaut is required to talk to the president midflight and is thus reminded that the point of the trip to the moon is actually political).

These last two levels of activity – aimed at goals and motives – are relevant here in seeing how consciousness may develop through joint activity. When an individual subject acts within a joint activity with others in a division of labour (e.g. the researcher works with the teachers and learners in a classroom project to develop pedagogy) each may act with a different subjective view and different consciousness of its goal, as described above. Over time, however, the participants in the joint activity – and of course through shared dialogue – may share and develop new perspectives and awareness of the societal motives of the activity, and furthermore the activity itself is always evolving.

Leont'ev (1981) famously described development in schooling this way: the adolescent begins to study history with others in the class with the goal to please their teacher, family or community, or maybe even to earn a grade; but if the activity is successfully developmental, the student becomes 'interested' and begins to study history for its 'true' societal motive, which is perhaps to understand humanity's condition and trajectory, to learn the lessons of history and so to live better lives. Thus, in joint activity there are multiple, sometimes contradictory consciousnesses and goals, and development involves learning new motives drawing on multiple perspectives (for a fuller account see Black *et al.*, 2010; Williams, 2011a, 2012).

This complexity suggests that actually it is a mistake to see any one of the aforementioned practices or activities (of school practice, policy making and research) as always and only involving a single, pure 'activity', but rather one should see each as a dynamic system that harbours contradictory actions, or even multiple activities. Modern activity theory says activity is multi-voiced in the Bakhtinian sense (Engeström, 1987, 1995). In a dynamic system individual and collective consciousness and knowledge can develop through dialogue, changing social relationships and evolving new forms and objects of activity, as contradictions within and between activities unfold.

This, we argue, can be the source for overcoming the contradictions we have discussed. In the next section we will analyse lesson study from this point of view.

Multiple activities and their contradictions: the case of classroom research and lesson study

We have described elsewhere some joint work of researchers and classroom teachers on 'lesson study', a model of continuing professional development that focuses attention on classroom practice, but uses the tools of research and enquiry to effect the study (Hart, Alston and Murata, 2011; Ryan and Williams, 2012). One can think of such an activity as involving 'brokering' between practices and systems: as Wenger (1998) puts it, brokering involves carrying (while sometimes transforming) elements of one practice into another. Thus researchers broker research practices in the lesson study or lessons, say, when they carefully observe and collect data about children's mathematical talk, inscriptions and 'thinking' mid-lesson. Similarly, in the post-lesson review the researchers may be identifying material of research interest, while the teachers may be focused on assessing progress and replanning the lesson for a second run. (A common practice in lesson study is that teachers jointly plan, observe and review a lesson leading to a second, improved lesson.)

However, what emerges in joint activity may go beyond this. As teachers and researchers we (authors) worked together in lesson study in one school in England over more than a year: we found that new forms of activity started to emerge, in which hybrid practices formed and took on new meanings. To illustrate, we will now examine three examples of hybridity from which we hope to generalise. The first is about meanings of dialogue in research and pedagogy; the second about the process of lesson study itself; and the third about policy and curriculum development.

1: The meaning of dialogue in pedagogy

Lesson study involves the teachers (and researchers of course) in the study group carefully observing and collecting evidence of the children's learning during the course of the lesson being studied. This might involve written work, jotted descriptions in a notebook, photographs and audio- or video-recordings. In our group we found it convenient for one adult to sit near a 'group table' (on which typically a group of four to six children would be working at problem-solving tasks). In many instances, the children engaged the adult or assistant in conversation, or their work. They knew that we were studying their problem solving and wanted to know about their mathematical ideas; simple curiosity might lead a child to ask what we were writing in our notebooks, and similarly we would ask them to clarify their reasoning or arguments. As such, the various adults were naturally drawn into dialogue and even the teaching, sometimes making observations and note-taking more difficult. We experienced a conflict of roles, as it were, between researcher and teacher: and in various ways we sometimes tried to achieve both.

Because there were, in a sense, two enquiries going on in the lesson (learning mathematics, say, and finding out what the children knew and what arguments they could produce), the children knew we were interested in their ideas – even the kind of activity and the tasks and models provided were somewhat different and, in particular, dialogue was explicitly being provoked between researchers, teachers and the children. For the teachers this was a new classroom practice, and one that they have come to adopt as part of their teaching. This was experienced by teachers who recognised that this 'listening to the children's mathematics' could be a powerful tool in assessment for learning (see Black and Wiliam, 1998). Now a year later in one of our interviews one of the teachers said of the school 'we are still working on standing back and listening to the children' and another reported that teaching should be 60 per cent listening. It is natural in retrospect that hybridising research in teaching practices should develop new pedagogy in this way. But we argue that research has been developed in a new hybrid form by lesson study too.

2: What have we learned from the process of lesson study?

In our lesson study discussions (planning and debriefings) we made a virtue of intervention in lesson dialogue (lesson study purists have told us this is NOT 'proper' lesson study!). We decided it might be very productive if the teachers' interventions could be a bit more like the researchers (that is, to listen more and teach less) and the researchers' interventions a bit more like the teachers (to ask the children what their arguments were and to make sure the teacher knew about some of them for the plenary part of the lesson). We reflected that, because our inquiry was interested in the children's arguments, we might *help them* to clarify their arguments, their differences, and so on: a key pedagogic strategy in dialogic teaching–learning activity (see also Williams and Ryan, 2012). As such the research hybridised with teaching, and thereby became helpful in developing the teaching.

But what did we learn for the research? By becoming more actively engaged with the children in learning (as well as the teachers in the lesson study planning) we claim we became engaged in a hybrid of research-and-pedagogy: we therefore believe the research knowledge we generate will be more likely to be 'developmental' in two crucial ways. First, our challenging of the learners' argumentation serves to develop it, and to feed it into the lesson. We therefore find out not what argumentation will 'naturally produce' under normal pedagogic conditions, but what it could perhaps ideally produce. The hybrid practice offers the learner a zone of proximal development, which is what we would ideally hope schooling can produce. Second, we also provide pedagogy with a zone of proximal development; that is, we try to generate together the sort of lesson that the teachers might ideally produce. Thus the hybrid research–teaching practice develops a new kind of research, by producing a new kind of joint pedagogy.

This kind of research in the context of change produces a different kind of knowledge from the usual research into 'what works', because it allows 'what works' to emerge in the research practice itself. We argue that by studying teaching in the context of development, we find a different kind of knowledge: we find out what might work, and how things might work, if dialogic teaching–learning develops.

3: What did we learn about curriculum and policy?

A vignette from one lesson study concerned a particular event in which learners were using the measurement system as a model for decimals and their ordering (see Ryan and Williams, 2012).

The Year 6 (10/11-year-old) children were asked to decide which children (given their heights to the nearest centimetre) would be allowed on a 'Big Ride' at the fairground, given a height requirement of 1.4 metres or more. In discussing the difference between 1.04 and 1.4, one of the children eventually mentioned 'tenths' in her argument, and there was much discussion of tenths of a metre, how big it was, compared with centimetres etc. In the post-lesson discussion, the lesson study team discussed the fact that (i) the metre rulers did not have decimetres marked out, and (ii) the 'decimetre' is not mentioned in the National Curriculum for England and was not known to some of the teachers. It was decided it would be important to rectify this situation if the intention becomes to teach the decimal system and its place value concept through the use of modelling with measurement. New metre rulers were ordered, decimetre strips were constructed and the decimetre was written into lesson plans and the school's scheme of work.

In one sense the school and the teachers were able to put this situation right: they made their own policy and developed their professional tools and practices. More importantly, they became teachers who make local policy, and who speak critically of national policy with a teacher–research perspective, that is ventriloquating policy with teacher–research voices. Perhaps, in a profession in which lesson study and development activity is taken seriously by policy, then such work could be generalised to the National Curriculum, to textbooks, and to educational suppliers and their designers. If policy makers were present in lesson study groups, perhaps this would be facilitated: at present probably the best we can say is that the teachers and researchers can use their voices to speak to policy. We think the deeper lesson is that when policy is made, the profession might in future hold policy to account: 'Show us your lesson study data first'!

The agenda and discourses of 'what works' and 'how things work'

What emerged from this experience of lesson study (extended over more than a year) regarding 'what works' and 'how things work' policy discourses and agendas? The focus of the joint activity on children's mathematical arguments allowed us to see that – given some caveats – a developmental pathway for children's conceptual growth (e.g. regarding decimals) required a change in curriculum, and an introduction of the 'decimetre' into the classroom via tools such as the metre and decimetre ruler, curricula and pedagogy. We argue that the joint activity involving learning, teaching and closely studying the classroom were all required to produce this proposed change in teaching–learning practice, and thus proposed policy.

However, other things begin to emerge from this lesson study: the children's learning is becoming constructed around their persuasive arguments and explanations (traditionally perhaps thought of as being the preserve of the teacher), while the teachers in turn are becoming more accustomed to listening carefully to the children's mathematics. As the researchers study the classroom, we/they become more active in engaging in dialogue with the children, probing their arguments and helping them to articulate and develop their ideas, while also of course learning from the children 'how things work'. The teachers are becoming more active enquirers too, and we have been told that the staff as a whole is reading much more, and that discussion in the staffroom about mathematics education has been growing. The management are convinced this 'can only be good' for education – and for their test results too: if nothing else, the management can claim to their governors and inspectors that they have a plan, and that it involves a policy of staff development.

We do not claim that the boundaries are disappearing. As one teacher told us, 'because of this project' they had space to talk, think and develop their ideas together (with us researchers) – but next week is 'assessment week again' and while the research team are writing research papers, the teachers will be back to assessing the children (who will perhaps be back to 'grade producing' for the accountability system). The joint activity of the project tends to overcome alienation and the division of labour, but only temporarily.

We suggest this 'lesson study' space is a third space where new hybrids of research, teaching-and-learning and maybe even policy making can be co-constructed. (For a longer account of other 'third spaces' see Williams *et al.*, under review.) The active agency and consciousness of learners, teachers and researchers together gave us a dynamic joint activity in which social learning processes and more joined-up practices of pedagogy, research and policy making could occur, developing learning-and-teaching and research, and critiquing policy.

It is particularly important here to see that we must first consider 'how things work' if we are to understand what the 'what' might be in the discourse of 'what works'. This occurred through dialogism in which voices from learners, teachers and researchers collided and ventriloquated: because researchers, teachers and learners came to develop together.

More importantly for our conclusion, 'what works' logically seems to imply an understanding of the 'what' by all those involved in mediating it. 'What works' then only makes sense in terms of 'how things work' and, in particular, how we can make things work locally. Truly dialogic policy, if there is such a thing, needs to grow out of dialogue with and between researchers and practitioners, which in turn needs to arise in conditions of developing pedagogy, in which teaching is engaged in dialogue with learning, which we named dialogic teaching-and-learning.

Thinking about brokering, hybridity and third spaces as sources of development

The social conditions required for some of these reflections involved a third space where multiple practices were involved, in a single system or activity, and in which multiple voices and perspectives could be shared. In principle, internalisation of the social contradictions between activities can lead to an internal dialogue, and hence through imagination of how things might be if contradictions were resolved, to creative solutions. In practice, we suggest we require the resources of dialogue out loud with other voices and discourses. Joint activity in a third space may provide a motive for this dialogue between contrasting or contradictory voices, out of which mutual understanding and hybridised discourses may emerge. The lesson study was one such third space, where the joint activity was an enquiry into dialogic teaching–learning in lesson study classrooms, where the normal requirements and norms of lesson activity were suspended. How might research and policy be similarly subsumed in joint activity in a third space, leading to hybridised practices and discourses? Or how about research-and-policy-and-teaching–learning?

Rather than work through the problem of how we might get from here to there, consider the implications of what being there might mean. The seeds of such a resolution of contradictions were arguably already there in the analysis of how teaching and learning might become a joint activity: through dialogism. Similarly, then, the process of dialogic reflection in and on policy might hybridise with research discourses. Insofar as policy is an activity of communication with the wider body politic, a dialogic policy making could become equitable in the sense that arbitrary power relations would disappear. The power of argument and evidence in policy would then ideally become supreme. In the meantime, in practice, we must face the fact of power imbalance: we must learn to manage the vertical conditions of accountability without which we will be denied the resources to research.

Conclusions

The conclusion we would like to draw is that the three activities posited, namely, 'policy/policy making', 'research' and 'teaching–learning' become alienated from each other to the extent that they become separate, divided by more or less impermeable boundaries, and controlled. Thus, teachers and learners may have little agency in policy making, or research may remain trapped in its own scholarly work, and policy may remain in a Westminster bubble (i.e. in a government circle) and so on. The danger with 'what works' as a policy agenda is that it becomes a separate and alienated activity: a government minister may decide to include long division in the new mathematics curriculum with no reference to the knowledge and expertise of teachers and researchers; or a research team may discover the pattern that single sex schools produce more physicists without revealing the processes that make this happen.

But joint activity can be productive in reducing these barriers: we claimed that learning and teaching can sometimes be hybridised into a joint activity of teaching-and-learning through joint, dialogic enquiry by teachers and learners. In such a view, the notion that teachers deliver a curriculum to learners alienates and separates teacher, learner and subject matter. On the contrary, a dialogic approach leads to joint teaching-and-learning of subject matter, where the object is to mutually understand the subject matter or problem at issue. Such an approach may require us to re-envisage and reconstruct the activity of the classroom, the curriculum, pedagogy, schooling, etc.; and this probably cannot in fact be achieved without the support of policy and research.

We argued that joint activity of research and teaching can be developmental for both, leading to these more dialogic practices of teaching and of research-ing. We suggested that this can happen in the third space of lesson study, where discourses and practices can hybridise. In particular, we want to challenge the division between discourses of 'what works' and 'how things work'. We need always to think about policy on practice as a reification of how things might work better, which will only work if professional agency is allowed to freely do its work. We argue for a dialogue between policy, research and practice: policy needs to be made reflexively accountable to practice at least as strongly as the reverse.

Notes

1 We gratefully acknowledge the support of the Economic and Social Research Council (ESRC) for support of our seminar series grant RES-451-26-0576.
2 The UK body National Institute for Health and Clinical Excellence (NICE).

Bibliography

2020 Public Service Hub (2011). *The further education and skills sector in 2020: A social productivity approach*. London: RSA.

Adler, P. (2006). From Labor process to activity theory. In P. H. Sawchuk, N. Duarte and M. Elhammoumi (eds) *Critical perspectives on activity: Explorations across education, work and everyday life*. (pp. 225–261). Cambridge: Cambridge University Press.

Adler, P. and Heckscher, C. (2006). Towards collaborative community. In C. Heckscher and P. Adler (eds) *The firm as a collaborative community* (pp. 11–15). Oxford: Oxford University Press.

Ainscow, M. (1999). *Understanding the development of inclusive schools*. London: Routledge.

Ainscow, M. (2003). Using teacher development to foster inclusive classroom practices. In T. Booth, K. Nes and M. Stromstad (eds) *Developing inclusive teacher education*. London: RoutledgeFalmer.

Ainscow, M. (2010). Achieving excellence and equity: reflections on the development of practices in one local district over 10 years. *School Effectiveness and School Improvement*, 21(1), 75–92.

Ainscow, M. (2012). Moving knowledge around: strategies for fostering equity within educational systems. *Journal of Educational Change*, 13(3), 289–310.

Ainscow, M. and Howes, A. (2007). Working together to improve urban secondary schools: a study of practice in one city. *School Leadership and Management*, 27(3), 285–300.

Ainscow, M. and Kaplan, I. (2006). Using evidence to encourage inclusive school development: possibilities and challenges. *Australasian Journal of Special Education*, 29(2), 106–116.

Ainscow, M. and West, M. (eds) (2006). *Improving urban schools: Leadership and collaboration*. London: Open University Press.

Ainscow, M., Booth, T., Dyson, A., with Farrell, P., Frankham, J., Gallannaugh, F., Howes, A. and Smith, R. (2006). *Improving schools, developing inclusion*. London: Routledge.

Ainscow, M., Dyson, A., Goldrick, S. and West, M. (2012). *Developing equitable education systems*. London: Routledge.

Ainscow, M., Muijs, D. and West, M. (2006). Collaboration as a strategy for improving schools in challenging circumstances. *Improving Schools*, 9(3), 192–202.

Akyeampong, K., Pryor, J. and Ampiah, J. G. (2006). A vision of successful schooling: Ghanaian teachers' understandings of learning, teaching and assessment. *Comparative Education*, 42, 155–176.

Allen, D., Wainwright, M., Mount, B. and Hutchinson, T. (2008). The wounding path to becoming healers: medical students' apprenticeship experiences. *Medical Teacher*, 30(3), 260–264.

Allman, P., Mclaren, P. and Rikowski, G. (2003). After the box people. In J. Freeman-Moir and A. Scott (eds) *Yesterday's dreams: International and critical perspectives on education and social class.* (pp. 149–179). Christchurch: Canterbury University Press.

Alsup, J. (2006). *Teacher identity discourses: Negotiating personal and professional spaces.* Mahwah, NJ: Lawrence Erlbaum Associates.

Antman, E. M., Lau, J., Kupelnick, B., Mosteller, F. and Chalmers, T. C. (1992). A comparison of results of meta-analyses of randomized control trials and recommendations of clinical experts. Treatment of myocardial infarction. *JAMA*, 268, 240–248.

Anyon, J. (1997). *Ghetto schooling: A political economy of urban educational reform.* New York: Teachers College Press.

Apple, M. W. (1996). *Cultural politics and education.* New York: Teachers College Press.

Askew, M., Brown, M., Rhodes, V., Wiliam, D. and Johnson, D. (1997). The contribution of professional development to the effectiveness in the teaching of numeracy. *Teacher Development*, 1(3), 335–356.

Astley, W. G. and Zammuto, R. F. (1992). Organization science, managers, and language games. *Organization Science*, 3, 443–460.

Atkinson, E. (2000). In defence of ideas, or why 'what works' is not enough. *British Journal of Sociology of Education*, 21(3), 317–330.

Avis, J. (1981). Social and technical relations: the case of FE. *British Journal of Sociology of Education*, 2(2), 145–161.

Avis, J. (2000). Policy talk: reflexive modernization and the construction of teaching and learning within post-compulsory education and lifelong learning in England. *Journal of Education Policy*, 15(2), 185–199.

Avis, J. (2007). Engeström's version of activity theory: a conservative praxis? *Journal of Education and Work*, 20(3), 161–177.

Avis, J. (2009a). Further Education: policy hysteria, competitiveness and performativity. *British Journal of Sociology of Education*, 30(5), 639–648.

Avis, J. (2009b). Transformation or transformism: Engeström's version of activity theory? *Educational Review*, 61(2), 151–165.

Avis, J. (2011). More of the same? New Labour, the Coalition and education: markets, localism and social justice. *Educational Review*, 63(4), 421–438.

Bakhtin, M. (1963). *Problems of Dostoevsky's poetics.* Minneapolis, MN: University of Minnesota Press.

Bakhtin, M. (1979). *The aesthetics of verbal creativity.* Moscow: Iskusstvo.

Bakhtin, M. (1981). *The dialogic imagination: Four essays by M. M. Bakhtin.* (Ed. M. Holquist, trans. C. Emerson and M. Holquist). Austin, TX: University of Texas Press.

Bakhtin, M. (1986). *Speech genres and other late essays* (trans. C. Emerson and M. Holquist). Slavic series, no. 8. Austin, TX: University of Texas Press.

Bakhtin, M. (1993). *Toward a philosophy of the act* (trans. V. Liapunov). Austin, TX: University of Texas Press.

Ball, S. J. (2003). The teacher's soul and the terrors of performativity. *Journal of Education Policy*, 18(2), 215–228.

Ball, S. J. and Vincent, C. (1998). I heard it on the grapevine: hot knowledge and school choice. *British Journal of Sociology of Education*, 19(3), 377–400.

Ball, S. J., Davies, J., David, M. and Reay, D. (2002). 'Classification' and 'judgement': social class and the 'cognitive structures' of choice of Higher Education. *British Journal of Sociology of Education*, 23(1), 51–72.

Barry, J. and Proops, J. (1999). Seeking sustainability discourses with Q methodology. *Ecological Economics*, 28(3), 337–345.

Barton, D. and Tusting, K. (2005). *Beyond communities of practice: Language, power, and social context*. Cambridge: Cambridge University Press.

Bayne, S. (2010). Academetron, automaton, phantom: uncanny digital pedagogies. *London Review of Education*, 8(1), 5–13.

BBC (2010). *Student loan bosses stand down*. Retrieved 25 May 2010 from: http://news.bbc.co.uk/1/hi/education/10157509.stm.

BBC (2011a). *England Riots*. Retrieved 15 August 2011 from: www.bbc.co.uk/news/uk-14452097.

BBC (2011b). *David Cameron to review policies after riots*. Retrieved 15 August 2011 from: www.bbc.co.uk/news/uk-politics-14526095.

Beach, K. D. (1999). Consequential transitions: a sociocultural expedition beyond transfer in education. *Review of Research in Education*, 24, 124–149.

Berliner, D. C. (2002). Educational research: the hardest science of all. *Educational Researcher*, 31(8), 18–20.

Bernstein, B. (1993). Foreword. In H. Daniels (ed.) (1993). *Charting the agenda: Educational activity after Vygotsky*. London: Routledge.

Bernstein, B. (2000). *Pedagogy, symbolic control and identity: Theory, research, critique (revised edition)*. Lanham, MD: Rowman & Littlefield Publishers Inc.

Biesta, G. (2007). Why 'what works' won't work: evidence-based practice and the democratic deficit in educational research. *Educational Theory*, 57(1), 1–22.

Billett, S. (2011). Subjectivity, self and personal agency in learning through and for work. In M. Malloch, L. Cairns, K. Evans and B. N. O'Connor (eds) *The Sage handbook of workplace learning* (pp. 60–72). London: Sage.

Black, L., Williams, J., Hernandez-Martinez, P., Davis, P., Pampaka, M. and Wake, G. (2010). Developing a 'Leading Identity': the relationship between students' mathematical identities and their career and Higher Education aspirations. *Educational Studies in Mathematics*, 73(1), 55–72.

Black, P. and Wiliam, D. (1998). Assessment and classroom learning. *Assessment in Education*, 5(1), 7–74.

Blair, T. (1998). *The Third Way: New politics for the new century*. London: Fabian Society.

Boggs, J. P. (1992). Implicit models of social knowledge use. *Knowledge: Creation, diffusion, utilization*, 14, 29–62.

Boudreau, J. D., Cruess, S. R., and Cruess, R. L. (2011). Physicianship: educating for professionalism in the post-Flexnarian era. *Perspectives in Biology and Medicine*, 54(1), 89–105.

Bourdieu, P. (1977). *Outline of a theory of practice* (trans. R. Nice). New York: Cambridge University Press.

Bourdieu, P. (1984). *Distinction: A social critique of the judgment of taste.* Cambridge, MA: Harvard University Press.

Bourdieu, P. (1991). *Language and symbolic power.* Cambridge: Polity Press.

Bourdieu, P. (1992). *The logic of practice.* Stanford, CA: Stanford University Press.

Bourdieu, P. (2002). *Distinction: A social critique of the judgement of taste.* London: Routledge.

Bourdieu, P. (2003). *Practical reason.* Cambridge: Polity Press.

Boyle-Baise, M. and McIntyre, D. J. (2008). What kind of experience? Preparing teachers in PDS or community settings. In M. Cochran-Smith, S. Feiman-Nemser, K. E. Demers and D. J. McIntyre (eds) *Handbook of research in teacher education: Enduring questions in changing contexts* (3rd ed.) (pp. 307–330). Mahwah, NJ: Lawrence Erlbaum Associates.

Bridges, D., Smeyers, P. and Smith, R. D. (eds) (2009). *'Evidence-based educational policy': What evidence? What basis? Whose policy?* Oxford: Wiley Blackwell.

Brighouse, T. (2007). The London Challenge: a personal view. In T. Brighouse and L. Fullick (eds) *Education in a global city.* (pp. 71–94). London: Institute of Education Bedford Way Papers.

Broekkamp, H. and van Hout-Wolters, B. (2007). The gap between educational research and practice: a literature review, symposium, and questionnaire. *Educational Research and Evaluation,* 13, 203–220.

Brown, S. R. (1971). The forced-free distinction in Q-technique. *Journal of Educational Measurement,* 8(4), 283–287.

Brown, S. R. (1980). *Political subjectivity: Applications of Q methodology in political science.* New Haven, CT and London: Yale University Press.

Brown, S. R. (2002). Q technique and questionnaires. *Operant Subjectivity,* 25(2), 117–126.

Brown, P., Lauder, H. and Ashton, D. (2011). *The global auction: The broken promises of education, jobs and incomes.* Oxford: Oxford University Press.

Brown, T., Hanley, U., Darby, S. and Calder, N. (2007). Teachers' conceptions of learning philosophies: discussing context and contextualising discussion. *Mathematics Teacher Education,* 10, 183–200.

Bruner, J. (1999). Postscript: some reflections on education research. In E. C. Lagemann and L. S. Shulman (eds) *Issues in education research: Problems and possibilities* (pp. 399–409). San Francisco, CA: Jossey-Bass.

Bruns, A. and Humphreys, S. (2005). Wikis in teaching and assessment: the MCyclopedia project. *WikiSym,* 16–18 October 2005, San Diego, CA.

Bryant, S., Forte, A. and Bruckman, A. (2005, November). Becoming Wikipedian: transformation of participation in a collaborative online encyclopedia. In W. Lutters and D. Sonnenwald (eds) *Proceedings of GROUP International Conference on Supporting Group Work* (pp. 1–10). New York: ACM Digital Library.

Bullock, S. and Russell, T. (2010). Does teacher education expect too much from field experience? In T. Falkenberg and H. Smits (eds) *Field experiences in the context of reform of Canadian teacher education programs,* 2 vols (pp. 91–100). Winnipeg: Faculty of Education of the University of Manitoba.

Bulterman-Bos, J. A. (2008). Will a clinical approach make education research more relevant for practice? *Educational Researcher,* 37, 412–420.

Burchill, F. (2001). The road to partnership: forcing change in the UK further education sector; from 'college incorporation' and 'competition' to 'accommodation and compliance'? *Employee Relations*, 23(2), 146–163.

Burkhardt, H. and Schoenfeld, A. (2003). Improving educational research: toward a more useful, more influential, and better-funded enterprise. *Educational Researcher*, 32(9), 3–14.

Cameron, D. (2011) PM's speech on the fightback after the riots. Retrieved 15 August 2011 from: www.number10.gov.uk/news/pms-speech-on-the-fightback-after-the-riots.

Campbell, D. T. (1984). Can we be scientific in applied social science? *Evaluation Studies Review Annual*, 9, 26–48.

Caplan, N. (1979). The two-communities theory and knowledge utilization. *American Behavioral Scientist*, 22, 459–470.

Chaiklin, S. (2001). The category of 'personality' in cultural–historical psychology. In S. Chaiklin (ed.) *The theory and practice of cultural–historical psychology* (pp. 238–259). Aarhus: Aarhus University Press.

Chaiklin, S. (2011). The role of 'practice' in cultural–historical science. In M. Kontopodis, C. Wulf and B. Fichtner (eds) *Children, development and education: Cultural, historical, anthropological perspectives* (pp. 227–246). Dordrecht: Springer.

Chaiklin, S. (2012). Dialectics, politics and contemporary cultural–historical research, exemplified through Marx and Vygotsky. In H. Daniels (ed.) *Vygotsky and sociology* (pp. 24–43). Abingdon: Routledge.

Cheyne, J. A. and Tarulli, D. (1999). Dialogue, difference and voice in the zone of proximal development. *Theory and Psychology*, 9(1), 5–28.

Cochrane, A. (1973). Effectiveness and efficiency: random reflections on health services. In A. Cochrane (ed.) *Effectiveness and efficiency: Random reflections on health services*. Oxford: Oxford University Press.

Cochrane Collaboration (n.d.). Retrieved 30 November 2011 from: www.cochrane.org.

Cohen, D. K. and Garet, M. S. (1975). Reforming educational policy with applied social research. *Harvard Educational Review*, 45(1), 17–43.

Cohen, D., McLaughlin, M. W. and Talbert, J. (1993). (eds) *Teaching for understanding: Challenges for policy and practice*. San Francisco, CA: Jossey-Bass.

Cole, M. and Engeström, Y. (1993). A cultural–historical approach to distributed cognition. In G. Salomon (ed.) *Distributed cognitions: Psychological and educational considerations*. New York: Cambridge University Press.

Commission on 2020 Public Services (2010) *From social security to social productivity: A vision for 2020 public services*. London: 2020 Public Services Trust.

Cook, D. A., Bordage, G. and Schmidt, H. G. (2008). Description, justification and clarification: a framework for classifying the purposes of research in medical education. [Review] *Medical Education*, 42(2), 128–133.

Cooke, M., Irby, D. M. and O'Brien, B. C. (2010). No Title. In M. Cooke, D. M. Irby and B. C. O'Brien (eds) *Educating physicians: A call for reform of medical school and residency. Carnegie Foundation for the advancement of teaching*. San Francisco, CA: Jossey-Bass.

Coulehan, J. and Williams, P. C. (2001). Vanquishing virtue: the impact of medical education. *Acad Med*, 76(6), 598–605.

Cox, R., McKendree, J., Tobin, R., Lee, J. and Mayes, T. (1999). Vicarious learning from dialogue and discourse: a controlled comparison. *Instructional Science*, 27(6), 431–457.

Crowley, T. (2001). Bakhtin and the history of the language. In K. Hirschkop and D. Shepherd (eds) *Bakhtin and cultural theory* (pp. 177–200). Manchester: Manchester University Press.

Crowther, D., Cummings, C., Dyson, A. and Millward, A. (2003). *Schools and area regeneration.* Bristol: The Policy Press.

Crowther, J. (2004). In and against lifelong learning: flexibility and the corrosion of character. *International Journal of Lifelong Education*, 23(2), 125–136.

Daniels, H. (2001). *Vygotsky and pedagogy.* London: Routledge.

Daniels, H. (2006). Analysing institutional effects in Activity Theory: first steps in the development of a language of description. *Outlines: Critical Social Studies*, 2, 43–58.

Daniels, H. (2008). *Vygotsky and research.* London: Routledge.

Daniels, H. (2010). The mutual shaping of human action and institutional settings: a study of the transformation of children's services and professional work. *British Journal of Sociology of Education*, 31(4), 377–393.

Daniels, H. and Warmington, P. (2007). Analysing third generation activity systems: labour power, subject position and personal transformation. *Journal of Workplace Learning*, 19(6), 377–391.

Daniels, H., Edwards, A., Engeström, Y. and Ludvigsen, R. S. (eds) (2010). *Activity theory in practice: promoting learning across boundaries and agencies.* London: Routledge.

Danielson, S. (2009). Q method and surveys: three ways to combine Q and R. *Field Methods*, 21(3), 219–237.

Datnow, A., Hubbard, L. and Mehan, H. (2002). *Extending school reform: From one school to many.* London and New York: Routledge/Falmer.

Davies, H., Nutley, S. and Walter, I. (2008). Why 'knowledge transfer' is misconceived for applied social research. *Journal of Health Services Research and Policy*, 13(3), 188–190.

Davis, P., Farnsworth, V., Farrell, P., Kalambouka, A., Ralph, S. and Shi, X. (2008, September). *Students' personal financial management life narratives: Revealing the notion of leading identity as a tool with which to understand changes in young people's financial practices.* Paper presented at the International Society for Cultural and Activity Research (ISCAR) International Congress, San Diego, CA.

Davydov, V. V. (2008). *Problems of developmental instruction: A theoretical and experimental psychological study* (trans. P. Moxhay). Hauppauge, NY: Nova Science. (Original work published 1986.)

Dean, M. (1999). *Governmentality: Power and rule in modern society.* London: Sage.

Deignan, T. (2005, September). *Transferable people: Reframing the object in UK post-compulsory education and training.* Paper presented at the University of Manchester conference on Sociocultural Theory in Educational Research and Practice, Manchester. Retrieved 3 July 2012 from the University of Manchester website: http://orgs.man.ac.uk/projects/include/experiment/tim_deignan.pdf.

Deignan, T. (2009). Enquiry-based learning: perspectives on practice. *Teaching in Higher Education*, 14(1), 13–28.

Deignan, T. (2012a). Modeling and developing a dyslexia support system. In D. Moore, A. Gorra, M. Adams, J. Reaney and H. Smith (eds) *Disabled students in education: Technology, transition and inclusivity* (pp. 239–271). Hershey, PA: IGI Global.

Deignan, T. (2012b). A novel way to develop policy and practice. *Operant Subjectivity: The International Journal of Q Methodology*, 35(2), 102–128.

Department for Education and Employment (2001). *Opportunities and skills in the knowledge economy: A final statement on the work of the national skills task force* Nottingham: DfEE.

Department for Education and Science (1991). *The parents' charter.* London: HMSO.

Department for Education and Skills (2005). *Skills: Getting on in business, getting on at work.* London: HMSO.

Department for Education and Skills (2006). *Further education: Raising skills, improving life chances* (Cm 6768). London: The Stationary Office.

Department for Industry, Universities and Skills (2008). *Higher education at work.* London: HMSO.

Department of Trade and Industry (1998). *Our competitive future: Building the knowledge driven economy.* London: DTI.

Dewey, J. (1929). *The sources of a science of education.* New York: Horace Liveright.

Dillenbourg, P. (2002). Over-scripting CSCL: the risks of blending collaborative learning with instructional design. Retrieved 14 April 2011 from: http://hal. archives-ouvertes.fr/hal-00190230.

Donner, J. C. (2001). Using Q-sorts in participatory processes: an introduction to the methodology. In R. A. Krueger, M. A. Casey, J. Donner, S. Kirsch and J. N. Maack (eds) *Social analysis, selected tools and techniques, social development papers, 36* (pp. 24–49). Washington, DC: The World Bank.

Dornan, T. (2008). Self-assessment in CPD: lessons from the UK undergraduate and postgraduate education domains. *Journal of Continuing Education in the Health Professions*, 28, 32–37.

Dornan, T. (2010). On complexity and craftsmanship. *Medical Education*, 44, 2–3.

Dornan, T. and Bundy, C. (2004). What can experience add to early medical education? Consensus survey. *BMJ*, 329(7470), 834.

Dornan, T. and Smithson, S. (2009). Clinical teaching in the early years. In J. Dent and R. A. Harden (eds) *Practical guide for medical teachers* (3rd ed.). Edinburgh: Elsevier.

Dornan, T., Boshuizen, H., King, N. and Scherpbier, A. (2007). Experience-based learning: a model linking the processes and outcomes of medical students' workplace learning. *Medical Education*, 41(1), 84–91.

Dornan, T., Mann, K., Scherpbier, A. and Spencer, J. (2010). Introduction. In T. Dornan, K. Mann, A. Scherpbier and J. Spencer (eds), *Medical Education: Theory and practice.* (pp. xv–xxix). Edinburgh: Churchill Livingstone (Elsevier Imprint).

DSA-QAG (2010, March). SFE recommendations: standard packages. DSA-QAG update. Retrieved 25 March 2010 from DSA-QAG website: www.dsa-qag.org. uk/assets/_managed/cms/files/MonthlyNewsletterMarch10.pdf.

Du Gay, P. (2000). Entrepreneurial governance and public management: the anti-bureaucrats. In J. Clarke, S. Gewirtz and E. McLaughlin (eds) *New managerialism new welfare?* Buckingham: Open University Press.

Edward, S., Coffield, F. and Steer, R. (2005, September). *Coping with endless change: The impact on teaching staff in the learning and skills sector.* Paper presented at the British Educational Research Association Annual Conference, Glamorgan, Wales.

Edwards, D. (1997). *Discourse and Cognition.* London: Sage.

Edwards, D. and Mercer, N. M. (1989). Reconstructing context: the conventionalization of classroom knowledge. *Discourse Processes*, 8, 229–259.

Edwards, D. and Potter, J. (1992). *Discursive psychology*. Newbury Park, CA: Sage.

Elmore, R. F. (1996). Getting to scale with good educational practice. *Harvard Educational Review*, 66(1), 1–26.

Emerson, C. (1983). The outer word and inner speech: Bakhtin, Vygotsky, and the internalization of language. *Critical Enquiry*, 10(2), 245–264.

Engeström, R. (1995). Voice as communicative action. *Mind, Culture, and Activity*, 2(3), 192–214.

Engeström, Y. (1987). *Learning by expanding: An activity-theoretical approach to developmental research*. Helsinki: Orienta-Konsultit. Retrieved 29 June 2004 from: http://ilch.ucsd.edu/mca/paper/Engestrom/expanding/toc.htm.

Engeström, Y. (1991). *Non scolae sed vitae discimus*: Toward overcoming the encapsulation of school learning. *Learning and Instruction*, 1(3), 243–259.

Engeström, Y. (1993). Developmental studies of work as a testbench of activity theory: the case of primary care medical practice. In S. Chaiklin and J. Lave (eds) *Understanding practice: Perspectives on activity and context* (pp. 64–103). Cambridge: Cambridge University Press.

Engeström, Y. (1999a). Innovative learning in work teams: analysing cycles of knowledge creation in practice. In Y. Engeström, R. Miettinen and R. L. Punamaki (eds) *Perspectives on activity theory*. Cambridge: Cambridge University Press.

Engeström, Y. (1999b). Activity theory and individual and social transformation. In Y. Engeström, R. M. Miettinen and R.-L. Punamäki (eds) *Perspectives on activity theory* (pp. 19–38). Cambridge: Cambridge University Press.

Engeström, Y. (2000). Activity theory as a framework for analyzing and redesigning work. *Ergonomics*, 43(7), 960–974.

Engeström, Y. (2001). Expansive learning at work: toward an activity theoretical reconceptualisation. *Journal of Education and Work*, 14(1), 133–156.

Engeström, Y. (2005). Knotworking to create collaborative intentionality capital in fluid organizational fields. In M. M. Beyerlein, S. T. Beyerlein and F. A. Kennedy (eds) *Collaborative capital: Creating intangible value*. Amsterdam: Elsevier.

Engeström, Y. (2007). Putting Vygotsky to work: the change laboratory as an application of double stimulation. In H. Daniels, M. Cole and J. V. Wertsch (eds) *The Cambridge companion to Vygotsky* (pp. 363–382). Cambridge: Cambridge University Press.

Engeström, Y. (2008). Enriching activity theory without shortcuts. *Interacting with Computers*, 20, 256–259.

Engeström, Y. (2009). The future of activity theory. In A. Sannino, H. Daniels and K. Gutiérrez (eds) *Learning and expanding with activity theory* (pp. 303–328). Cambridge: Cambridge University Press.

Engeström, Y. (2010a). Studies of expansive learning: foundations, findings and future challenges. *Educational Research Review*, 5, 1–24.

Engeström, Y. (2010b). *From teams to knots: Activity-theoretical studies of collaboration and learning at work*. Cambridge: Cambridge University Press.

Engeström, Y. (2010c). Activity theory and learning at work. In M. Malloch, L. Cairns, K. Evans and B.N. O'Connor (eds) *The Sage handbook of workplace learning* (pp. 86–104). London: Sage.

Erben, M. (1998). Biography and research method. In M. Erben (ed.) *Biography and education: A reader*. London: Falmer Press.

Erickson, F. and Gutierrez, K. (2002). Culture, rigor, and science in educational research. *Educational Researcher*, 31(8), 21–24.

Ewick, P. and Silbey, S. S. (1995). Subversive stories and hegemonic tales: towards a sociology of narrative. *Law and Society Review*, 29(2), 197–226.

Fairclough, N. (2000). *New Labour, new language?* New York: Routledge.

Farmer, J. D., Gerretson, H. and Lassak, M. (2003) What teachers take from professional development: cases and implications. *Journal of Mathematics Teacher Education*, 6, 331–360.

Farnsworth, V. (2006). *Learning to learn about communities in teacher education: Constructing identities and confronting ideologies*. Dissertations and theses: A and I. Ref. No. AAT 3234545.

Farnsworth, V. (2010). Conceptualizing identity, learning and social justice in community-based learning. *Teaching and Teacher Education*, 26(7), 1481–1489.

Farnsworth, V., Davis, P., Farrell, P., Kalambouka, A., Ralph, S. and Shi, X. (2008, September). Weaving narratives: the dialogue between leading activity and a course narrative? Paper presented at the International Society for Cultural and Activity Research (ISCAR) International Congress, San Diego, CA.

Farnsworth, V., Davis, P., Kalambouka, A., Farrell, P., Ralph, S. and Shi, X. (2011). Students' production of curricular knowledge: perspectives on empowerment in financial capability education. *Education, Citizenship and Social Justice*, 6(2), 153–167.

Feuer, M. J., Towne, L. and Shavelson, R. J. (2002). Scientific culture and educational research. *Educational Researcher*, 31(8), 4–14.

Fischer, F. (2003). *Reframing public policy*. Oxford: Oxford University Press.

Fitzgibbon, C. T. (2001). The outcomes of education. In C. Teddlie and D. Reynolds (eds) *The international handbook on school effectiveness research*. London: Falmer.

Flyvbjerg, B. (2006). Five misunderstandings about case-study research. *Qualitative Inquiry*, 12(2), 219–245.

Foucault, M. (1972). *The archaeology of knowledge*. New York: Harper Colophon.

Fraser, N. (1997). *Justice interruptus: Critical reflections on the 'postsocialist' condition*. New York: Routledge.

Fullan, M. (2007). *The new meaning of educational change* (4th ed.). New York: Teachers College Press.

Furlong, J. and Oancea, A. (2006). Assessing quality in applied and practice-based research in education: a framework for discussion. *Review of Australian Research in Education*, 89–104.

Garrison, R., Anderson, T. and Archer, W. (2001). Critical thinking, cognitive presence and computer conferencing in distance education. *American Journal of Distance Education*, 5, 7–23

Gaufberg, E. H., Batalden, M., Sands, R. and Bell, S. K. (2010). The hidden curriculum: what can we learn from third-year medical student narrative reflections?' *Academic Medicine*, 85(11), 1709–1716.

Gee, J. P. (1999). *An introduction to discourse analysis*. London: Routledge.

Gee, J. P. (2003). *What video games have to teach us about learning and literacy*. Basingstoke: Palgrave Macmillan.

Gee, J. P. (2004). Discourse analysis: What makes it critical? In R. Rogers (ed.), *An introduction to critical discourse analysis in education*. (pp. 19–50). Mahwah, NJ: Lawrence Erlbaum Associates.

Gee, J. P. (2007). Semiotic social spaces and affinity spaces. In D. Barton and K. Tusting (eds) *Beyond communities of practice: Language, power, and social context*. Cambridge: Cambridge University Press.

Gibbons, M. (2000). Mode 2 society and the emergence of context-sensitive science. *Science and Public Policy*, 27, 159–163.

Giddens, A. (1984). *The constitution of society: Outline of the theory of structuration*. Cambridge: Polity Press.

Giddens, A. (1991). *Modernity and self-identity: Self and society in the late modern age*. Cambridge: Polity Press.

Gideonse, H. D. (1968). Research, development, and the improvement of education. *Science*, 162, 541–545.

Gleeson, D. and Husbands, C. (2003). Modernising schooling through performance management: a critical appraisal. *Journal of Education Policy*, 18(5), 499–511.

Gleeson, D. and James, D. (2007). The paradox of professionalism in English Further Education. *Educational Review*, 59(4), 451–467.

Gleeson, D. and Shain, F. (1999). Managing ambiguity: between markets and managerialism, *Sociological Review*, 57(3), 461–490.

Gleeson, D., Davies, J. and Wheeler, E. (2005). On the making and taking of professionalism in the further education (FE) workplace. *British Journal of Sociology of Education*, 26(4), 445–460.

Godin, B. (2006). The linear model of innovation. *Science, Technology and Human Values*, 31, 639–667.

Goldstein, H. and Thomas, S. (1996). Using examination results as indicators of school and college performance. *Journal of Royal Statistical Society*, 159(1), 149–163.

Goodson, I. (2008). *Investigating the teacher's life and work*. Rotterdam: Sense Publishers.

Goodson, I. and Sikes, P. (2001). *Life history research in educational settings*. Buckingham: Open University Press.

Gorz, A. (2010). *The immaterial*. London: Seagull books.

Goulding, M. (2002). Cognitive acceleration in mathematics education: teachers' views. *Evaluation and Research in Education*, 16(2), 104–119.

Gramsci, A. (1971). *Selections from the prison notebooks*. London: Lawrence & Wishart.

Gray, J. (2010). Probing the limits of systemic reform: the English case. In A. Hargreaves, A. Lieberman, M. Fullan and D. Hopkins (eds) *Second international handbook of educational change*. (pp. 293–307). Dordrecht: Springer.

Griffith, C. H. and Wilson, J. F. (2001). The loss of idealism in the 3rd-year clinical clerkships. *Evaluation and the Health Professions*, 24(1), 61–67.

Gutierrez, K. D., Baquedano-Lopez, P. and Tejeda, C. (1999). Rethinking diversity: hybridity and hybrid language practices in the third space. *Mind, Culture, and Activity*, 6(4), 286–303.

Hackman, J. R. (2003). Learning more by crossing levels: evidence from airplanes, hospitals, and orchestras. *Journal of Organizational Behavior*, 24, 905–922.

Hafferty, F. W. and Franks, R. (1994). The hidden curriculum, ethics teaching, and the structure of medical education. *Academic Medicine*, 69, 861–871.

Hammersley, M. (1997). Educational research and teaching: a response to David Hargreaves' TTA lecture. *British Educational Research Journal*, 23(2), 141–162.

Hammersley, M. (2000). The relevance of qualitative research. *Oxford Review of Education*, 26 (3/4), 393–405.

Hammersley, M. (2003). Can and should educational research be educative? *Oxford Review of Education*, 29(1), 3–25.

Hanley, U. and Darby, S. (2006). Working with curriculum innovation: teacher identity and the development of viable practice. *Research in Mathematics Education*, 8, 53–66.

Harden, R. M., Crosby, J. R. and Davis, M. H. (1999). AMEE guide no. 14: outcome-based education: part 1 – an introduction to outcome-based education. *Medical Teacher*, 21, 7–14.

Hardt, M. and Negri, A. (2009). *Commonwealth*. Harvard: Harvard University Press.

Hargreaves, D. H. (1996). *Teaching as a research based profession: Possibilities and prospects*. London: Teacher Training Agency.

Hargreaves, D. H. (1997). In defence of research for evidence-based teaching: a rejoinder to Martyn Hammersley. *British Educational Research Journal*, 23(4), 405–419.

Harré, R. and Gillett, G. (1995). *The discursive mind*. Thousand Oaks, CA: Sage.

Harris, A. and Chapman, C. (2002). *Leadership in schools in challenging circumstances*. Report to the National College for School Leadership.

Hart, L.C., Alston, A. and Murata, A. (eds) (2011). *Lesson study research and practice in mathematics education*. London: Springer.

Hasan, R. (2002). Semiotic mediation and mental development in pluralistic societies: some implications for tomorrow's schooling. In G. Wells and G. Claxton (eds) *Learning for life in the 21st century: Socio-cultural perspectives on the future of education*. (pp. 32–67). Oxford: Blackwell.

Hayes, D. (2003). New Labour, new professionalism. In K. Satterthwaite, E. Atkinson and K. Gale (eds) *Discourse, power, resistance: Challenging the rhetoric of contemporary education*. (pp. 27–42). Stoke-on-Trent: Trentham.

Haythornthwaite, C. and Andrew, R. (2011). *E-Learning theory and practice*. London: Sage.

Hayward, G., Hodgson, A., Janson, J., Oancea, A., Pring, R., Spours, K., Wilde, S. and Wright, S. (2006). *The Nuffield Review of 14–19 education and training: Annual report 2005–6*. London: Nuffield Foundation.

Hedegaard, M. (1988). *Skolebørns personlighedsudvikling set gennem orienteringsfagene*. Aarhus: Aarhus Universitetsforlag.

Hedegaard, M. (2002). *Child development and learning*. Aarhus: Aarhus University Press.

Hedegaard, M. and Chaiklin, S. (2005). *Radical-local teaching and learning*. Aarhus: Aarhus University Press.

Heyd-Metzuyanim, E. (2012). Emotional aspects of learning mathematics: how the interaction between identifying and mathematizing influences the effectiveness of learning. Unpublished PhD dissertation. Haifa: University of Haifa.

Heyd-Metzuyanim, E. and Sfard, A. (2012). On learning mathematics as an interplay of mathematizing and identifying. *International Journal of Educational Research*, 51/52, 128–145.

Higham, J. J. S. and Farnsworth, V. L. (2012). What makes a course vocational? School-based work-related programmes in Canada in dialogue with a community of practice. *Journal of Education and Work*, 25(4), 443–471.

Hillage, J., Pearson, R., Anderson, A. and Tamkin, P. (1998). *Excellence in research on schools*. London: DfEE.

Hilton, S. R. and Slotnick, H. B. (2005). Proto-professionalism: how professionalisation occurs across the continuum of medical education. *Medical Education*, 39(1), 58–65.

Hodge, S. (2007). The origins of competency-based training. *Australian Journal of Adult Learning*, 47, 179–209.

Hodges, B. D. (2010). A tea-steeping or i-Doc model for medical education? *Academic Medicine*, 85(9), S34–44.

Hodgson, A., Edward, S. and Gregson, M. (2006, September). *Riding the waves of policy in adult and community learning in England: The case of basic skills*. Paper presented at the British Educational Research Association Annual Conference, Warwick.

Holland, D. and Quinn, N. (1987). *Cultural models in language and thought*. New York: Cambridge University Press.

Holland, D., Lachicotte Jr, W., Skinner, D. and Cain, C. (1998). *Identity and agency in cultural worlds*. Cambridge, MA: Harvard University Press.

Holmboe, E., Ginsburg, S. and Bernabeo, E. (2011). The rotational approach to medical education: time to confront our assumptions? *Medical Education*, 45(1), 69–80.

Holmes Group (1990). *Tomorrow's schools: Principles for the design of professional development schools*. East Lansing, MI: Author.

Holquist, M. (1990). *Dialogism: Bakhtin and his world*. London: Routledge.

Holquist, M. (1998). *The dialogic imagination*. Austin, TX: University of Texas Press.

Hopayian, K., Howe, A. and Dagley, V. (2007). A survey of UK medical schools' arrangements for early patient contact. *Medical Teacher*, 29(8), 806–813.

Hopkins, D. (2001). *School improvement for real*. London: Routledge/Falmer.

House of Commons Innovation, Universities, Science and Skills Committee (2009). *Re-Skilling for recovery: After Leitch, implementing skills and training policies*. First Report of Session 2008–09, Volume I, London: House of Commons.

Howes, A. and Ainscow, M. (2006). Collaboration with a city-wide purpose: making paths for sustainable educational improvement. In M. Ainscow and M. West (eds) *Improving urban school: Leadership and collaboration* (pp. 104–116). Maidenhead: Open University Press.

Hutchings, M., Hollingworth, S., Mansaray, A., Rose, R. and Greenwood, C. (2012). *Research report DFE-RR215: Evaluation of the city challenge programme*. London: DfE.

Hutchins, E. (1995). *Cognition in the wild*. London: MIT Press.

Hutchinson, J. R. and Huberman, M. (1994). Knowledge dissemination and use in science and mathematics education: a literature review. *Journal of Science Education and Technology*, 3, 27–47.

Innovation Unit (undated). An overview of best practice vs next practice. Retrieved 18 August 2008 from: www.innovation-unit.co.uk/images/stories/bp_and_np.ppt.

ISIS-2 (1988). Randomised trial of intravenous streptokinase, oral aspirin, both, or neither among 17,187 cases of suspected acute myocardial infarction: ISIS-2. ISIS-2 (Second International Study of Infarct Survival) Collaborative Group. *Lancet*, 2(8607), 349–360.

Jacobson, N. (2007). Social epistemology: theory for the 'fourth wave' of knowledge transfer and exchange research. *Science Communication*, 29, 116–127.

Jarvis-Selinger, S., Pratt, D. D. and Regehr, G. (2012). Is competency-based medical education enough? Adding identity formation to the conversation about physician development. *Academic Medicine*, 87(9), 1185–1190.

Jenkins, R., (2004). *Social identity*. London: Routledge

Kangasoja, J. (2002). *Complex design problems: An impetus for learning and knotworking*. Helsinki: Center for Activity Theory and Developmental Work Research. Retrieved 14 December 2009 from University of Helsinki website: www.edu.helsinki.fi/activity/publications/files/47/ICLS2002_Kangasoja.pdf.

Kasman, D. L., Fryer-Edwards, K. and Braddock, C. H., 3rd. (2003). Educating for professionalism: trainees' emotional experiences on IM and pediatrics inpatient wards. *Academic Medicine*, 78(7), 730–741.

Kieser, A. and Leiner, L. (2009). Why the rigour–relevance gap in management research is unbridgeable. *Journal of Management Studies*, 46, 516–533.

King, J. E. (1991). Dysconscious racism: ideology, identity, and miseducation of teachers. *Journal of Negro Education*, 60(2), 133–146.

Kornhaber, M. L. and Gardner, H. (2006). Multiple intelligences: developments in implementation and theory. In M. A. Constas and R. J. Sternberg (eds) *Translating theory and research into educational practice: Developments in content domains, large scale reform, and intellectual capacity* (pp. 255–276). Mahwah, NJ: Lawrence Erlbaum Associates.

Kuhn, T. (1962). *The Structure of scientific revolutions*. Chicago, IL: University of Chicago Press.

Kuper, A. and D'Eon, M. (2011). Rethinking the basis of medical knowledge. *Medical Education*, 45(1), 36–43.

Labaree, D. F. (2008). The dysfunctional pursuit of relevance in education research. *Educational Researcher*, 37, 421–423.

Ladson-Billings, G. (1994). *The dreamkeepers: Successful teachers of African American children*. San Francisco, CA: Jossey-Bass.

Lambert, P. (2003). Promoting developmental transfer in vocational teacher education. In T. Tuomi-Gröhn and Y. Engeström (eds) *Between school and work: New perspectives on transfer and boundary-crossing*. (pp. 233–254). Boston, MA: Pergamon.

Langemeyer, I. and Roth, W.-M. (2006). Is cultural–historical activity theory threatened to fall short of its own principles and possibilities as a dialectical social science. *Outlines*, 2, 20–42.

Latour, B. and Woolgar, S. (1979). *Laboratory life: The social construction of scientific facts*. Thousand Oaks, CA: Sage.

Laudan, L. (1977). *Progress and its problems: Towards a theory of scientific growth*. Berkeley, CA: University of California Press.

Lave, J. (1988). *Cognition in practice*. Cambridge: Cambridge University Press.

Lave, J. and Wenger, E. (1991). *Situated learning: Legitimate peripheral participation*. Cambridge: Cambridge University Press.

Leont'ev, A. N. (1978). *Activity, consciousness, and personality*. Englewood Cliffs, NJ: Prentice-Hall.

Leont'ev, A. N. (1981). *Problems of the development of the mind*. Moscow: Progress.

Leont'ev, A. N. (2009). *The development of mind*. Pacifica, CA: Marxists Internet Archive.

Levin, B. (2004). Making research matter more. *Education Policy Analysis Archives*, 12(56), 1–20. Retrieved 4 January 2012 from: http://epaa.asu.edu/epaa/v12n56.

Levin, B. (2005, April). *Thinking about improvements in schools in challenging circumstances.* Paper presented at the American Educational Research Association, Montreal.

Lindblom, C. E. and Cohen, D. K. (1979). *Usable knowledge: Social science and social problem solving.* New Haven, CT: Yale University Press.

Lingwood, D. A. (1979). Producing usable research: 'The first step in dissemination'. *American Behavioral Scientist*, 22, 339–362.

Lipman, P. (2004). *High stakes education: Inequality, globalisation and urban school reform.* New York: Routledge.

Livingstone, D. W. (2006). Contradictory class relations in work and learning: some resources of hope. In P. H. Sawchuk, N. Duarte and M. Elhammoumi (eds) *Critical perspectives on activity; explorations across education, work and everyday life.* (pp. 145–159). Cambridge: Cambridge University Press.

Llorente, R. (2006). Analytical Marxism and the division of labor. *Science and Society*, 70, 232–251.

Lombard, M. and Ditton, T. (1997). At the heart of it all: the concept of presence. *Journal of Computer Mediated Communication*, 3(2). Retrieved 3 September 2012 from: http://jcmc.indiana.edu/vol3/issue2/lombard.html.

Luckett, K. (2012). Disciplinarity in question: comparing knowledge and knower codes in sociology. *Research Papers in Education*, 27(1), 19–40.

Lyotard, J.-F. (1979). *The postmodern condition: A report on knowledge.* Minneapolis, MN: University of Minnesota Press.

McAteer, E., Crook, C., Macleod, H., Tolmie, A. and Musselbrook, I. (2002). Learning networks and the issue of communication skills. In C. Steeples and C. Jones (eds) *Networked learning: Perspectives and issues.* London: Springer-Verlag.

McConnell, D. (2000). *Implementing computer supported cooperative learning* (2nd ed.). London: Kogan Page.

MacIntyre, A. C. (1981). *After virtue: A study in moral theory.* Notre Dame, IN: University of Notre Dame Press.

McKeown, B. and Thomas, D. (1988). *Q Methodology.* Thousand Oaks, CA: Sage.

McLachlan, E., King, N., Wenger, E. and Dornan, T. (2012). Phenomenological analysis of patients' experiences of medical student teaching encounters. *Medical Education*, 46(10), 963–973.

McLaughlin, M. W. (1991). Learning from experience: lessons from policy implementation. In A. R. Odden (ed.) *Education policy implementation* (pp. 185–195). Albany, NY: State University of New York Press.

MacLeod, A. (2011). Caring, competence and professional identities in medical education. *Advances in Health Sciences Education*, 16(3), 375–394.

McNamara, O. and Corbin, B. (2001). Warranting practices: teachers embedding the National Numeracy Strategy. *British Journal of Educational Studies*, 49(3), 260–284.

Makitalo, A. and Saljo, R. (2002). Talk in institutional context and institutional context in talk: categories as situated practices. *Text*, 22(1), 57–82.

Martin, I. (2003). Adult education, lifelong learning and citizenship: some ifs and buts. *International Journal of Lifelong Education*, 22(6), 566–579.

Martin, J. R. (1996). There's too much to teach: cultural wealth in an age of scarcity. *Educational Researcher*, 25(2), 4–16.

Marx, K. (1973). *Grundrisse*. Harmondsworth: Penguin.

Marx, K. (2007). Estranged labour. In M. Milligan (ed.) *K. Marx: Economic and philosophic manuscripts of 1844* (pp. 67–83). Mineola, NY: Dover Publications Inc.

Marx, K. and Engels, F. (1973). Manifesto of the Communist Party. In K. Marx and F. Engels, *Selected works*. London: Lawrence & Wishart.

Matusov, E. (2010). *Journey into dialogic pedagogy*. Hauppauge, NY: Nova Science Publishers.

Meadows, S., Herrick, D. and Feiler, A. (2007). Improvements in national test reading scores at Key Stage 1: grade inflation or better achievement? *British Educational Research Journals* 33 (1), 47–59.

Mennin, S. (2010). Self-organisation, integration and curriculum in the complex world of medical education. *Medical Education*, 44(1), 20–30.

Messiou, K. (2006). Understanding marginalisation in education: the voice of children. *European Journal of Psychology of Education*, 21(3), 305–318.

Meszaros, I. (2005). *Marx's theory of alienation*. London: Merlin.

Mezirow, J. (1991). *Transformative dimensions of adult learning*. San Francisco, CA: Jossey-Bass.

Mezirow, J. (1997). Transformative learning: theory to practice. *New Directions for Adult and Continuing Education*, 74, 5–12.

Middleton, D. (2004). Concepts, learning and the constitution of objects and events in discursive practice. In A.-N. Perret-Clermont, C. Pontecorvo, L. Resnick, T. Zittoun and B. Burge (eds) *Joining society: Social interaction in adolescence and youth* (pp. 204–215). Cambridge: Cambridge University Press.

Middleton, D., Brown, S., Daniels, H., Edwards, A., Leadbetter, J. and Warmington, P. (2008). Making the difference in interagency working: analytic challenges in studying professional learning in communicating what matters. In C. Candlin and S. Sarangi (eds) *Handbook of applied linguistics communication in professions and organisations*. (pp. 103–145). Berlin: Mouton de Gruyter.

Miettinen, R. (2009). Contradictions of high-technology capitalism and the emergence of new forms of work. In A. Sannino, H. Daniels and K. Gutiérrez (eds) *Learning and expanding with activity theory* (pp. 160–175). Cambridge: Cambridge University Press.

Miles, S. and Kaplan, I. (2005). Using images to promote reflection: an action research study in Zambia and Tanzania. *Journal of Research in Special Educational Needs*, 5(2), 77–83.

Miller, M., Godfrey, N., Levesque, B. and Stark, E. (2009). *The case for financial literacy in developing countries: Promoting access to finance by empowering consumers*. Washington, DC: The International Bank for Reconstruction and Development/ The World Bank. Retrieved 13 October 2009 from: www.financial-education. org/dataoecd/35/32/43245359.pdf.

Monrouxe, L. V. (2010). Identity, identification and medical education: why should we care? *Medical Education*, 44(1), 40–49.

Moore, M. and Kearlsey, G. (1996). *Distance education: A systems view*. Belmont, CA: Wadsworth Publishing.

Mørcke, A., Dornan, T. and Eika, B. (2012). Competency and outcome based education: an exploration of its origins, theoretical basis, and empirical evidence. *Advances in Health Sciences Education: Theory and Practice*.

Morris, P. (1997). *The Bakhtin reader*. London: Arnold.

Mourshed, M., Chijioke, C. and Barber, M. (2010). *How the world's most improved school systems keep getting better*. London: McKinsey & Company.

Mulford, B. (2007). Building social capital in professional learning communities: importance, challenges and a way forward. In L. Stoll and K. Seashore Louis (eds) *Professional learning communities: Divergence, depth and dilemmas*. London: Open University Press.

NADP (2009, November). *Report on disabled students allowances [DSAs] situation from the National Association of Disability Practitioners [NADP]*. Retrieved 29 March 2010 from NADP website: www.nadp-uk.org/docs/resources/nadp-dsa-report-nov2009.doc.

National Audit Office (2010). *The Customer First programme: Delivery of student finance*. London: NAO/BIS.

National Research Council (1999). *Improving student learning: A strategic plan for education research and its utilization*. Washington, DC: National Academy Press.

Newman, J. (2001). *Modernising governance*. London: Sage.

Nolan, K. (2008). Imagine there's no haven: exploring the desires and dilemmas of a mathematics education researcher. In T. Brown (ed.) *The psychology of mathematics education: A psychoanalytical displacement* (pp. 159–181). The Netherlands: Sense Publishers.

Nolan, K. (2012). Dispositions in the field: viewing mathematics teacher education through the lens of Bourdieu's social field theory. *Educational Studies in Mathematics*, 80, 201–215.

Norman, G. (2006). Editorial: outcomes, objectives, and the seductive appeal of simple solutions. *Advances in Health Sciences Education*, 11(3), 217–220.

O'Leary, D. and Craig, J. (2007). *Systems leadership: Lessons from the literature*. Nottingham: NCSL.

Oancea, A. (2005). Criticisms of educational research: key topics and levels of analysis. *British Educational Research Journal*, 31(2), 157–183.

Ochberg, R. (1994). Life stories and storied lives. In A. Lieblich and R. Josselson (eds) *The narrative study of lives: Exploring identity and gender*. London: Sage.

OECD (2007). *No more failures: Ten steps to equity in education*. Paris: OECD.

OECD (2010). *PISA 2009 results: Overcoming social background – equity in learning opportunities and outcomes (Volume II)*. Paris: OECD.

Orwell, G. (1949). *Nineteen Eighty-Four*. London: Martin Secker and Warburg Ltd.

Page, D. (2011a). Fundamentalists, priests, martyrs, and converts: a typology of first tier management in Further Education. *Research in Post-Compulsory Education*, 16(1), 101–121.

Page, D. (2011b). From principled dissent to cognitive escape: managerial resistance in the English further education sector. *Journal of Vocational Education and Training*, 63(1), 1–13.

Payne, C. M. (2008). *So much reform, so little change: The persistence of failure in urban schools*. Cambridge, MA: Harvard Education Press.

Pearson, E. J. (2011). *Investigating the psychological and contextual factors affecting the experience of emotion by medical students in the clinical workplace.* Unpublished PhD Thesis.

Pelz, D. C. (1978). Some expanded perspectives on the use of social science in public policy. In J. M. Yinger and S. J. Cutler (eds) *Major social issues: A multidisciplinary view* (pp. 346–357). New York: Free Press.

Pollard, A. (2006). Challenges facing educational research: Educational Review Guest Lecture 2005. *Educational Review,* 58(3), 251–267.

Pope, C., Mays, N. and Popay, J. (2007). (eds) *Synthesising qualitative and quantitative health evidence.* Maidenhead: Open University Press.

Potter, J. and Wetherell, M. (1987). *Discourse and social psychology beyond attitudes and behaviour.* London: Sage.

Putnam, L. L. and Boys, S. (2006). Revisiting metaphors of organizational communication. In S. R. Clegg, C. Hardy and W. R. Nord (eds) *The Sage handbook of organization studies* (pp. 541–576). London: Sage.

Putnam, R. D. (2000). *Bowling alone.* New York: Simon & Schuster.

Qasim, S. and Williams, J. (2012). *A critical appraisal of Holland et al.'s (1998) appropriation of Bourdieu.* Presented at The European Conference on Educational Research (ECER). Cadiz, Spain.

Randle, K. and Brady, N. (1997). Managerialism and professionalism in the 'Cinderella Service'. *Journal of Vocational Education and Training,* 49(1), 121–140.

Ratner, C. (1997). *Cultural psychology and qualitative methodology: Theoretical and empirical considerations.* London: Plenum Press.

Rein, M. and White, S. H. (1981). Knowledge for practice. *Social Service Review,* 55(1), 1–41.

Rikowski, G. (1999). Education, capital and the transhuman. In D. Hill, P. McLaren, M. Cole and G. Rikowski (eds) *Postmodernism in educational theory: Education and the politics of human resistance.* London: Tufnell.

Robbins, P. (2005). Q Methodology. In K. Kempf-Leonard (ed.) *Encyclopedia of social measurement* (pp. 209–215). Amsterdam: Elsevier.

Roberts, G. (2002). *SET for success: The supply of people with science, technology, engineering and mathematics skills.* London: DfES.

Robson, B., Deas, I. and Lymperopoulou, K. (2009). *Schools and pupil performance in Greater Manchester: A key driver of social polarization.* Manchester: University of Manchester Press.

Rorty, R. (1979). *Philosophy and the mirror of nature.* Princeton, NJ: Princeton University Press.

Rose, N. and Miller, P. (1992). Political power beyond the state: problematics of government. *British Journal of Sociology,* 43, 172–205.

Rose, N. (1999). *Powers of freedom: Reframing political thought.* Cambridge: Cambridge University Press.

Roth, W.-M., Tobin, K., Elmesky, R., Carambo, C., McKnight, Y.-M. and Beers, J. (2004). Re/making identities in the praxis of urban schooling: a cultural historical perspective. *Mind, Culture and Activity,* 11(1), 48–69.

Rourke, L., Anderson, T. and Garrison, D. R. (1999). Assessing social presence in asynchronous text-based computer conferencing. *Journal of Distance Education,* 14(2), 50–71.

Ryan, J. and Williams, J. (2007). *Children's mathematics 4–15: Learning from errors and misconceptions.* Maidenhead: Open University Press/McGraw-Hill.

Ryan, J. and Williams, J. (2012, September). *Children's argumentation in primary school mathematics: The use of models and tools to support reasoning and explanation.* Paper presented to the Annual Conference of the British Educational Research Association, Manchester.

Sackett, D. L., Richardson, W. S., Rosenberg, W. and Haynes, R. B. (1997). *Evidence-based medicine: How to practice and teach EBM.* Edinburgh: Churchill Livingstone.

Sainsbury (2007). *The race to the top: A review of government's science and innovation policies.* London: HMSO.

Sammons, P. (2008). Zero tolerance of failure and New Labour approaches to school improvement in England. *Oxford Review of Education,* 34(6), 651–664.

Sannino, A. (2008a). Sustaining a non-dominant activity in school: only a utopia? *Journal of Educational Change,* 9(4), 329–338.

Sannino, A. (2008b). From talk to action: experiencing interlocution in developmental interventions. *Mind, Culture and Activity,* 15(3), 234–257.

Sawchuk, P. H. (2006). Activity and power: everyday life and development of working-class groups. In P. H. Sawchuk, N. Duarte and M. Elhammoumi (eds) *Critical perspectives on activity: Explorations across education, work and everyday life.* Cambridge: Cambridge University Press.

Sawyer, K. (2002). Unresolved tensions in sociocultural theory: analogies with contemporary sociological debates. *Culture and Psychology,* 8(3), 283–305.

Schmidt, J. P. and Glott, R. (2009). Wikipedia survey results. *Wikimania,* 26–28 August 2009, Buenos Aires. Retrieved from: http://wikimania2009.wikimedia.org/wiki/Proceedings:290.

Schmolck, P. (2010). *PQMethod Software.* Retrieved 13 June 2010 from: www.lrz-muenchen.de/~schmolck/qmethod.

Scott, R. A. and Shore, A. R. (1979). *Why sociology does not apply: A study of the use of sociology in public policy.* New York: Elsevier.

Seddon, T. (1997). Education: deprofessionalised? Or reregulated, reorganised and reauthorised? *Australian Journal of Education,* 41(3), 228–246.

Sennett, R. (2008). *The craftsman.* London: Allen Lane.

Sfard, A. (1998). On two metaphors for learning and the dangers of choosing just one. *Educational Researcher,* 27, 4–13.

Sfard, A. (2008). *Thinking as communicating: Human development, the growth of discourses, and mathematizing.* Cambridge: Cambridge University Press.

Sfard, A. (2009). Metaphors in education. In H. Daniels, J. Porter and H. Lauder (eds) *Educational theories, cultures and learning: A critical perspective* (pp. 39–49). London: Routledge.

Shacklady, J., Holmes, E., Mason, G., Davies, I. and Dornan, T. (2009). Maturity and medical students' ease of transition into the clinical environment. *Medical Teacher,* 31(7), 621–626.

Shah, P., Smithies, A., Dexter, H., Snowden, N. and Dornan, T. (in preparation). How do residents learn through work? Case study in rheumatology.

Shain, F. and Gleeson, D. (1999). Under new management: changing conceptions of teacher professionalism and policy in the further education sector. *Journal of Educational Policy,* 14(4), 445–462.

Shove, E. and Rip, A. (2000). Users and unicorns: a discussion of mythical beasts in interactive science. *Science and Public Policy*, 27, 175–182.

Simon, H. A. (1967). The business school: a problem in organizational design. *Journal of Management Studies*, 4(1), 1–16.

Simon, M. and Tzur, R. (1999). Explicating the teacher's perspective from the researchers' perspective: generating accounts of mathematics teachers' practice. *Journal for Research in Mathematics Education*, 30(3), 252–264.

Sinclair, S. (1997). *Making doctors: An institutional apprenticeship.* Oxford: Berg.

Skeggs, B. (1997). *Formations of class and gender.* London: Sage.

Skemp, R. R. (1976). Relational and instrumental understanding. *Mathematics Teaching*, 77, 20–26.

Skill: National Bureau for Students with Disabilities (2009). *Evidence for BIS/Professor Hopkin Review of Student Loans Company with specific reference to disabled students applying for Disabled Students' Allowance for entry October 2009 and onwards.* Retrieved March 29 2010 from SKILL website: www.skill.org.uk/uploads/Skill_Hopkin%20Review_submission%20part%201.doc.

Skinner, D., Valsiner, J. and Holland, D. (2001). Discerning the dialogical self: a theoretical and methodological examination of a Nepali adolescent's narrative. *Forum: Qualitative Social Research*, 2(3), 1–17. Retrieved 20 November 2011 from: www.qualitative-research.net/fqs-texte/3-01/3-01skinneretal-e.htm.

Smith, A. (2004). *Making mathematics count.* London: HMSO.

Somers, M. (1994). The narrative constitution of identity: a relational and network approach. *Theory and Society*, 23, 605–649.

Spillane, J., Reiser, B.J. and Reiner, T. (2002). Policy implementation and cognition: reframing and refocusing implementation. *Review of Educational Research*, 72(3), 387–431.

Spours, K., Coffield, F. and Gregson, M. (2006, September). *Translation problems: FE colleges, policy levers and local ecologies in the learning and skills sector.* Paper presented at the British Educational Research Association Annual Conference, Warwick.

Steeples, C. and Jones, C. (eds) (2002). *Networked learning: Perspectives and issues.* London: Springer-Verlag.

Stenner, P., Watts, S. and Worrell, M. (2008). Q Methodology. In C. Willig and W. Stainton-Rogers (eds), *The Sage handbook of qualitative research in psychology* (pp. 215–239). London: Sage.

Stephenson, W. (1953). *The study of behaviour: Q-technique and its methodology.* Chicago, IL: University of Chicago Press.

Stephenson, W. (1980). Consciring: a general theory for subjective communicability. In D. Nimmo (ed.) *Communication Yearbook 4* (pp. 7–36). New Brunswick, NJ: Transaction.

Stokes, D. E. (1997). *Pasteur's quadrant: Basic science and technological innovation.* Washington, DC: Brookings Institution Press.

Stronach, I. and MacLure, M. (1997). *Educational research undone, the postmodern embrace.* Buckingham: Open University Press.

Student Finance England (SFE) (2010). *Bridging the gap: A guide to the disabled students' allowances (DSAs) in higher education 2011/2012.* Retrieved 29 June 2012 from the UK government website: www.direct.gov.uk/prod_consum_dg/groups/dg_digitalassets/@dg/@en/documents/digitalasset/dg_194349.pdf.

Suppes, P. (ed.) (1978). *Impact of research on education: Some case studies.* Washington, DC: National Academy of Education.

Testerman, J. K., Morton, K. R., Loo, L. K., Worthley, J. S. and Lamberton, H. H. (1996). The natural history of cynicism in physicians. *Academic Medicine*, 71(10 Suppl), S43–45.

Thistlethwaite, J. and Hammick, M. (2010). The best evidence medical education (BEME) collaboration: into the next decade. *Medical Teacher*, 32(11), 880–882.

Thistlethwaite, J., Davies, H., Dornan, T., Greenhalgh, T., Hammick, M. and Scalese, R. (2012). What is evidence? Reflections on the AMEE symposium, Vienna, August 2011. *Medical Teacher*, 34(6), 454–457.

Thomas, E. J. and Rothman, J. (1994). An integrative perspective on intervention research. In J. Rothman and E. J. Thomas (eds) *Intervention research: Design and development for human service* (pp. 3–23). Binghamton, NY: Haworth Press.

Thorpe, M. (2009). Technology-mediated learning contexts. In R. Edwards, G. Biesta and M. Thorpe (eds) *Rethinking contexts for learning and teaching* (pp. 119–32). London: Routledge.

Thorpe, M. and Edmunds, R. (2011). Practices with technology: learning at the boundary between study and work. *Journal of Computer Assisted Learning*, 27, 385–398.

Todorov, T. (1998). *Mikhail Bakhtin: The dialogical principle.* Minneapolis, MN: University of Minnesota Press.

Todres, M., Stephenson, A. and Jones, R. (2007). Medical education research remains the poor relation. *BMJ*, 335(7615), 333–335.

Tooley, J. and Darby, D. (1998). *Educational research: A critique.* London: Ofsted.

Towers, J. (2010). Learning to teach mathematics through inquiry: a focus on the relationship between describing and enacting inquiry-oriented teaching. *Journal of Mathematics Teacher Education*, 13, 243–263.

Trent, S. C., Artiles, A. J. and Englert, C. S. (1998). From deficit thinking to social constructivism: a review of theory, research and practice in special education. *Review of Research in Education*, 23, 277–307.

Troman, G., (2008). Primary teacher identity, commitment and career in performative school cultures. *British Educational Research Journal*, 34(5), 619–663.

Tymms, P. (2004). Are standards rising in British primary schools? *British Educational Research Journal*, 30(4), 477–494.

Tzur, R., Simon, M., Heinz, K. and Kinzel, M. (2001). An account of a teacher's perspectives on learning and teaching mathematics: implications for teacher development. *Journal of Mathematics Teacher Education*, 4(3), 227–254.

U.S. Department of Education (2002). *No child left behind: A desktop reference.* Washington, DC: Author. Available at www.ed.gov/offices/OESE/reference.html.

U.S. House of Representatives (2000). *Scientifically based education research, statistics, evaluation, and Information Act of 2000.* Washington, DC: Author.

Vagan, A. (2011). Towards a sociocultural perspective on identity formation in education. *Mind, Culture, and Activity*, 18(1), 43–57.

Valsiner, J. (2008). Ornamented worlds and textures of feeling: the power of abundance. *Critical Social Studies*, 1, 67–78.

van der Zwet, J., Zwietering, P. J., Teunissen, P. W., van der Vleuten, C. P. M. and Scherpbier, A. J. J. A. (2011). Workplace learning from a socio-cultural perspective: creating developmental space during the general practice clerkship. *Advances in health sciences education: Theory and practice*, 16(3), 359–373.

Van Dijk, T. A. (1998) *Ideology: A multidisciplinary approach*. London: Sage.

Van Zoest, L. R. and Bohl, J. V. (2002). The role of reform curricular materials in an internship: the case of Alice and Gregory. *Journal of Mathematics Teacher Education*, 5, 265–288.

Vann, K. and Bowker, G. (2001). Instrumentalizing the truth of practice. *Social Epistemology*, 15(3), 247–262.

Vasilyuk, F. (1988). *The psychology of experiencing*. Moscow: Progress.

Victor, B. and Boynton, A. (1998). *Invented here: Maximizing your organization's internal growth and profitability*. Boston, MA: Harvard Business School Press.

Vignoles, V. L., Schwartz, S. J. and Luyckx, K. (2011). Introduction: towards an integrative view of identity. In S. J. Schwartz, K. Luyckx and V. L. Vignoles (eds) *Handbook of identity theory and research* (pp. 1–27). New York: Springer.

Virkkunen, J. (2009). Two theories of knowledge creation. In A. Sannino, H. Daniels and K. Gutiérrez (eds) *Learning and expanding with activity theory* (pp. 144–159). Cambridge: Cambridge University Press.

Vygotsky, L. S. (1978). *Mind in society: The development of higher psychological processes*. Cambridge, MA: Harvard University Press.

Vygotsky, L. S. (1987). *The collected works of L. S. Vygotsky. Vol.1: Problems of general psychology, including the volume Thinking and Speech*. (Eds R. W. Rieber and A. S. Carton, trans. N. Minick. New York: Plenum Press.

Wall, K., McAteer, E. and Miller, O. (2008). *Evaluation of the on-line delivery pilot of the RNIB 'Partners in Learning' programme (Units 1–3)*. Internal Report to RNIB. London: Institute of Education.

Warmington, P. (2005, September). *From activity to labour: Commodification, labour power and contradiction in activity*. Paper presented at the 1st International Society for Cultural and Activity Research (ISCAR) International Congress, Seville.

Watson, A. and De Geest, E. (2005). Principled teaching for deep progress: improving mathematical learning beyond methods and materials. *Educational Studies in Mathematics*, 58, 209–234.

Watts, S. and Stenner, P. (2012). *Doing Q methodological research*. London: Sage.

Weatherall, D. (2011). Science and medical education: is it time to revisit Flexner? *Medical Education*, 45(1), 44–50.

Wegerif, R. (2008). Dialogic or dialectic? The significance of ontological assumptions in research on educational dialogue. *British Educational Research Journal*, 3(34), 347–361.

Weiss, C. H. (1995). The four 'I's' of school reform: how interests, ideology, information, and institution affect teachers and principals. *Harvard Educational Review*, 65(4), 571–592.

Weiss, C. H. with Bucuvalas, M. J. (1980). *Social science research and decision-making*. New York: Columbia University Press.

Wenger, E. (1998). *Communities of practice: Learning, meaning and identity*. Cambridge: Cambridge University Press.

Wenger, E. (2006). *Learning for a small planet: A research agenda*. Retrieved from: http://wenger-trayner.com/map-of-resources. Accessed 26 March 2013.

Wenger, E. (2009). *Social learning capability: Four essays on innovation and learning in social systems*. Social Innovation, Sociedade e Trabalho booklets, 12 – separate supplement. Lisbon: MTSS/GEP and EQUAL.

Wenger, E., McDermott, R. and Snyder, W. M. (2002). *Cultivating communities of practice*. Harvard, MA: Harvard School Press.

Wenger-Trayner, E. and Wenger-Trayner, B. (2012). *Social learning capability*. Retrieved from: http://wenger-trayner.com/resources/social-learning-capability. Accessed 26 March 2013

Wenger-Trayner, E. and Wenger-Trayner, B. (in preparation). Learning in landscapes of practice: a framework. In E. Wenger-Trayner, M. Fenton-O'Creevy, S. Hutchinson, C. Kubiak and B. Wenger-Trayner (eds) *Learning in landscapes of practice*.

Wertsch, J. V. (1991). *Voices of the mind*. Cambridge, MA: Harvard University Press.

Wertsch, J. V. (2007). Mediation. In H. Daniels, M. Cole and J. V. Wertsch (eds) *The Cambridge companion to Vygotsky*. New York: Cambridge University Press.

West, M., Ainscow, M. and Stanford, J. (2005). Sustaining improvement in schools in challenging circumstances: a study of successful practice. *School Leadership and Management*, 25(1), 77–93.

Whitty, G. (2010). Marketization and post-marketization in education. In A. Hargreaves, A. Lieberman, M. Fullan and D. Hopkins (eds) *Second international of educational change*. (pp. 405–413). Dordrecht: Springer.

Wickman, P. and Ostman, L. (2002). Learning as discourse change: a sociocultural mechanism. *Science Education*, 86, 601–623.

Williams, J. (2011a). Toward a political economic theory of education: use and exchange values of enhanced labor power. *Mind, Culture, and Activity*, 18(3), 276–292.

Williams, J. (2011b). Audit and evaluation of pedagogy: towards a cultural–historical perspective. In T. Rowland and K. Ruthven (eds) *Mathematical knowledge in teaching* (pp. 161–178). New York: Springer.

Williams, J. (2012). Use and exchange value in mathematics education: contemporary CHAT meets Bourdieu's sociology. *Educational Studies in Mathematics*, 80(1), 57–72.

Williams, J., Corbin, B. and McNamara, O. (2007). Finding inquiry in discourses of audit and reform in primary schools. *International Journal of Educational Research*, 46(1–2), 57–67.

Williams, J., Hernandez-Martinez, P., Black, P., Davis, P., Farnsworth, V., Harris, D., Hutcheson, G., Jooganah, K., Kleanthous, I., Pampaka, M., Pepin, B. and Wake, G. (under review). Mathematics education in university transition: boundary crossers, brokers and third spaces. *British Educational Research Journal*.

Williams, P. (2008). *Independent Review of Mathematics Teaching in Early Years Settings and Primary Schools*. DCSF-00433-2008.

Willinsky, J. (2001). The strategic education research program and the public value of research. *Educational Researcher*, 30(1), 5–14.

Willis, P. (1977). *Learning to labour: How working class kids get working-class jobs*. New York: Columbia University Press.

Wingens, M. (1990). Toward a general utilization theory: a systems theory reformulation of the two-communities metaphor. *Knowledge: Creation, diffusion, utilization*, 12, 27–42.

Wittgenstein, L. (1953/2003). *Philosophical investigations: The German text, with a revised English translation* (trans. G. E. M. Anscombe) (3rd ed.). Malden, MA: Blackwell Publishing.

Yardley, S. and Dornan, T. (2012). Kirkpatrick's levels and education 'evidence'. *Medical Education*, 46(1), 97–106.

Index